BADER'S WAR

BADER'S WAR

'HAVE A GO AT EVERYTHING'

by

S.P. MACKENZIE

SPELLMOUNT

British Library Cataloguing in Publication Data:
A catalogue record for this book is available
from the British Library

Copyright © S.P. Mackenzie 2008
ISBN 978 1 86227 467 9
First published in the UK in 2008 by
Spellmount Limited
Cirencester Road, Chalford
Stroud, Gloucestershire. GL6 8PE
www.thehistorypress.co.uk

Spellmount Limited is an imprint of The History Press

1 3 5 7 9 8 6 4 2

Printed in Great Britain

Contents

ACKNOWLEDGEMENTS

This book would not have been possible without the help of diligent staff members at the following archives: the BBC Written Archive, Caversham Park; Churchill College, Cambridge; the Imperial War Museum Department of Documents and Department of Sound, London; the Liddell Hart Centre, Archives, King's College London; the National Archives (formerly the Public Record Office), Kew; the Royal Air Force Museum Department of Research and Information Services, Hendon; the Royal Canadian Air Force Memorial Museum, Trenton, Ontario; the Liddle Collection, University of Leeds; and, last but not least, Dr J.C. Perkins as overseer of the archive of St Edward's School, Oxford. The help provided by Mary Guy and Tim Pierce as librarians at the Royal Air Force College, Cranwell, proved to be of great value, as did the patient assistance of the inter-library loan staff at Thomas Cooper Library, University of South Carolina.

I would also like to thank Ruth Parr, who suggested that there might be more to say about Douglas Bader, and Jamie Wilson, and others employees of Spellmount for their enthusiasm and support. The two anonymous readers who read an earlier version of the typescript provided helpful feedback and suggestions. Dr Jeremy Crang deserves special mention for placing me in touch with former fighter pilot Wallace Cunningham. I wish in addition to express my gratitude to Mr Cunningham himself for his willingness to correspond concerning his encounters with Douglas Bader both before and after his capture, and to Bill Macot for sharing his memories of what his father-in-law, Helmut Swantje, had to say about guarding Bader at St Omer. Last but not least, I wish to acknowledge the suggestions of Charles Rollings regarding what I have to say about Bader's time as a POW. Though we disagree on the value of certain sources, his knowledge of the RAF prisoner-of-war experience remains peerless. Any errors of fact that may appear in the following pages are, of course, wholly my responsibility.

ABBREVIATIONS

AOC – Air Officer Commanding
AOC-in-C – Air Officer Commander-in-Chief
BBC – British Broadcasting Corporation, People's War website
BFI – British Film Institute library
CAS – Chief of Air Staff
CCC – Archive of Churchill College, Cambridge
CFS – Central Flying School
CO – Commanding Officer
DCAS – Deputy Chief of Air Staff
DFC – Distinguished Flying Cross
DSO – Distinguished Service Order
E/A – Enemy aircraft
F/O – Flying Officer
HQ – Headquarters
IWM – Imperial War Museum, Department of Documents
IMWSA – Imperial War Museum, Sound Archive
ORB – Operations Record Book
RAAF – Royal Australian Air Force
RAF – Royal Air Force
RAFCA – Cranwell archives
RAFM – Royal Air Force Museum, Department of Research and Information Services
RAFVR – Royal Air Force Volunteer Reserve
RCAFM – Royal Canadian Air Force Memorial Museum
RDF – Radio Direction Finding [radar]
RSM – Regimental Sergeant Major
R/T – radio telephone
SESA – Archive of St Edwards School, Oxford
UNB – Archives and Special Collections, Harriet Irving Library, University of New Brunswick
VHF – Very High Frequency

Introduction

*It's a wonderful achievement, to fight and lead in battle,
with no legs.*

Wallace 'Jock' Cunningham, 2005[1]

A quarter of a century after his death, Douglas Bader remains the most famous fighter pilot that Britain has ever known. A school, various centres, a charitable foundation, several scholarships and awards, a number of streets, a garden, a housing estate, plus two pubs have been named after him. His personal effects have generated much interest at major auctions, and some of his official papers were considered valuable enough to be targeted for theft from the Public Record Office. He is a potent symbol of human triumph over adversity (especially for those who have lost limbs), and still the most widely recognised leader of The Few in the Battle of Britain. A dozen volumes – along with a hugely popular feature film – have been devoted to either his life or aspects of his career, many of them selling briskly in mass-market form. Douglas Bader, in short, is a name that continues to resonate in the public imagination.[2]

Given that this is so, and in view of how much ink has already been spilled on the subject, why expend effort on yet another book about Bader? The answer is essentially twofold. Firstly, new memoirs, interviews, and old documents have become available which help shed further light on various episodes in his life. Secondly, and perhaps more importantly, those who have written about Bader in the past have, with few exceptions, either focused on particular points in his career – albeit in some cases with considerable skill – or have written from the perspective of friends of their subject during his lifetime. Biographers in this latter category were able to record a great deal of what Bader had to say about himself and his deeds that will prove invaluable to future generations. In getting close to the man, however, such authors were, as they usually admitted quite freely, inherently biased in his favour.[3]

There is, of course, a tremendous amount to admire from a more objective standpoint as well. Douglas Bader, after all, overcame a physical disability that would have left lesser mortals either using sticks or in a wheelchair, became one of the most inspiring fighter aces of the early war years, and set a shining example to those unfortunate enough to lose limbs. Nevertheless in the years since his death enough evidence has accumulated and enough time has now passed to call into question some of what Bader accomplished as an RAF leader during the Second World War.

To actually do so, of course, is to run the risk of being accused of attacking someone who was physically disabled as well as a long-cherished national hero. As the authors of a biography of Guy Gibson – the bomber-pilot equivalent to Douglas Bader within the pantheon of ultra-famous RAF figures – explained more than a decade ago, 'historians tamper with legends at their peril.'[4] The aim here, however, is to neither praise nor bury Bader; it is, rather, to put what he accomplished in perspective and provide a portrait that deals with his flaws as well as his more positive features without the result being a hatchet job. Bader's bravery in the air, as will become clear, was not always matched by operational or even sometimes tactical acumen. Moreover as a leader of men, both on RAF stations and in POW camps, he made bitter enemies as well as lifelong admirers. As the following chapters will show, the character traits that made Douglas Bader strong enough to rise the way he did – his determination, single-mindedness, power of decision, and overall forcefulness – could sometimes lead him and those he led astray. In order to understand the man, however, it is first necessary to get to know the youth.

Notes

[1]W. Cunningham in *Britain's War Heroes: Douglas Bader, Fighter Ace* (Blakeway Associates, 2005).

[2]On the books (a number currently available in paperback) and film (available on DVD) see the Bibliography. On Bader as national hero see A. Bowdoin Van Riper, *Imagining Flight* (College Station, TX: Texas A&M Press, 2004), p. 34. On Bader as instantly associated with The Few see http://www.raf.mod.uk/history/recall. html (accessed 27 August 2003), 'Recalling the Few Who Saved Britain From Invasion', p. 1; Patrick Bishop, *Fighter Boys* (London: HarperCollins, 2003), p. 323.

On Bader as an inspiration to the disabled see http://www.rsdalert.co.uk/stories/
PushingPain.htm (accessed 12 February 2004). There is a Douglas Bader Close in
North Walsham, a Douglas Bader Gardens in Fife, a Douglas Bader primary
school near Norwich, a Douglas Bader Day Centre for the disabled in Leicester, a
Douglas Bader Foundation for the disabled, a Douglas Bader Sports Centre at St
Edward's School in Oxford (his alma mater), a Royal International Air Tattoo Flying
Scholarship for the disabled in memory of Douglas Bader, a Douglas Bader Award
for Inspiration from the Limbless Association, a Douglas Bader housing estate in
London, a Douglas Bader family pub and restaurant at Martlesham Heath, and a
Bader Arms at Tangmere. (There is also a Douglas Bader Toby Mug and a 1/72nd
scale Corgi model Spitfire done up in Bader's personal markings, plus assorted
renderings in paint of his aircraft in flight.) On the auctioning of Bader's personal
effects, see 165 HC Deb. 6th Series, 25 June 1990, col. 795; *Mail on Sunday*, 13 May
1999; http://news.bbc.co.uk/hi/uk/509916.stm (accessed 12 February 2004). On
the theft of papers from the PRO see *Daily Telegraph*, 23 February 1991. Bader has
also featured in various novels, including Frederick Forsyth's *Avenger* (New York:
St. Marton's, 2003), pp. 26–28.

[3]On biographers getting close to their subject see Laddie Lucas, *Flying Colours*
(London: Wordsworth, 2001 edn), prologue; John Frayn Turner, *Douglas Bader*
(Shrewsbury: Airlife, 2001 edn), pp. 155, 245. On studies published since his death
that focus in the main on specific episodes in Bader's war see Andy Saunders,
Bader's Last Flight (London: Grub Street, 2007); Michael G. Burns, *Bader* (London:
Cassell, 1998 edn); Dilip Sarkar, *Bader's Duxford Fighters* (Worcester: Ramrod,
1997); Dilip Sarker, *Bader's Tangmere Spitfires* (Sparkford: Patrick Stephens, 1996).
This is not to suggest any attempt at deception on the part of those who have writ-
ten about Bader in the past: indeed, as the notes will show, this book quite literally
could not have been written without the published work of everyone from Paul
Brickhill to Dilip Sarkar.

[4]Richard Morris with Colin Dobinson, *Guy Gibson* (London: Penguin, 1994), xxvi.

CHAPTER ONE

Headstrong Youth

I'm fed up with you. If you don't change considerably I shall take steps to have you and your friends removed from the college.

Squadron commander in conversation with Flight Cadet D.R.S. Bader, Crawnell, September 1929[1]

In one sense the defining moment in the life of Douglas Bader came at age twenty when he lost his legs in a flying accident. The rest of his life, after all, would be largely defined by his efforts to overcome the effects of the resulting physical loss, the battle for which he is admired and remembered the most. In another sense, though, the events that made Bader what he was – indeed that gave him the qualities that enabled him to survive and then triumph over physical adversity – had already occurred. It was during the first two decades of his life that the wilfulness, tenacity, voluble self-confidence, pugnacity and personal loyalties characteristic of Bader the man first manifested themselves. In a very real sense the circumstances of his childhood and adolescence would mark him for life.[2]

Douglas Bader was born in St John's Wood on 21 February 1910, the second son of Frederick and Jessie Bader (*nee* McKenzie). Within days mother and son came down with the measles. Then Jessie required a major operation. By the time she had recovered, the furlough Frederick had been granted from his job as a civil engineer in India had expired. The family returned to the subcontinent minus Douglas, who was farmed out to relatives on the Isle of Man on the grounds that a recovering baby would not be able to cope with the harsh Indian climate. When he was two years old Douglas was reunited with his family in India, but by then he was clearly something of an intruder. Derick, two years older than Douglas, was very much the favoured son. Sibling rivalry soon set in, the two brothers fighting constantly as children with their mother always taking the side of her first-born in any dispute. Whether or not Jessie 'hated' her second child, as a cousin later claimed, there was no question that Douglas lacked parental affection. His mother did not seem to love him. His father, a gruff, remote figure twenty years older than his wife – with whom he fought constantly – went off to war when Douglas was only five, and was seen thereafter only while on leave from service in France to the time of his death from old wounds seven years later. 'The only times he cried', biographer Paul Brickhill related, 'were when his father and mother and Derick went visiting in the car and left him behind, which they often did.'[3]

The family moved to Kew on the outskirts of London when Douglas was three, where sibling rivalry, in the form of potentially dangerous dares, continued at home and at Colet Court, a nearby prep school. Struggling to assert himself against Derick, the younger brother began to fight other, bigger, boys as well when he felt his self-worth was under threat. When the boys went on to another prep school, Temple Grove, Douglas found a new outlet for his growing energy and pent-up aggression in sport. At age twelve he had become captain of the rugby, football, and cricket teams, and won every foot race he ran. Made aware that family funds were short after the death of his father, Douglas also took time to swot up for and win a scholarship to St Edward's School, Oxford.[4]

Family relations, however, remained strained. 'Douglas had a very unhappy childhood,' his future sister-in-law recalled. What family money there was had gone towards keeping Derick at another public school, King's at Canterbury. After the death of the boys' father in France their mother – still only thirty-two – had married again, this time to a clergyman, the Reverend Ernest William Hobbs. His stepsons resented moving to his parish in Yorkshire, and the rather gentle Hobbs does not seem to have become the father-figure Douglas in particular sorely lacked. In the summer of 1923 Douglas was packed off alone to spend a week with in-laws; luckily ones able to provide the kind of human warmth lacking at home.[5]

Though sibling rivalry initially continued in the summer holidays – culminating in the older brother shooting the younger brother in the shoulder with an air-gun pellet at close range – it was the public-school world of St Edward's that soon became the centre of his life. Either through callow youthfulness or as psychological defence mechanism, Douglas was able to ignore potentially stressful emotions and focus both his attention and his aggressive energy on competitive sports. Lack of interest characterised his attitude to academic subjects, particularly maths, but on the playing fields he shone in every sport going. He got a beating from an older boy, Laurence Olivier, after he bowled him out in a house cricket match, but was clearly an athletic star. At age fifteen he became the youngest member of the school rugby team, rather inclined to hog the ball but always willing to mix it with older and bigger opponents. As time passed his relations with his older brother seem to have improved. Moreover, the first in a series of older men whom Douglas could look up to appeared in his life. The headmaster at St Edward's, Warden H.E. Kendall, adopted a tolerant view of Bader's sometimes wild behaviour, and took the risk of making him a prefect despite what others saw as a strong streak of conceit in the boy. 'In his formative and impressionable years, and indeed, for much longer,' observed a future in-law who knew him well, 'Douglas was unusually susceptible to example – good and bad.' Luckily this particular father-substitute provided him with a steadying influence.[6]

Meanwhile, as the terms passed, Bader was developing as an athlete if not a scholar, and in his last year was made captain of the First Fifteen. Arthur Tilley, the school sports master, witnessed Douglas in an early command position, later commenting on his self-assurance and breezy commitment, his ability to infect others with his enthusiasm, as well as his tendency to treat the other members as younger brothers.

Being captain of the team, assuming the mantle of big brother, was clearly a role that Bader relished. In the spring of 1928 he became captain of cricket as well. It also seems to have dampened his ego somewhat, insofar as he was no longer quite so selfish about handling the rugby ball. But it was the element of contest, the struggle to assert his authority, that still animated the boy now on the verge of young manhood; that was why he enjoyed debating as well as sports: 'he always dominated every society he was in', a close school chum recalled.[7]

By the time Douglas Bader was in his final year at school the central elements of his essential nature were already manifesting themselves. There was the urge to compete and win; the desire to lead; the need to prove himself; the blustery self-confidence that masked a certain loneliness; and the need to show loyalty to all those who demonstrated faith in him, not least authority figures.

Now, though, there arose the inevitable question: what to do after leaving St Edward's?

At first he did not have a clue. 'I remember in my last year at school at the age of 17 wondering what it was I wanted to do when I left school', he reminisced almost thirty years later. A visit to the school by an old boy, now a cadet at the RAF College, prompted him to recall his own days at Cranwell staying with his uncle and aunt five years previously.

> As soon as I recalled those days my mind was made up. Indeed I cannot truthfully say whether it was the excitement of flying, or watching, as I did that time, the triangular sports between Cranwell, the Royal Military Academy, Woolwich, and the Royal Military College, Sandhurst, which struck in my mind more deeply. In fact what I wanted to do was to go to Cranwell – I think that was the truth.[8]

Douglas therefore wrote at the end of 1927 to his well-liked uncle about the possibility of becoming an air force officer. As personal assistant to the Chief of the Air Staff the uncle, Cyril Burge, was in a position to help. He knew the sort of answers the selection board liked to hear, and sent his nephew a list of the things he should say in response to questions. Moreover, once it became clear that the family could not afford the fees – Jessie disliked the idea of her second son joining the Air Force anyway – Uncle Cyril gave the kind of competitive challenge to which he knew his nephew would instinctively rise. Each year the RAF college at Cranwell offered six prize cadetships through competitive examination to potential new entrants: perhaps Douglas was up to winning one of these? Suitably primed, Douglas did well. In the selection board interview he scored 235 out of a maximum of 250 points. And in the wake of a good deal of cramming in maths and other subjects that he had previously neglected, he sat the exam and managed to win the fifth of the six cadetships.[9]

The two years Bader spent at Cranwell (1928–30) were important in a number of ways. Cadets, of course, were taught to fly, and Bader found that he loved being a pilot (see chapter two). But in setting up the Royal Air Force College in the early twenties, Air Chief Marshal Sir Hugh Trenchard and his staff saw it as far more than simply a school for pilots wearing Air Force blue. The college, drawing its intake from the public schools, was to be the source for RAF regular officers – men who would form the permanent nucleus of the new service – the best of whom would rise to senior command positions. That meant education in service subjects as well as ground school and flying. The fact that Bader was a product of a college with such goals in mind would have a positive impact on his career prospects later on when relatively few pilots had passed through Cranwell because of the forced expansion of the RAF in the late 1930s.[10]

Bader found he liked Cranwell a lot. 'The life in the R.A.F.,' he reflected in a letter to one of his former masters at St Edward's, 'I think is ideal.' The flying aspect apart, in some respects it was very much like a public school, with plenty of games as well as more adult opportunities to let off steam. Bader continued to excel at rugby and cricket, and added hockey and boxing to his repertoire of sports. Motorcycling was tolerated, but the more daring cadets took to banned activities such as speeding, pillion riding, plus owning – and then racing – personal cars. A number of minor mishaps occurred. 'I may say that we had more accidents on motor cycles while I was at Cranwell than we ever did in aeroplanes', he fondly remembered. Bader, boisterous and, as always, keen to assert himself, gained the reputation among the staff of being something of an *enfant terrible*. More serious in the short run was his attitude to the academic side of the curriculum during his first year. It has been argued that Cranwell 'turned Bader into a total professional', but while he certainly developed an interest in the aces of the Great War there was little sign that he took such subjects as maths or accountancy with any seriousness. At the end of his first year Flight Cadet Douglas Bader was in fact in danger of being expelled, having been caught joy riding in a banned car once too often and having come nineteenth out of twenty-one in his class on the written exams. Luckily for him the commandant, Air Vice-Marshal Frederick Halahan, like the Warden at St Edward's, thought that leadership talent underlay youthful rebelliousness and warned Bader quietly that the RAF wanted adults, not overgrown adolescents, as officers.[11]

The interview with Halahan sobered Bader up quite noticeably. A senior authority figure had placed faith in him despite his failings, and the chastened flight cadet was not about to let him down by showing that the boy could not become a man. But there were limits to the subsequent change in character. While he took academic subjects a bit more seriously, he could not entirely abstain from what he called 'messing about with motor bikes', a pastime in which he more than matched the dare-devilry of his friends. And he channelled his restless energy – the need to prove himself, to dominate, to win – even more into sports. Rupert Leigh, a more junior cadet, later recalled how Bader seemed almost godlike in his apparently effortless ability to play and excel at every individual and team sport. Excellence in cricket, rugby, and boxing were what he was particularly noted for; though his style, at least in the boxing ring, focused on aggression more than technique. Bader would invariably rush forward and attempt to floor his opponent with a blizzard of punches in what an observer called his 'usual "no-time-to-spare" manner'. This worked most of the time, though when he tried to box above his weight the result was instructive. 'He went out for all he was worth against his opponent,' the college magazine recorded of a bout with a light heavy-weight, adding that the opponent, 'stepping back from a rush, shot out a short right to the chin' that sent Bader 'down and out for the count.' Though relations with his mother had got better since Derick had moved to South Africa, Douglas clearly still had something to prove. 'The reactions', as his brother-in-law put it in reference to Bader's difficult early life, 'were to rumble on and on.'[12]

And prove himself he did. By the spring of 1930 his flying ability, sporting activities, and record as an under-officer of one of the two training squadrons, placed him second overall among the graduating class. In later years Bader took no umbrage at not managing to come out on top and win the coveted Sword of Honour. 'I didn't really mind', he said. 'Paddy [Coote] was a splendid man, very good all round – at games, at work, at flying, at everything.' As for Bader himself, a later Air Ministry brief noted that 'he showed strong personality and determination, and had a great deal of influence in the College'; but added that – apparently in spite of efforts to improve – his 'academic subjects were weak!' The commandant, responding to a request for information on how Bader was getting on in the RAF, admitted that while excellent at games during his time at Cranwell, the young man in question 'did not take a genuine interest in subjects such as Science, Engineering and Workshop practice.' This was reflected in his class standing in July 1930: he placed 17 in order of academic merit within his graduating class of 21. His final report, providing a further clue as to why he did not gain first place overall, summed up the freshly minted Pilot Officer D.R.S. Bader in three very accurate words: 'Plucky, capable, headstrong.'[13]

Notes

[1]Paul Brickhill, *Reach for the Sky* (London, 1954), p. 36.

[2]The hypothesis that the accident does not fully explain the thrusting, loud, and indeed bellicose aspects of Bader's personality is supported by the equally determined but otherwise different natures of other pilots who lost limbs and fought their way back to operational squadrons during the war. These included Colin 'Hoppy' Hodgkinson, who also lost both legs in a flying accident, B. F. Rose (RAAF), who lost an arm while bailing out, and James MacLachlan, who lost an arm in air combat. See Brian Cull and Roland Symonds, *One-Armed Mac* (London: Grub Street, 2003); *New York Times*, 5 October 1941, p. 35; Colin Hodgkinson, *Best Foot Forward* (London: Odams, 1957); on Hodgkinson see also R.W. F. Sampson with Norman Franks, *Spitfire Offensive* (London: Grub Street, 1994), p. 60; Vincent Orange, *The Road to Biggin Hill* (Shrewsbury: Ailife, 1986), p. 77. There were also the Soviet pilots Alexei Maresyev and Zakhar Sorokin, both of whom lost both their feet, and Graham West, a USAAF pilot who, like Hodgkinson, was inspired by Bader's example to push for a return to combat duty after losing his legs to a booby trap. On West see *New York Times*, 22 August 1943, p. 12. On the Soviet pilots see Albert Axell, *Russia's Heroes* (London: Constable, 2001), pp. 187–92.

[3]Brickhill, *Reach for the Sky*, p. 12. The claim that Jessie hated Douglas was made by a cousin Suzanne Goodhew in an interview for *Secret Lives: Douglas Bader* (Twenty-Twenty Productions, 1996).

[4]Brickhill, *Reach for the Sky*, pp. 12–14.

[5]Jill Lucas in *Britain's War Heroes: Douglas Bader, Fighter Ace* (Blakeway Associates, 2005); see Brickhill, *Reach for the Sky*, pp. 16–17; Laddie Lucas, *Flying Colours* (London: Wordsworth, 2001 edn), p. 25.

[6]Lucas, *Flying Colours*, p. 26; see Brickhill, *Reach for the Sky*, p. 23. On Bader as sportsman see *St. Edward's School Chronicle*, May 1924, p. 152, February 1925, p. 209, March 1925, pp. 219–220, May 1925, p. 232, July 1925, pp. 248–53, April 1926, pp. 299, 303, June 1926, pp. 311–312, July 1926, p. 321, October 1926, p. 343, December 1926, pp. 354–55, February 1927, p. 372, May 1927, p. 395. On Bader hogging the ball see *St. Edward's School Chronicle*, December 1925, p. 278. On Bader being beaten by Olivier see Terry Coleman, *Olivier* (New York: Henry Holt, 2005), p. 18.

[7]St Edward's School Archive, Bader collection [hereafter SESA], Dan to Jack, 22 November 1982; see Brickhill, *Reach for the Sky*, p. 25.

[8]Douglas Bader, 'Fighter Pilot', in E. Leyland and T.E. Scott-Chard (eds), *The Boys' Book of the Air* (London: Edmund Ward, 1957), p. 59; see Brickhill, *Reach for the Sky*, p. 25.

[9]It was while Douglas was contemplating an air force career that he learned from

his mother that the bursar at St Edward's had been helping pay his fees. Precisely what motivated Walter Dingwall, a rather reserved history master whom Bader never took a class from, is unclear, though he would not be the last authority figure to be charmed by the extrovert qualities he himself lacked. When Bader left St Edward's for Cranwell, his patron insisted on buying and giving him a second-hand motorcycle, and subsequently provided him with a £12 cheque every twelve weeks. See Brickhill, *Reach for the Sky*, 23, 26–29, 33–34. It should be noted that this was not an isolated case: Al Reid, another master at St Edward's, assisted with the fees for the father of Oliver Dashwood in the 1930s when his father ran into financial difficulties; apparently a not uncommon occurrence. Oliver M. Dashwood to Author, 5 June 2005. On Dingwall at St Edward's see R.D. Hill, *A History of St. Edward's School* (Oxford: St Edward's School Society, 1962), pp. 204, 216, 218, 229, 240, 246, 251, 254.

[10]On Cranwell see R. De La Bère, *A History of the Royal Air Force College Cranwell* (Aldershot: Poldin, 1934); E.B. Haslam, *The History of Royal Air Force Cranwell* (London: HMSO, 1982), pp. 32–33; John James, *The Paladins* (London: Macdonald, 1990), pp. 137–41, 143, 145; Andrew Boyle, *Trenchard* (London: Collins, 1962), p. 363.

[11]Bader in *Boys' Book of the Air*, p. 61. For the 'total professional' quote see Michael G. Burns, *Bader* (London: Cassell, 1998 edn), p. 6. On Bader as *enfant terrible* see Brickhill, *Reach for the Sky*, pp. 33–36. On Bader and sports at Cranwell see *The Journal of the Royal Air Force College*, vol. 9, no. 1, Spring 1929, pp. 50–51, vol. 9, no. 2, Autumn 1929, pp. 154, 156, vol. 10, no. 1, Spring 1930, pp. 52–59, vol. 10, no. 2, Autumn 1930, pp. 180–86. For the 'ideal' comment see SESA, Bader to Kendall [or Dingwall?], 21 April 1930.

[12]Lucas, *Flying Colours*, p. 24; *Journal of the Royal Air Force College* 10 (1930), pp. 59, 186. On the 'motor bikes' comment, see Lucas, *Flying Colours*, p. 35. On Bader as boxer and the Rupert Leigh comment see Brickhill, *Reach for the Sky*, p. 37; see also SESA, Bader to Kendall [or Dingwall?], 21 April 1930. On Bader as a rugby player and cricketer see *Journal of the Royal Air Force College* 9 (1920), pp. 49, 50, 51; *Journal of the Royal Air Force College* 10 (1930), pp. 52, 55, 182. On the Halahan interview and its effect see Brickhill, *Reach for the Sky*, pp. 36–38; Lucas, *Flying Colours*, pp. 27–28, 33, 37–38.

[13]Brickhill, *Reach for the Sky*, p. 39; SESA, Adjutant for Commandant to Kendall, 23 September 1930; Churchill College Cambridge, Churchill Papers, CHUR 2/180, Group Captain Douglas R. S. Bader, D.S.O., D.F.C., Brief Note, p. 1; see also CHUR 2/180, Montague Browne to James, 15 March 1954. For information on Bader's class standing in July 1930 I am indebted to the library staff at the Royal Air Force College, Cranwell. For the comment on Paddy Coote see Lucas, *Flying Colours*, p. 32.

CHAPTER TWO

Fighter Pilot

I know I'll be able to fly still.

Douglas Bader in conversation with well-wishers, Royal Berkshire Hospital, February 1932[1]

It was the prospect of games that first attracted young Douglas to the idea of going to Cranwell. Within a few days of arriving at the college in 1928, though, he was taken aloft for the first time and was hooked for life. The joy of flying, the sense of being carried by a machine under one's personal command into a three-dimensional world where 'the surly bonds of earth' were broken, was like a drug to him. His skill at it, in combination with his character, would lead first to Icarus-like ruin and then to an astonishing feat of resurrection.

His instructor at Cranwell was Flying Officer Wilfred Pearson, another of the quiet older men that Douglas could look up to. With Pearson seated behind him in the open rear cockpit of an Avro 504 biplane, Flight Cadet D.R.S. Bader quickly learned the art of smooth and simultaneous movement of stick and rudder. As September gave way to October he progressed through takeoffs and landings, what to do in the event of engine failure, various kinds of turns, and how to recover from a spin. Helped by the excellent hand-foot-eye co-ordination that made him a fine sportsman, as well as his ingrained willingness to rise to a challenge, Bader was ready to solo after little more than eleven hours of dual instruction. Further lessons on how to deal with various emergencies and cross-country challenges followed, but it was already clear that this particular flight cadet had real talent as a pilot. Bader passed his end-of-year test under the eye of the Senior Flying Instructor in the spring of 1929 with ease.[2]

Even at this early stage in his flying career there were signs that, good as Bader was, in the search to prove that he was the best he was willing to push the envelope. Once one cadet had invented the dare of climbing out of the rear cockpit while in the air and crawling forward to tie a handkerchief round the joystick in the empty front cockpit, others had to try it. It was Bader who developed the technique of straddling the fuselage between the cockpits while tying the handkerchief. An official report noted that he was rather too fond of aerobatics and predicted that as a pilot Bader 'might neglect accuracy when no longer under instruction'. Shortly before he died Bader recalled that neither he nor his friends were at all concerned about getting into a situation where the parachute might have to be used: 'It never occurred to any of us that abandoning an aircraft would present a problem.' Not long after he left Cranwell the commandant, in a letter to the Warden of St Edward's concerning Bader, praised the former cadet for having 'developed into a very good pilot'; but went on to wonder if he had not also accumulated 'almost too much confidence.'[3]

Given his combative nature it was hardly surprising that Bader wanted to be a fighter pilot. As he later remembered, 'In those days the fastest aeroplane was the single-seater fighter so that the element of speed was one attraction, and secondly it was more controllable and interesting to fly than other types. In a fighter you could loop the loop and do all those amusing things which in later flying jargon became known as "aerobatics".'[4]

Though he was not judged the best all-round pilot of his term, he was rated 'above average' as a flyer, and in the summer of 1930 the freshly minted Pilot Officer D.R.S. Bader was happy enough to find himself posted along with his friend Geoffrey Stephenson to Kenley. This was the home of No. 23 Squadron, a unit equipped with the Gloster Gamecock, an agile, single-seat biplane fighter: exactly the sort of aeroplane the new pilot officer wanted to fly. The CO, Squadron Leader Henry Woollett, was a World War I ace who believed strongly in individual initiative; and the squadron itself was known as a breeding ground for pilots who could aerobat to perfection in the annual Hendon air pageant. Life in those days for a young RAF officer was pleasant, indeed almost idyllic. Servants were constantly at hand to keep rooms and uniforms clean and tidy and to serve food and drink. Marriage was forbidden until age thirty, but young women were naturally attracted to the dashing young men with wings on their tunics who roared about the area in sports cars. (Bader soon traded up from an Austin to an MG.) Conversation in the mess, the comfortingly routine round of daily duty, and of course flying, were the be-all and end-all of their lives. 'It was truly a man's life,' Bader fondly recalled many years later.

> We all lived in the mess, dined-in four nights a week and spent the weekends playing sport. There were no women on the station. We all knew each other, went out together, played games together, flew together. Life was great, and flying was what we all loved.

Relations with his parent and step-father had meanwhile improved to the point where, with typical bravado, he saw fit to deliver a birthday gift to his mother by flying low over their house in Sprotsbrough and dropping the wrapped present on the rectory lawn. 'It was enormous fun', Bader reflected later concerning his life at this stage. 'The most enormous fun.'[5]

This did not mean, however, that the need to excel, to do better than his peers, had in any way abated. Having been chosen for the RAF cricket team and then asked to play rugby for the Harlequins as centre-three-quarter, Bader set his sights on joining the Hendon team. He was a fine pilot who loved aerobatics – 'stunting' as it was then known – and always would. As he enthusiastically asserted many years later:

> I think there is no more graceful or exhilarating sight than three or four fighters stunting in formation. To see these aeroplanes looping and rolling with their wings overlapping and only a few feet apart never fails to give me the most tremendous thrill. I think it is the finest form of flying that has ever been invented.

Back in 1930, Bader had more than watching from the ground on his mind: he wanted to be among the select band of pilots who flew formation aerobatics during the annual public air display at RAF Hendon. Luck was with him when it transpired that he was a member of the very last flight in the RAF to operate the Gamecock. The rest of the force, including the other flights in No. 23 Squadron, had by the spring of 1931 been re-equipped with the faster but less agile Bristol Bulldog. The Gamecock was a better aerobatic machine than the Bulldog, and it was decided that the plane being retired should thrill the crowds one last time in June 1931. It was thus up to Flight Lieutenant Harry 'Pricky' Day, commanding the Gamecock flight, to choose a Hendon partner from among the pilots of the squadron. Douglas Bader was his wingman in a series of synchronised loops, rolls, and head-on passes that thrilled the crowds and gave the twenty-one year-old pilot officer the satisfaction of knowing he was among the best in the business.[6]

Though he did not know it, Bader was now in real peril. He had done every authorised aerobatic manoeuvre in the book well enough to perform at Hendon. Once that particular peak had been scaled, what new worlds were there to conquer? This was no idle question with such a driven man. Laddie Lucas, a fighter pilot who knew Bader well, put the problem thus:

> There arrives a time in a pilot's career – and this was certainly true of Douglas – when the exhilaration of flying begins to lose its strength. It is not that the allure of flying is lessened, for to be alone in a man-made machine in God's sky will ever retain its sensation. Intercourse with the air will always remain one of man's indulgent pleasures. It is when the natural orgasm of flight ceases to be regularly achieved that troubles begin and satisfaction is sought in what the sexologists rather picturesquely call 'deviations of aim'.

To put it another way, having experienced the thrill, or natural head rush, of carrying out authorised aerobatics, the pilot in question 'will start turning to the hard stuff'; that is, start doing more dangerous and therefore forbidden manoeuvres.[7]

Bader was already something of a daredevil when it came to low flying. Pilots were not supposed to do aerobatics in the Gamecock below 500 feet, but with his flight commander turning a blind eye Bader took to doing slow rolls at near-ground level. The danger was made greater after the remainder of No. 23 Squadron converted to the Bristol Bulldog. Though a fine fighter for its day, the Bulldog had problems of directional stability at low speeds. This made low-level aerobatics particularly hazardous, and strict orders were issued forbidding aerobatic manoeuvres below two thousand feet. To Bader this became another safety rule to be proven unnecessary rather than an order to be obeyed. There was no doubt in his mind by now that he knew best. 'My first impression', a pilot from another squadron who met him in the spring of 1931 remembered, 'was of a young man with complete confidence in himself and with absolutely no doubt that all his beliefs and opinions were correct.' What was more, he was not slow to demonstrate his skill in the air if he thought his talent and accomplishments were being maligned. During gunnery training exercises held at Sutton Bridge the pilots of No. 25 Squadron took to pointing out to the pilots of No. 23 Squadron their weaknesses in this area. Bader, no doubt frustrated by his own poor gunnery performance – he scored only 38 per cent overall – refused to let this pass without a display of his piloting skill. The jibes 'made Douglas even more angry and one of his ways of expressing annoyance was to dive on the airfield in his Bulldog on return from the ranges and do a vigorous upward roll starting at ground level', Kenneth Cross recalled. 'This was a continuing cause of amusement to us [in No. 25 Squadron], but such manoeuvres were absolutely forbidden by regulations.'[8]

The survival rate among former Hendon pairs was already poor, and no less than twenty-three accidents –seven of them fatal – occurred in the second half of the year because of standing orders being ignored. A more disciplined unit might have been able to slow Bader down before he misjudged what he could get away with. The CO of No. 25 Squadron, H. M. 'Daddy' Probyn, seeing Bader pull one of his stunts at Sutton Bridge, remarked to his pilots that if he were in their squadron he would court-martial the man, adding 'I would probably be saving his life if I did.'[9] But the CO of No. 23 Squadron encouraged his pilots to be individuals and favoured Bader. As for his flight commander, Harry Day was himself an aficionado of aerobatics who tended towards indulgence when his pilots broke the rules. Even after another pilot crashed and was killed, Day – who became temporary CO of the squadron after the departure of Wollett – was less than emphatic in stressing the need to fly by the rulebook. Perhaps resigned to the fact that official regulations would be ignored, Day sought to emphasise to his assembled pilots the need to judge their height and speed carefully before doing any low-level aerobatics and to avoid showing off when senior officers were likely to be on the field. This approach, though, especially when linked with Day's well-known opinion that regulations were necessary only for those too stupid to understand their own limits, was not the way to deter a man who 'always knew best – in his own opinion.'[10]

On the other hand Harry Day did subsequently issue a specific warning to Bader against 'showing off', and it was Bader himself who refused to heed the rules when challenged again at the end of the year. In November came the news that he had been selected as fly-half for the Combined Services rugby team, and he seemed set to play for England. On 14 December 1931 he tagged along with two other No. 23 Squadron pilots, Geoffrey Stephenson and Geoffrey Phillips, who had decided to fly over to Woodley near Reading and have lunch with Phillips's brother, who ran the aero club at this civilian aerodrome. As they were about to depart from Woodley, Bader was pressed by some of the civilian pilots present to do a few aerobatics for them. Some accounts indicate that he at first demurred on the grounds that it would be contrary to regulations, but then took umbrage at comment that suggested he might be 'windy'. Other accounts stress that as a guest Bader felt it impolite to refuse and was keen to show his stuff once more. It was even apparently suggested at the subsequent RAF court of enquiry – wrongly in view of the fact that he was known to be abstemious – that Bader had overindulged during lunch. Whatever the case, it was clear that Bader was going to do something, and the senior man present, Flying Officer Phillips, was later blamed by higher authority for not holding him back: a judgment which assumed, of course, that this could be done. The three RAF pilots took off, having agreed to carry out a Prince of Wales's feathers display. This involved three aircraft climbing steeply together; then, while the centre aircraft continued to climb straight up and over, the aircraft to the left and right peeled away on either side. Bader, as expected, broke off to the left; and then – quite unexpectedly – headed back toward the field at low level. He commenced a roll in which his wingtips would at best be no more than ten feet off the ground. Bader had flown solo in the Bulldog now for 115 hours, and had done this trick before. But this time something went horribly wrong: he misjudged the necessary speed, the left wingtip hit the ground, and the Bulldog cart-wheeled into the earth. *'Crashed slow-rolling near ground'*, Bader would write with emphasis many weeks later in his logbook. *'Bad show.'*[11]

Hubris had finally caught up with him. His face was gashed, a tooth had sliced through his upper lip, two ribs were broken, and – more serious by far – both his legs were badly smashed up. His left leg had buckled under him, the shin broken and splintered. A piece of rudder bar had buried itself in his right knee and he was bleeding profusely from a severed leg artery. Bader would have to have the right leg amputated above the knee at once, and his left leg cut off below the knee shortly thereafter. Only a series of lucky breaks prevented him from expiring entirely. One of the civilian student pilots was among the first to arrive at the crash site and he knew enough to hold on the femoral artery in the right leg and prevent Bader from bleeding to death. Bader arrived at the hospital just in time to catch one of the best surgeons in the country, Leonard Joyce, before he left for the day. Despite the expert care he was given, there were several occasions when it seemed inevitable that the young pilot would die from loss of blood and shock. There was also a frightening amount of physical agony at various times. 'What mattered was the pain', as another pilot who found himself in remarkably similar circumstances would relate. 'It became worse as my body fought back and the effects of the drugs wore off.'[12]

What ultimately saved Bader was his physical fitness prior to the crash and, rather paradoxically, the kind of unwavering determination that had got him into such trouble in the first place. Once the worst was over he at once began pushing himself and those around him to provide the tools and skills he would need – both literally and metaphorically – to get back on his feet again in the early months of 1932 while convalescing at the RAF hospital at Uxbridge or being fitted for the latest aluminium artificial legs at a Ministry of Pensions facility for the limbless based at Roehampton hospital in London. 'I suppose the most important decision I ever made in my life was at the beginning of 1932 after I lost both my legs in December 1931,' he later wrote. 'I determined to go it alone and not be a bore to other people.' Bader was often frustrated that he could not be fitted with, and use, his new legs more quickly, and sometimes his impatience allowed gravity to get the better of him. But he refused to slow down or compromise. Told that he would never walk without support, Bader pugnaciously replied 'I'll never, *never*, walk *with* a stick!' He never did, and learned to perambulate again in record time.[13]

Bader made it abundantly clear then and ever after that he was not going to allow what had happened to him to prevent him from doing what he wanted to do. He would not remain 'Supernumerary Non-Effective Sick', as the No. 23 Squadron operations record book listed him in the wake of the crash. Walking, driving, romancing, playing (with golf replacing cricket and rugby) unaided, and, ulti-mately, flying, would all still be on the agenda. It was to prove an unparalleled triumph of determination and willpower over physi-cal adversity.[14]

Getting back into the cockpit, however, was what preoccupied Bader most even before he had learned to walk again. The court of enquiry, aware of the price he had paid for his recklessness, placed the blame for what had happened elsewhere. And as his friends were quick to remind him, there were plenty of examples of men with missing limbs who had continued to serve their country in uniform. Bader, however, was set on proving that he could still be a fighter pilot. Thanks to a personal intervention by Sir Philip Sassoon, the urbane Under-Secretary of State for Air, Bader was given the opportunity to prove to his own satisfaction in the sum-mer of 1932 that, tin legs or not, he still had the right stuff in an Avro 504. In the autumn of the same he spent four weeks proving to friendly instructors at the RAF Central Flying School that he could still fly a variety of dual-control service aircraft. The Air Ministry, however, had apparently already decided that, whatever the state of his flying skills, Pilot Officer D.R.S. Bader would not be allowed to fly again in a service aircraft. The stated reason was that there was nothing in King's Regulations governing a case such as his. An alternative explanation is that, with his record of hazardous flying and the appearance of an article in a Sunday paper questioning the safety of anyone sent up in a plane piloted by a man with tin legs, allowing Bader to return to flying duties was considered an unac-ceptable risk.[15]

All that was offered him was a job as officer in charge of the RAF station ground transport at Duxford. He seems to have got on well with the airmen under his command and continued courting Thelma Edwards, the woman who would soon become his wife and constant supporter. 'As far as I am concerned,' he wrote almost forty years later, 'the greatest influence in my life has been my wife, whom I did not meet until after I had lost my legs in 1931.' Yet there was no doubt that Bader was uncharacteristically subdued in the first few months of his twenty-third year. 'I don't think he wanted to be in the MT section,' one of his drivers later recounted, 'he wanted to fly.'[16]

Bader did manage in March 1933 to wangle a couple of flights on a dual control Atlas aircraft from Flying Officer Joe Cox, one of the instructors for the Cambridge University Air Squadron. Asked why he had agreed to this, in spite of his own reservations about anyone flying with artificial legs, Cox replied that he liked Bader and knew that 'he was so desperately keen to go up in the air to prove to people [on the station] that he could fly.' As before, Bader rapidly showed that even on an unfamiliar aircraft he could take off, fly, do loops, and land with astonishing skill. In the mess that evening some officers apparently queried whether it had been Bader or Cox who had been at the controls. Bader later seems to have remembered that it was Cox who suggested they go up again and land with Cox holding his hands in the air to prove Bader's skill beyond a shadow of a doubt; Cox recalled that it was Bader's idea. Either way the second flight took place. Bader later appears to have embellished the neatness of his second Atlas landing – according to Cox the idea that they had landed on the tarmac rather than the grass was 'absolute rubbish' – but there was no question that Bader was 'beautiful' at the controls. Unfortunately, this second landing, with Cox's hands raised high as advertised, was observed by the station commander, who knew quite well that Bader was not authorised to take the controls. Bader, to his credit, refused to let Cox take the blame – 'I'm terribly sorry, Sir, but I quite forgot to warn Cox' – and got away with a verbal reprimand.[17]

That was that, as far as flying went. Unfortunately, this was not the only run-in with the station CO. Though he would never try and shift the blame for the crash – 'I just made a balls of it, old boy', was how he put it to Laddie Lucas, 'that's all there was to it'[18] – Bader still possessed absolute confidence in his own judgement. When four of his MT lorries were involved in a pile-up on a wet road, his report on the incident castigated the RAF for fitting the vehicles with skid-friendly solid rubber tires. The station commander tersely reminded his MT officer that it was not his job to tell the Air Ministry what equipment it should use. In any event his days in the Air Force were numbered.

One biographer has written that 'he resigned from the RAF.' An Air Ministry letter forwarded to the station commander suggests that it was the Air Force that made the decision that Bader could no longer be employed and ought to be retired. If so, why was it necessary to give him the push? While most general duties officers were active pilots this was not universally the case, and there were administrative jobs of the kind that Bader had already undertaken.

If artificial legs were considered a long-term impediment even on the ground in general duties, then a post in either the stores or the accounts branch might have been offered. But even if a permanent ground job was an option, Bader made it clear that this was not what he wanted: it was to be flying or nothing. So in a sense perhaps the decision to retire was his after all.[19]

'I felt in 1933 when the R.A.F. chucked me out', Bader reflected later in a letter to his old sponsor, Walter Dingwall, 'that all you had done for me had been wasted.' Yet in certain respects the years that followed were good to Douglas Bader. In spite of the poor state of the economy it did not take him long to find a job with the aviation fuel sales section of the Asiatic Petroleum Company, soon to be part of Shell Oil, and he was able to marry Thelma. He learned to play golf, which became one of his passions, as well as tennis. He still drove a sports car, and, as fortune would have it, entirely escaped injury in the several accidents in which he was involved that resulted from a combination of speed and impatience. (Bader would not be the first or the last pilot to wrongly believe that handling one kind of high-performance craft with skill meant that one could handle any other kind of speeding machine with equal competence.) The essential problem was that Bader was temperamentally not suited to an office job that required a certain degree of tactfulness and a mastery of detail. Bader disliked the minutia of paperwork and still communicated his opinions with an air of absolute certainty. And there was no question that he missed being a fighter pilot.[20]

When the RAF began to expand in 1935, therefore, Bader decided to write a letter to the Air Member for Personnel at the Air Ministry requesting that he be reinstated. Air Marshal Sir Frederick Bowhill was personally sympathetic but turned down Bader's petition on the grounds that nobody else would agree with him that employing a legless pilot was an acceptable risk. In the aftermath of the march into Prague by Hitler's troops in April 1939, Bader tried again. He called on his old friend Geoffrey Stephenson, along with other Old Cranwellians now at the Air Ministry, to plead the case that he should be among the former pilots whose names were being added to the new Auxiliary Air Force Reserve. In late August 1939 he attempted to make his case directly with the Air Member for Personnel, but with war about to break out Air Marshal Sir Charles Portal was too busy to see him. 'I am afraid that during peace-time it is not possible for me to permit you to enter a flying class of the

Reserve', Portal wrote in reply to a letter from Bader on 31 August. There was, however, an important positive caveat to this negative decision: 'you can rest assured that if war came we would almost certainly be only too glad of your services in a flying capacity after a short time, if the doctors agree.'[21]

War of course was only a few days away, and as soon as it began, Bader started bombarding the Air Ministry with phone calls and messages to his old pals at the Air Ministry demanding an interview. 'They'll have to have me now,' he thought. When his father-in-law tried to suggest that the doctors would never agree, Bader fiercely replied that he would never accept no for an answer: 'by God, I'll sit on their doorsteps till I do get in.' A month later the summons to Whitehall finally arrived. The senior officer who saw him at first assumed that Bader would be content with a ground posting: not so, of course. It was to be flying or nothing. Luckily for Bader, Air Vice-Marshal Frederick Halahan, who had been commandant at Cranwell in his first year as a cadet, was sufficiently impressed by Bader's tenacity to give him a chance. As long as he was fit, then Bader would be given the opportunity to prove himself again at the Central Flying School.[22]

Bader had no doubt that he could fly. What the RAF medical staff members who examined him would say, though, was sufficiently worrying for him to remember in detail how the examination unfolded. The first hurdle was the reflex test. Bader could not be tapped on the knee, but the man who wielded the rubber hammer was flexible enough to test his elbows instead. The ear, nose, and throat exam, along with the recording of his blood pressure and the state of his lungs, went well, though the examinee was a little put out when one examiner simply laughed when he asked if he was fit to fly. Luckily for him Air Vice Marshal Halahan had pressed his thumb into the scales by appending a note to his medical file suggesting that if he was sound in body other than his legs then Bader ought to be passed on to CFS for evaluation. He was thrilled, of course, and so eager that within days he was pestering his contacts at the Air Ministry to get him posted at once.[23]

It was over seven years since he had last flown, and as he prepared to report to the CFS at Uphavon in mid-October 1939 he was uncharacteristically nervous. Happily the man assigned to test his flying skill was none other than Rupert Leigh, who as a junior cadet had viewed the more senior Bader almost as a god. Bader, it emerged, had retained his stick and rudder skills. The aircraft on which he was tested, however, the North American Harvard, had foot brakes that Bader could not operate with his tin legs. Leigh decided that, since other service aircraft had hand brakes, this failing did not really matter. Weeks then passed, and Bader once more began to pepper the Air Ministry with demands for action. Finally in late November he learned that he was to be reinstated in the RAF at the rank of Flying Officer and was to report for a refresher course at Uphavon. After only a single twenty-five minute flight in an Avro Tutor biplane under the supervision of Flight Lieutenant Christopher Clarkson – another admirer from the past – Bader went solo. Rupert Leigh bore the brunt of the chief flying instructor's ire when Bader's Tutor was observed flying inverted below 600 feet. Over the next several weeks, during the day and then at night, he flew a variety of aircraft types both dual and solo. By the third week of December 1939 he had graduated to the single-seat Hawker Hurricane fighter, in which he promptly did 'Aerobatics', according to his logbook. When his refresher course ended in January 1940, Flying Officer Bader had racked up fifty-four hours of flight time: most of it solo. There was no question as to his desire to fly or ability in the air. 'I have never met a more enthusiastic pilot', wrote Joe Cox, who had allowed him to fly an Atlas 504 back in 1933 and was now one of his nominal instructors. 'He lives for flying.' There was also no question that, given his temperament and possible concerns about his legs if he was part of an aircrew, Bader ought to be posted to a Hurricane or Spitfire fighter squadron. Leigh wrote in his final report on Bader that he was highly motivated and best suited to fly single-seat fighters. The subject of this report could not agree more, and once again badgered Geoffrey Stephenson – now commanding a squadron of Spitfires at Duxford – to help arrange a posting. It was probably no coincidence that Bader chose to take a CFS Hurricane over to Duxford on a day that the Air Officer Commanding 12 (Fighter) Group, Air Vice-Marshal Trafford Leigh-Mallory, was due to visit this sector station. 'I introduced Douglas to the AOC,' A.B. 'Woody' Woodhall, then squadron leader in charge of flying operations at Duxford, later recalled, 'and over lunch Douglas used all his considerable charm in persuading Leigh-Mallory to take him into one of his operational squadrons.' After lunch Bader put on a display of aerobatics that confirmed for Leigh-Mallory that this was a pilot whose career was worth fostering. On 7 February 1940 a posting to 19 Squadron duly arrived. In his logbook the same day the CO of the CFS refresher squadron, Wing Commander G. H. Stainforth, rated Flying Officer D.R.S. Bader as an 'Exceptional' pilot.[24]

Bader had achieved his long sought-after goal. 'I must say that getting back into the R.A.F. was a masterpiece of persistence', he wrote with evident self-satisfaction many months later in a letter to Dingwall. And, though he did not know it yet, Bader had set an example for a flier a decade or so younger in age whose personal circumstances almost exactly matched his own at that age. Colin Hodgkinson had been training to be a pilot in the Fleet Air Arm when, through no fault of his own, his aircraft had crashed in May 1939 and left both his legs very badly mangled. One had to come off immediately above the knee, and the other refused to heal properly and was eventually lopped off below the knee. Though he possessed the physical stamina to see the operations through and survive – he too was a keen sportsman – Hodgkinson, as he admitted in his memoirs, was psychologically traumatised by what had happened and desperately unsure about his future. On Christmas Eve 1939 he had an epiphany:

> I was thumbing listlessly through the *Sunday Express* when the caption of a short paragraph caught my eye. A young man named Douglas Bader, I read, who had lost both his legs in an air crash ten years before at Woodley Aerodrome, near Reading, had talked his way into the R.A.F. and was now flying Hurricanes on operational duties [*sic*]. I dropped the paper and pulled myself up on the pillow [in hospital], the invalid's equivalent of sitting bolt upright. I collected the paper and read the paragraph again. Bader, it said, not only flew but danced, played golf and swam. He was married. He drove a car. I didn't mind about the dancing, the swimming and the golf. The essential point was that Bader was in the war. He was doing something significant at this significant time, as were my friends... To prove to myself that I could still be a man among men I had to get into the war, and in a fighting role... The only flying role possible for me, as for Bader, was as a pilot in an operational squadron.

Though prone to private self-doubt, Hodgkinson set about achieving his goal with a determination that would have made his role model proud. Even when Bader, replying to a letter in which the younger man announced his intentions, wrote something that turned out to be 'candid in its refusal to underestimate my difficulties', Hodgkinson persisted. With the help of one or two sympathetic admirers he managed to talk his way back into the Fleet Air Arm and eventually to a Spitfire squadron by the end of 1942.[25]

The role model himself, meanwhile, was not entirely happy in 19 Squadron during the first months of 1940. On arrival his spirits had been high, as onlookers witnessed when on his first flight Bader had beat up the aerodrome in order to demonstrate his talent. Relations with ground crew were at this stage of the war also apparently quite good, Bader winning points through his willingness to take 'erks' up on joyrides in the station Miles Magister. But he was acutely conscious of the fact that he was almost thirty, about the same age as the squadron CO and a decade older than the other junior pilots. He also came to believe that he knew more about flying than most of the young officers with whom he had contact. As a fellow fighter pilot later reflected, 'it was not an easy time for him.'[26]

According to his own later account Bader was poorly briefed in preparation for his initial Spitfire solo. 'I sat in the cockpit while a young pilot officer, with little experience, showed me the knobs. He omitted to tell me one important thing about the undercarriage that embarrassed me in due course, fortunately without damage.' It was true enough that pilots who were used to relatively slow, fixed-undercart biplane fighters often found it hard at first to master the relatively complex cockpit layout and procedures of the fast new monoplane fighters with their retractable undercarriages, flap controls, and radio communications. But Bader had already flown the Hurricane, had complete faith in himself, and likely was not paying full attention to what the young pilot officer – who in fact would have been flying Spitfires for many months – was saying. He had already impatiently cut the young man off when he tried to explain the unfamiliar and relatively complicated Radio/Telephone (R/T) procedure. As the pilot officer concerned, Frank Brinsden, later argued, 'the crew room had an ample supply of Pilot's Handling Notes and anyone who embarked upon his first solo in such a (for that time) radical aircraft without fully understanding its controls was a complete B.F.!' Whatever the cause, Bader found that, after carrying out what one observer described as 'an impeccable display of aerobatics', he could not lower the undercarriage and was unable to contact the ground for help. Through a mixture of trial and error he got the right action sequence and landed safely.[27]

That incident confirmed Bader's sense, justified or otherwise, that he should be leading the sprogs, not the other way round. So too did an incident that occurred a few days later. Six days after joining the squadron Bader went aloft for the first time as part of a Spitfire formation, a three-aircraft 'vic' led by his twenty-five year-old flight commander, Flight Lieutenant Brian Lane. Determined to demonstrate his flying prowess, and disregarding the fact that he was piloting a much faster and still relatively unfamiliar plane, Bader tucked his aircraft in only three feet or so behind the leading Spitfire's wing as if they were flying Gamecocks at Hendon. This required so much concentration, however, that Bader nearly crashed on landing after noticing only at the last moment that there was a hut in front of him. As it was, the tail wheel of the Spitfire was torn away. In Bader's view this was Lane's fault for choosing a glide path so close to a building, and despite being junior in rank he was not shy about commenting on his flight commander's family ancestry to his face.[28]

In his own mind Bader was a damn sight better pilot than many of the others in 19 Squadron in the first months of 1940. His ebullient belligerence in the mess and utter unwillingness to let artificial legs prevent him from doing what he wanted inspired something like awe in some observers, but those who had to fly with him as February gave way to March were sometimes less than impressed. For despite his great natural talent, it took Bader longer than he was willing to admit to fully adjust to flying the Spitfire in varying conditions. Pilot Officer Michael Lyne, who with a friend of his were detailed to give Bader some experience of the number one position in a 'vic', found that Bader could become disoriented when flying through clouds. More than once they followed Bader out of cloud 'only to find ourselves in a steep diving turn!' Bader was also not always the best judge of height, as he proved when, in carrying out a dummy line-astern attack on a RAF Wellington bomber during an exercise, he clipped a treetop at 250 mph and damaged one of his ailerons. On this occasion he managed to land without mishap, but shortly thereafter he would be involved in an actual crash. On 31 March he was detailed to lead a section of 19 Squadron aircraft deployed to Horsham St Faith in Norfolk on convoy patrol duty. As the section scrambled, its leader forgot one of the major differences between a Bulldog and the Spitfire I: the latter had a two-pitch propeller. Lyne recalled that 'Douglas forgot to put the airscrew into fine pitch for take-off, and cartwheeled across the main road and into a ploughed field.' Ironically, the absence of flesh and bone below the knee saved him on this occasion from likely trauma: when the Spitfire came to rest the shins of Bader's tin limbs were badly mangled. 'The ignominy was horrible,' as Laddie Lucas put it.[29]

Perhaps in order to compensate for this sort of *faux pas* – which happened to other new pilots but was not the kind of thing this particular old hand believed he was susceptible to – Bader not only constantly adjusted his new tin legs to get them in perfect working order but also once again took to doing dangerous aerobatics. Opinion on such flying was mixed. Some pilots believed that confidence in one's ability to control the machine under the unusual G-forces arising through aerobatic manoeuvres made one a better all-round flier which, they argued, in turn had a direct applicability to success in combat. Others wondered if Hendon-style aerobatics really had much correlation to the life-and-death business of avoiding enemy bullets and shells. There was general agreement, however, that low-level stunting, however personally satisfying, could easily lead to disaster. When he thought no one was watching, Bader did a couple of slow rolls right on the deck. As it happened he was indeed being observed, and by the Tangmere station commander no less. Happily for all concerned, Wing Commander 'Pingo' Lester knew that a standard dressing down would have no positive impact on a man as obstinate as Bader. 'Oh Douglas,' he said with feigned but effective artlessness, 'I *do* wish you wouldn't do that. You had *such* a nasty accident the last time.'[30]

Then there was the matter of tactics. In the years Bader had been away from the Air Force, Fighter Command had developed a numbered series of highly choreographed attack formations designed to deal with single or multiple enemy bomber formations coming unescorted across the North Sea. The relatively simple Fighter Attack No. 1, for example, involved a series of set commands and actions to bring a section of three aircraft into line-astern formation and then into an attack against a single bomber from behind. Fighter Attack No. 6, the most complicated of all, set out in detail the multiple commands and actions necessary to bring an entire squadron into an attack against a formation of nine bombers. As it happened much of what was contained in the regulations governing attacks underestimated the chaos that ensued once contact with the enemy was made. Just as important, the premises on which the numbered attacks were based – that the bombers would be without escorts and would come in smallish numbers – were rendered null and void when the German conquest of France provided the Luftwaffe with a plethora of bases just across the Channel. But it was these attacks that 19 Squadron and the rest of Fighter Command practised week after week during the Phoney War.[31]

Despite any evidence (as yet) to the contrary, Bader was not shy about voicing his disdain for the official tactical instructions: 'they struck me as absurd', he wrote later on. In part this was just a matter of personality. Bader was not a team player unless he was leading the team, and the old need to dominate and triumph was still there. 'There's only one damn way to do it,' he argued in front of Geoffrey Stephenson, 'and that's for everyone to pile in together from each side as close to the Hun as they can and let him have the lot'. In part, though, Bader was echoing the views of the First World War aces he had read about and admired at Cranwell – men like Billy Bishop, Albert Ball, and James McCudden – concerning the importance of good positioning before an attack: above the enemy, with the sun behind you, and near enough for a certain kill. 'Their methods and tactics', he later related, 'stayed in my mind when I started to fight in the air myself'. At least some of what Bader was advocating would prove to be very sound in light of large-scale air combat experience. But as Stephenson defensively remarked, in March 1940 there was no way of telling if the Air Ministry had got it wrong or not about tactics: 'you don't *know*, do you? *No* one knows.'[32]

To reiterate, Bader was not a happy man while serving in 19 Squadron, despite the fact that Stephenson had overlooked the Horsham prang and rated him 'Exceptional' as a Spitfire pilot.[33] According to the account Bader gave to biographer Paul Brickhill, this unhappy state of affairs ended in April 1940 when another friend from Cranwell days, Squadron Leader H. W. 'Tubby' Mermagen, asked him to take over one of the flights of 222 Squadron, also stationed at Duxford and also flying Spitfires. According to Mermagen himself, it was Bader 'who asked me if I would approach the AOC, Leigh-Mallory, regarding the possibility of him being transferred to 222 as a flight commander.' Either way, Mermagen certainly wanted to get rid of a flight commander he suspected of being a bit windy, and Leigh-Mallory consented to the transfer. In mid-April 1940, despite fears that the Horsham incident would blot his copybook, Bader was promoted to the rank of flight lieutenant and assumed command of 'A' Flight in 222 Squadron.[34]

Now that he held a command position, albeit a subordinate one, Bader started to feel better. Thelma stayed at a pub nearby, and as Gordon Sinclair recalled her husband 'was always holding court there', buying drinks and generally taking charge 'as though he was a sort of commanding officer – which he wasn't!' Bader began immediately to drill it into the heads of the 'A' Flight pilots that the textbook attacks they had been practising 'were no damn good' and show them how things ought to be done: up-sun and more-or-less line abreast. He did, however, continue to stress Hendon-style close-formation flying, as two newly arrived officers quickly discovered. Tim Vigors later remembered:

> As instructed Hilary [Eldridge] and I waited for Douglas to get airborne before we took off behind him. We could see him ahead of us and he slowed to allow us to catch up as planned. I gradually eased my Spitfire in towards him and Hilary was doing the same on his left. When I was about twenty feet away from him, with my wing tip slightly behind his, I straightened out and held my position. Hilary did the same. Douglas looked over first at me and then at Hilary. Then his voice came over [the radio] loud and clear. 'What the bloody hell do you boys think you're doing, dancing the old fashioned waltz? Come on get in really snug like you would if you were smooching with your girlfriend, cheek to cheek.' Hilary and I began to edge in closer until our wing tips were no more than five feet from our leader. 'OK, that's better,' Douglas said. 'I'll expect both of you to be a lot closer than that in a couple of days.'

Bader also positively revelled in demonstrating to a new audience his prowess in aerobatics, up to and including low-level work that broke several regulations. Best of all, at the end of May and on into June 1940 his new squadron was drawn into the air defence of the Dunkirk evacuation and thereby 222's first serious combat. Bader was utterly confident that he would prove equal to the test.[35]

When his squadron was sent down to Martlesham Heath in the early hours of 28 May in preparation for a patrol over the Channel, his self-confidence grated on the leader of another Spitfire squadron waiting for the green light. As his squadron hung about without orders an impatient Bader, stumping along with his characteristic sailor's gait, pipe jammed between his teeth, buttonholed a rather tense Robert Stanford Tuck, then a 92 Squadron pilot who had already seen more than enough friends killed over the Dunkirk beaches. 'What's the score, old boy?' Bader peremptorily demanded. Irritated by the belligerence of this unknown flight lieutenant from a squadron that had not yet been in action, Tuck snapped back 'Haven't a clue', adding, irritably: 'We're *all* waiting to find out, aren't we? It's all right – we know you're bloody keen types.' The two future aces, pilots who had never met or heard of each other, stared at one another angrily. Tuck added insult to injury by gratuitously suggesting that Bader tuck his raffish scarf into his tunic: 'if you bail out that loose end's liable to get caught on something and you'll hang your silly self.' Bader let loose a series of choice oaths, quietly but at length. In part this was simply a matter of two strong characters sparking off one another, or of like repelling like: both men, for example, were avid practitioners of low-level aerobatics. But on Bader's part it was also a reflection of his almost instinctive need to dominate a situation. 'I remember that my immediate reaction to this rather obstreperous man who came up to me that morning was that he was too cocky', Tuck recalled, 'and ought to be taken down a few pegs.'[36]

If this was the intent then his words had no long-lasting effect. When 222 Squadron returned from its first – and disappointingly uneventful – Dunkirk patrol out of Matlesham Heath on the morning of 28 May, it was diverted to Hornchurch, where the pilots of 54 and 65 Squadrons got their first taste of the Bader persona over lunch. Flight Lieutenant Gordon Olive recalled many years later how in the mess that day 'he walked somewhat stiffly across, sat down at table and immediately took charge of the conversation.' Bader, along with other 222 pilots, gazed with mild derision on the pilots from 54 Squadron they saw with stubble on their chins and carrying pistols. This was taken to be a sign of Hollywood-style showing off rather than – as was in fact the case – long hours and the sight of friends being forced to parachute into enemy-held territory. 'He was desperately keen to get to grips with the enemy', remembered Al Deere, another future ace who, like Tuck before him, was encountering the Bader persona for the first time. After peppering Deere and his CO with questions about the fighting over Dunkirk, Bader walked away and left his interlocutors with the feeling that he was not impressed with what they had to say. For someone who had not yet met the enemy this was a bit rich: yet that of course may have been part of the problem. Bader had not yet been blooded, but he was not about to concede for a moment that anyone who had might have the edge on him.[37]

On 29 May, 222 Squadron finally saw action, though much to his frustration Bader was not involved. There was a sudden and very brief head-on encounter with a group of Messerschmitt 110s, in which only the leader, Tubby Mermagen, was able to loose off a burst of machine-gun fire and see one of the enemy go down in flames. Mermagen frankly admitted after the squadron had returned to Northolt that he had been surprised at how effective his actions had been. Bader could not forbear from commenting that he too had been greatly surprised: a gratuitous dig at the CO's normal marksmanship from a man who, to his intense chagrin, had yet to find an enemy plane in his sights.[38]

Finally, on the first day of June 1940, Bader got his chance. Operating with three other squadrons, 222's Spitfires encountered twin-engine Me 110s again and, for the first time, the single-seat Me 109. Bader was in the thick of things, wheeling, diving, and firing with joyful eagerness. In the life-and-death struggles of mass aerial combat, with dozens of aircraft individually climbing, diving, banking, wheeling, and shooting at each other, it was not always possible for a pilot to tell for certain what damage he had inflicted. It was dangerous to follow a burning plane down until it crashed because of the risk of being bounced from above, and not easy to know if it was one's own fire or someone else's that had caused an aircraft to start falling apart or blow up in the air. Over-claiming, therefore, was always a problem for Fighter Command in assessing the damage it was inflicting on the Luftwaffe. There was no doubt in Tubby Mermagen's mind – and doubtless later in the mind of the squadron intelligence officer – that Bader vastly overstated the scale of his success in his first day of real dog-fighting. 'I got five for certain, Tubby, five for cert!' he exulted. The battle had been brief, and the CO was sceptical; privately he thought Bader was shooting a line. The man himself may have had second thoughts, given that Tim Vigors remembered him saying only that 'I definitely got one.' Whatever the truth of the matter, Bader was only credited with one Me 109 destroyed and one Me 110 damaged.[39]

This was only the beginning, of course, and Bader damaged a Heinkel 111 in the next patrol. He flew, with the rest of the squadron, several further patrols over Dunkirk, the last on 4 June. On one of these excursions, he later conceded, his impatience got the better of him.

I saw a Dornier bomber bombing one of our ships. He was about a mile away and I rushed at him with the throttle wide open giving myself just enough time for a hurried burst which silenced the rear gunner [a damage claim for which he was not apparently credited]. I had to pull up quickly to avoid a collision. Thinking about it later in the evening I got the message which every fighter pilot assimilates early in his career – if he hopes for a career at all. It is this: overtake your target slowly and relax before you start shooting; you will never get him in a hurry.[40]

By the end of the air operations over Dunkirk he had not only scored his first kill but also grown more certain about his tactical thinking. His three principles – 'he who has the height, controls the battle; he who has the sun, achieves surprise; he who goes in close, shoots them down'[41] – were unquestionably sound. But it is worth bearing in mind that other pilots were reaching similar conclusions in the context of the Dunkirk air battles. A. G. 'Sailor' Malan, for example, had started pushing 74 Squadron patrols up to between 20,000 and 24,000 feet over the beaches in order not to be bounced by Me 109s. Fighting leaders such as Malan, Tuck, and Deere were also thinking through problems concerning section formations and gun harmonisation ranges that had yet to occur to Bader.[42]

Impatience, along with competitiveness, would continue to shape Bader's behaviour. When the squadron was detailed to try and intercept night raiders in June 1940 from Kirton-in-Lindsey, he was determined to get his section off the ground faster than anyone else, as Tim Vigors later explained:

On the sound of the alarm bell my first responsibility was to seize Douglas's [right] leg and place it onto the stump of his thigh which would be sticking over the end of the bed. Hilary would be helping him with his left leg. At the same time his fitter and rigger, the two mechanics who were responsible for the maintenance of the engine and airframe of his aircraft, would have rushed through the door [of the dispersal hut]. Seizing him under the arms they would carry him bodily out of the door and down the steps onto the grass. Lifted by them onto the rear edge of the wing he would grab the sides of the cockpit and lever himself into his seat.

With practice Bader was able to scramble in two minutes and fifty seconds.[43]

In the meantime the leader of 'A' Flight in 222 Squadron found himself in the embarrassing position of having inadvertently pranged another Spitfire. Bader was coming in to land after a night patrol on 12 June but misjudged his approach: 'Douglas came in far too high and far too fast', according to his CO. He skidded off the flare path and crashed into a hedge, seriously damaging his aircraft (a 'Category 1' accident in RAF parlance). Though uninjured, Bader was, as he later admitted, infuriated at this turn of events and at the time apparently loath to admit responsibility. Mermagen was not impressed when Bader came away shouting that 'the bloody flare path is laid out badly.' In the CO's judgement the approach and landing had been 'sheer bad flying.'[44]

Despite this unhappy incident, which Bader feared might lead him to be grounded, Mermagen still thought that Bader was both a fine flier – he officially rated him 'Exceptional' eleven days later – and 'quite an outstanding personality' among the pilots of Fighter Command. Whether he still believed that Bader was the best of subordinates as a flight commander, however, is questionable. According to his own account the accolades the 222 Squadron CO provided to higher authority helped speed Bader's promotion, and therefore posting; as Bader recounted to Paul Brickhill, Mermagen was grinning when he greeted him one day with the news that he was leaving. The word was out that Douglas Bader was to be promoted again and given the type of command he really yearned for: a squadron of his own.[45]

Notes

[1]Paul Brickhill, *Reach for the Sky* (London: Collins, 1954), p. 68.

[2]On Bader learning to fly see Royal Air Force Museum Department of Research and Information Services [hereafter RAFM], X002–5731, D.R.S. Bader logbook, 1928; Michael G. Burns, *Bader* (London: Cassell, 1998 edn), pp. 12–16; Brickhill, *Reach for the Sky*, pp. 31–33.

[3]St Edward's School Archives, Bader Collection [hereafter SESA], Adjutant for Commandant to Kendall, 23 September 1930; D. Bader foreword to Peter Hearn, *Sky High Irvin* (London: Hale, 1983), p. 9; Churchill College Cambridge [hereafter CCC], Churchill Papers, CHUR 2/180, Brief Note on Group Captain Douglas R. S. Bader, p. 1; see Brickhill, *Reach for the Sky*, p. 34.

[4]Douglas Bader, 'Fighter Pilot', in E. Leyland and T.E. Scott-Chard (eds), *The Boys' Book of the Air* (London: Edmund Ward, 1957), p. 60. New pilots coming out of Cranwell were sent to fly the various types of service aircraft on the basis of capability and interest. R. De La Bère, *A History of the Royal Air Force College Cranwell* (Aldershot: Poloden, 1934), p. 27.

[5]http://members.lycos.co.uk/jadastra/Bader.html (accessed 30 September 2003), John Behague, 'Douglas Bader: The Man behind the Legend', p. 3; Laddie Lucas, *Flying Colours* (London: Wordsworth, 2001 edn), p. 49; see Brickhill, *Reach for the Sky*, pp. 40–41. On delivering the birthday present see *Yorkshire Post Magazine*, 1 January 2005; On Woollett see also Kenneth Cross and Vincent Orange, *Straight and Level* (London: Grub Street, 1993), p. 36.

[6]Bader, 'Fighter Pilot', *Boys' Book*, p. 62; see Burns, *Bader*, pp. 17–22. On the importance of the annual Hendon display to the RAF see David Enrico Omissi, 'The Hendon Air Pageant, 1920–37' in John M. Mackenzie (ed.), *Popular Imperialism and the Military* (Manchester: Manchester University Press, 1991), pp. 201–02.

[7]Lucas, *Flying Colours*, p. 49.

[8]Cross and Orange, *Straight and Level*, p. 36; see Brickhill, *Reach for the Sky*, p. 42. On the accident rate see The National Archives [hereafter NA], AIR 10/1482, Half-yearly report on flying accidents in the Royal Air Force No. 16, July–December 1931, p. 17.

[9]Cross and Orange, *Straight and Level*, p. 37

[10]Ibid., p. 38; Brickhill, *Reach for the Sky*, pp. 44, 42.

[11]RAFM, X002–5731, Bader logbook, 14 December 1931. For varying accounts of what exactly happened at Woodley see Brickhill, *Reach for the Sky*, pp. 46–47; Burns, *Bader*, pp. 24–25; Lucas, *Flying Colours*, pp. 51–53; John Frayn Turner, *Douglas Bader* (Shrewsbury: Airlife, 2001 edn), p. 7; Richard Garrett, *Sky High* (London: Weidenfeld and Nicolson, 1991), p. 157. On Phillips being blamed for not stopping Bader see NA, AIR 43/7, M&AFD 8/99/HF, Colonel i/c Military and Air Force Dept., JAG's Office, to AOC Fighting Area, *re* Flying Officer G. W. Phillips case, 5 February 1932. On the unlikely tale that Bader was drunk at the time see Imperial War Museum Sound Archive [hereafter IWMSA] 11544, G.C. Unwin TS, pp. 30–31. RAF aircraft were not supposed to land at civilian aerodromes, but Phillips claimed that they had been forced to land because a map had fallen in his cockpit and he feared it might foul the controls. See NA, AIR 43//7, Colonel i/c Military & Air Force Dept., JAG's Office, to AOC Fighting Area, M&AFD3/108/

FGC, 9 March 1932. He was nevertheless court-martialled for not stopping Bader and for doing the Prince of Wales' Feathers at low level. See ibid., Colonel i/c Military & Air Force Dept., JAG's Office, to AOC Fighting Area, M&AFD 1/111/ HF, 21 March 1932. Not that it mattered much, but the RAF were given the impression, either by Bader or witnesses, that he had begun his role at 200 feet rather than at a lower height. See AIR 10/1482, Half-yearly report on flying accidents in the Royal Air Force No. 16, July–December 1931, p. 18.

[12]Colin Hodgkinson, *Best Foot Forward* (London: Odams, 1957), p. 75; see Brickhill, *Reach for the Sky*, pp. 48–60, 66. See also Bader's comments on the case of Peter Spencer in Eileen Waugh, *No Man an Island* (London: Triton, 1970), pp. 9, 36.

[13]Liddell Hart Centre [hereafter LHC], Nicholas Eadon papers, box 3, Bader to Eadon, 4 April 1968; Brickhill, *Reach for the Sky*, pp. 81, 84–85, *et al*. On the artificial legs see Ministry of Pensions, *Artificial Limbs and their Relation to Amputations* (London: HMSO, 1939), pp. 23–25. On the normal reactions to the loss of limbs see R.D. Langdale Kelhan, *Artificial Limbs in the Rehabilitation of the Disabled* (London: HMSO, 1957), pp. 3, 4, 6.

[14]NA, AIR 27/287, 23 Sqn ORB, 14 December 1931; see Brickhill, *Reach for the Sky*, chs.5–7, *et al*.

[15]Brickhill, *Reach for the Sky*, pp. 100–03, 105–06, 107–08, 111–13.

[16]IWMSA 6487/2, E. M. Woolley; LHC, Nicholas Eadon Papers, Box 3, Bader to Eadon, 27 April 1970; see Brickhill, *Reach for the Sky*, p. 114.

[17]IWMSA 6630/6, J. Cox; see Brickhill, *Reach for the Sky*, pp. 114–16.

[18]Lucas, *Flying Colours*, p. 53; see also http://members.lycos.co.uk/jadastra/ Bader.html (accessed 30 September 2003), John Behague, 'Douglas Bader: The Man behind the Myth', p. 3.

[19]Burns, *Bader*, p. 27. On the Air Ministry letter, which Brickhill seems to have seen, see Brickhill, *Reach for the Sky*, pp. 116–17. On the lorry incident see ibid., p. 116. On Bader voicing disdain for a possible ground job see ibid., pp. 117, 68. On the branch options in the RAF at this time see John James, *The Paladins* (London: Macdonald, 1990), pp. 133–34. It is perhaps worth noting that there *was* in fact a precedent for keeping a pilot with two tin legs in a flying role. Captain David Drummond had flown with the Royal Flying Corps in World War I despite having two tin legs. See *The Times*, 11 September 1982.

[20]SESA, Bader to Dingwall, 3 January 1941. On Bader as a civilian see Brickhill, *Reach for the Sky*, pp. 117–44. On Bader at Shell see also Jeremy Treglown, *Roald Dahl* (London: Faber, 1994), pp. 30–31.

[21]RAFM, MF 10027/4, Portal to Bader, 31 August 1939; Brickhill, *Reach for the Sky*, p. 144; see ibid., pp. 137–38; Denis Richards, *Portal of Hungerford* (London: Heinemann, 1977), p. 136.

[22]Brickhill, *Reach for the Sky*, pp. 145–46; Jill Lucas in *Britain's War Heroes: Douglas Bader, Fighter Ace* (Blakeway Associates, 2005).

[23]Turner, *Douglas Bader*, pp. 20–21; Brickhill, *Reach for the Sky*, p. 148.

[24]See NA, AIR 27/252, 19 Sqn ORB, 7 February 1940; Woodhall quoted in Dilip Sarkar, *Bader's Duxford Fighters* (Worcester: Ramrod, 1997), pp. 34–35; RAFM, B 354, Bader logbook, 27 November 1939–7 February 1940; Burns, *Bader*, p. 31; Brickhill, *Reach for the Sky*, pp. 151–55; see also NA, AIR 29/604.

[25]Hodgkinson, *Best Foot Forward*, pp. 107, 89–90, *passim*; SESA, Bader to Dingwall, 3 January 1941.

[26]SESA, C. Foxley-Norris address at St Edward's School, 4 December 1984. On trips in the Magister see E. French in Sarkar, *Duxford Fighters*, p. 36. On beating up the field on arrival see F. Roberts in Dilip Sarkar, *Battle of Britain: Last Look Back* (Worcester: Ramrod, 2002), p. 114.

[27]Briden quoted in Sarkar, *Duxford Fighters*, pp. 35–36; Douglas Bader, *Fight for the Sky* (London: Sidgwick and Jackson, 1975 edn), p. 12; see Brickhill, *Reach for the Sky*, pp. 156–7. On the Spitfire solo aerobatic display see Bobby Oxspring, *Spitfire Command* (London: Kimber, 1984), p. 42. On the kind of cockpit briefing Bader would likely have got see Geoffrey Page, *Shot Down in Flames* (London: Grub Street, 1999 edn), p. 21; Paul Richey and Norman Franks, *Fighter Pilot's Summer* (London: Grub Street, 1993), p. 73. On pilots used to relatively simple biplanes having trouble adjusting to relatively complicated monoplane fighters see IWMSA 20486/1, J.R.C. Young; Barry Sutton, *The Way of a Pilot* (London: Macmillan, 1943), p. 34; Peter Townsend, *Time and Chance* (London: Collins, 1978), p. 99. Even compared to advanced trainers the Spitfire could be intimidating: 'The jump from the Harvard to the Spitfire was immense', as one pilot put it (D. Green in *Spitfire: Power, Grace and Glory* [DD Video, 1998]).

[28]Brickhill, *Reach for the Sky*, pp. 157–58.

[29]Lucas, *Flying Colours*, p. 93; Lyne quoted in Sarkar, *Duxford Fighters*, pp. 36–37; see IWMSA 11544, G.C. Unwin TS, 29; Imperial War Museum Department of Documents [hereafter IWM], P.I. Howard-Williams, p. 3; RAFM, B 354, Bader logbook, 31 March 1940; Brickhill, *Reach for the Sky*, p. 160. On being in awe of Bader because of his legs see Oxspring, *Spitfire Command*, p. 42.

[30]Lucas, *Flying Colours*, p. 91. On the argument in favour of aerobatics see Brian Kingcome, *A Willingness to Die* (Stroud: Tempus, 1999), pp. 49–50; W.G.G. Duncan Smith, *Spitfire into Battle* (London: John Murray, 1981), p. 24; Athol Forbes and Hubert Allen (eds), *Ten Fighter Boys* (London: Collins, 1942), p. 14; see also Roland Beamont, *Phoenix into Ashes* (London: Kimber, 1968), pp. 32–33; IWMSA 006663 TS, H. Broadhurst, pp. 20–21, 22–23, 24. On dangerous aerobatics as a substitute challenge when combat was not in the offing see Anthony Bartley, *Smoke Trails in the Sky* (London: Kimber, 1984), p. 26; H. Welford in Dilip Sarkar, *A Few of the Many*

(Worcester: Ramrod, 1995), p. 24; Richard C. Smith, *Hornchurch Scramble* (London: Grub Street, 2000), p. 59. Aerobatics had, it is worth noting, been a major source of rivalry between squadrons before the war. See Sutton, *Way of a Pilot*, p. 33. On the dangers of low-level aerobatics in particular see Colin Gray, *Spitfire Patrol* (London: Hutchinson, 1988), p. 13; Victor Houart (ed.), *Lonely Warrior* (London: Souvenir, 1956), p. 94; Page, *Shot Down in Flames*, p. 40; Noel Monks, *Squadrons Up!* (London: Gollancz, 1940), pp. 13–15. On pilot errors among those new to the Spitfire or Hurricane see Dennis David, *My Autobiography* (London: Grub Street, 2000), p. 47; Alan C. Deere, *Nine Lives* (Canterbury: Wingham, 1999 edn), p. 37 [Deere, another soon-to-be ace, made the same mistake as Bader concerning propeller pitch]; Neville Duke, *Test Pilot* (London: Grub Street, 1992), p. 33. On Bader fiddling with his new legs see G. Unwin in Sarkar, *Battle of Britain: Last Look Back*, p. 51.

[31]For the numbered attacks see NA, AIR 2/3601, Fighter Command Attacks, 1939; see also AIR 16/74, encl. 5A; AIR 16/83, encl. D1, HQ 12 Group to HQ Bomber Command, 7 February 1939, App. A; Norman Franks, *RAF Fighter Command, 1936–1938* (Sparkford: Patrick Stephens, 1992), pp. 38–41.

[32]Brickhill, *Reach for the Sky*, p. 159; Bader foreword to James M. Dudgeon, '*Mick*' (London: Hale, 1981), p. 15; Bader, *Fight for the Sky*, p. 14; see http://home. tiscali.be/ed.ragas/awshistory/awsbader.html (accessed 12 February 2004), B. Cunningham interview with Bader for *Code One*, p. 1. Stephenson would discover how wrong the area attacks were when he tried them over Dunkirk and was among the resultant casualties. See IWMSA 11544, G.C. Unwin TS, p. 6; Unwin in Dilip Sarkar, *Spitfire Squadron* (New Malden: Air Research, 1990), p. 111; see also Deere, *Nine Lives*, p. 54; K. Lee in Steve Darlow, *Five of the Few* (London: Grub Street, 2006), p. 28. The books on the Great War aces to which Bader had access in the Cranwell library included Walter A. Briscoe and H. Russell Stannard, *Captain Ball, V.C.* (London: Jenkins, 1918); Floyd Phillips Gibbons, *The Red Knight of Germany* (London: Heinemann, 1927); James Thomas Byford McCudden, *Five Years in the Royal Flying Corps* (London: The Aeroplane, 1919); Manfred von Richthofen, *The Red Air Fighter*, C.G. Grey, ed. (London: The Aeroplane, 1918).

[33]RAFM, B 354, Bader logbook, 31 March 1940.

[34]NA, AIR 27/252, 19 Sqn ORB, 16 March 1940; AIR 27/1371, 222 Sqn ORB, 17 April 1940; Mermagen in Sarkar, *Duxford Fighters*, p. 38; Brickhill, *Reach for the Sky*, p. 161.

[35]Tim Vigors, *Life's Too Short to Cry* (London: Grub Street, 2006), p. 113; G. Sinclair in *Britain's War Heroes: Douglas Bader, Fighter Ace* (Blakeway Associates, 2005); Brickhill, *Reach for the Sky*, pp. 164–68; see Burns, *Bader*, p. 37.

[36]Larry Forrester, *Fly for Your Life* (Garden City, NY: Nelson Doubleday, 1978 edn), p. 105. On Tuck as an aerobatic type see Bartley, *Smoke Trails*, p. 19. The account of this incident given to Paul Brickhill by Bader suggested that Tuck was laconic

rather than abrasive (see Brickhill, *Reach for the Sky*, p. 169): but then Bader was not always a good judge of how his ebullient persona was being received.

[37]Deere, *Nine Lives*, p. 58; Gordon Olive and Dennis Newton, *The Devil at 6 O'clock* (Loftus, NSW: Australian Military History Publications, 2001), p. 68; see Richard C. Smith, *Al Deere* (London: Grub Street, 2003), p. 32; Brickhill, *Reach for the Sky*, p. 170.

[38]Brickhill, *Reach for the Sky*, p. 172.

[39]Vigors, *Life's Too Short*, p. 128; Mermagen in *Secret Lives: Douglas Bader* (Twenty Twenty Productions, 1996); Mermagen quoted in Sarkar, *Duxford Fighters*, p. 38. The account of this combat in *Reach for the Sky* mentions encounters with only two enemy aircraft, an Me 109 and an Me 110. See Brickhill, *Reach for the Sky*, p. 173.

[40]Bader, *Fight for the Sky*, p. 15.

[41]Burns, *Bader*, p. 44; see Bader foreword to Dudgeon, *'Mick'*. On the air operations over Dunkirk as a whole see Norman L.R. Franks, *Air Battle Dunkirk, 26 May–3 June 1940* (London: Grub Street, 2000).

[42]Norman L.R. Franks, *Sky Tiger* (London: Kimber, 1980), pp. 44–45; see Ira Jones, *Tiger Squadron* (London: Allen, 1954), pp. 281–2; see also,, N. Weir to Father, 28 May 1940, in Norman L.R. Franks, *Wings of Freedom* (London: Kimber, 1980), p. 35.

[43]Vigors, *Life's Too Short*, pp. 142–43.

[44]Mermagen in *Secret Lives: Douglas Bader* (Twenty Twenty Productions, 1996); Mermagen in Sarkar, *Duxford Fighters*, p. 38; Brickhill, *Reach for the Sky*, p. 176; see NA, AIR 27/1371, 222 Sqn ORB, 13 June 1940; AIR 22/255, Aircraft casualties as flying accidents for the week ended 15 June 1940. To be fair, Bader did not try and shift the blame when relating this incident to his first biographer (see Brickhill, *Reach for the Sky*, p. 176) and according to Tim Vigors – in contrast to the recollection of Tubby Mermagen – Bader was quite contrite and self-accusatory at the time (see Vigors, *Life's Too Short*, p. 144–45).

[45]Brickhill, *Reach for the Sky*, p. 176; Mermagen in Sarkar, *Duxford Fighters*, p. 39; RAFM, B 354, Bader logbook, 23 June 1940. On Bader fearing that he would be grounded see also J. Lucas in *Douglas Bader: Secret Lives* (Twenty Twenty Productions, 1996).

CHAPTER THREE

Squadron Commander

This is going to be the best squadron in the command if it kills me.

Douglas Bader in conversation with Warrant Officer Bernard West,
Coltishall, July 1940[1]

Bader, according to Tubby Mermagen, 'nearly fell through the floor'
when told he would get to command his own squadron. In his own
mind his most recent flying accident had seriously jeopardised his
chances. And, unbeknownst to this officer now thirty years of age,
the AOC-in-C of Fighter Command, Air Chief Marshal Sir Hugh
Dowding, was of the opinion that the upper age limit for fighter
squadron commanders ought to be twenty-six. What counted in
his favour was the support of a number of commanders within
12 Group, and above that of the AOC himself, Air Vice-Marshal
Trafford Leigh-Mallory. It was his patronage, starting with the gift
of 242 Squadron, which would allow Bader to achieve just about
everything he wanted as a leader in the sky.[2]

Leigh-Mallory was very different in character and background
from the officer whose fortunes he would oversee. He was not a
fighter pilot, his flying career having been built in the less-than-
glamorous world of army co-operation. He was not an extrovert,
the aloofness and pomposity noted by some of those who worked
with him masking a considerable shyness. He was also not an
instinctual commander, relying instead on a mastery of administrative and logistical detail. 'Leigh-Mallory was a staff officer, pure
and simple', Tom Neil of 249 Squadron remembered. Yet having
conversed with Bader on several occasions and consulted both his
squadron and station commanders as to his abilities, Leigh-Mallory
was clearly most impressed. The decision to promote Bader was in
part a simple matter of command logic. 242 Squadron, which had

been badly mauled in France and suffered from low morale, clearly needed a strong leader. Bader was a Cranwell graduate, had seen combat as a pilot, was a proven flight commander, and above all possessed the self-confidence and the drive necessary to go in and ginger up a badly shaken unit. It is clear that Leigh-Mallory also warmed to a personality so unlike his own. Over time Bader would become something akin to a surrogate son – they were two decades apart in age – and achieve the kind of heroic status accorded Leigh-Mallory's dead brother, the famous Everest climber, which had eluded Trafford himself. And, last but not least, there was personal advancement. Leigh-Mallory was ambitious, and wanted to make full use of his power, granted only the previous month, to appoint station and squadron commanders who would ipso facto feel a sense of loyalty and obligation to him which might someday come in useful. The AOC, for his part, would in turn become another, and arguably the most important, of the admired father figures who featured in Bader's life.[3]

On 23 June 1940, after hearing from Mermagen what was in the wind, Bader drove to Hucknall to be briefed by Leigh-Mallory on his new job. Informed by a still-smarting Bader that the man he was about to promote had pranged another Spitfire, the AOC was uncharacteristically jolly, pointing out with a smile that he was about to take command of a Hurricane rather than a Spitfire squadron. On a more serious note, Bader obtained a quick rundown on his new job. 242 (Canadian) Squadron had been formed in the autumn of the previous year using some of the many Canadian officers then serving in the Royal Air Force. It had served beside other Hurricane squadrons in France and become badly disorganised and disoriented as Allied forces fell back before the German onslaught in May 1940. Pilots had been killed, kit and spares had been lost, and cohesion had broken up as the squadron command structure buckled under the strain of a fighting retreat. According to the relevant operations record book, only 'remnants' of 242 arrived at Coltishall on 20 June. To what extent this was the result of poor leadership by the first CO, who became separated from his men, remains open to debate. But when the AOC inspected the unit the day after it landed, he was certain that something had to be done to rally and reorganise pilots who had done their best but were clearly feeling browned off. The newly promoted Squadron Leader D.R.S. Bader was to 'talk tough' and beat the Hurricane squadron back into shape. The AOC wished him luck and stressed that he could ask for anyone he wanted if replacements were needed.[4]

Bader's first instinct was to ask the members of the section he led to join him. After lengthy discussion, however, the pilots concerned decided to decline the invitation. 'That mad bugger will get us all killed when the real war starts!' Hilary Eldridge laughingly remarked.[5]

Bader learned more about the state of his new squadron after he arrived at Coltishall on 24 June. At first he found he could not enter the aerodrome because he did not know the password. Bader roared at the sentry that he could not know the password since he was arriving for the first time; but it was only after the duty officer had been contacted that he was finally allowed onto the station. He quickly ran into his old pal Rupert Leigh, now commanding 66 Squadron, who commented that since they were now of equal rank Bader could be rude to him without, as had been the case in the past, contravening regulations on how a junior officer should address a more senior officer.

On a more practical note Leigh filled him in on his new squadron, as did the station commander, Wing Commander Walter 'Bike' Beisiegel, and the veteran Tory MP who was serving as adjutant to 242 Squadron, Flight Lieutenant Peter Macdonald. What they had to tell him confirmed Bader in his view that he had to act quickly and decisively even before assuming formal command on 26 June.[6]

His first attempt at exerting authority, Bader had to admit, went awry. Accompanied by the squadron adjutant, he went to inspect the 242 pilots at standby readiness in the dispersal huts. He was shocked to discover that 'Leigh-Mallory had understated the situation.' After announcing his arrival through the adjutant Bader found the sullen Canadians, rather than standing in his presence and quickly answering his questions as to who was in charge, continued to lounge about, reluctant to respond and barely acknowledging his presence at all. 'In fact most of them, still lying flat on their backs, lowered their comics, looked over the tops and did not like what they saw', Bader later remembered. 'They raised their comics again and went on reading.' Furious, the new CO had the adjutant assemble the pilots for what he described as 'a reasonable three-minute talk' on dress and deportment. This did not go down well. When Bader finished his tirade and asked if anyone had anything to say, a particularly insubordinate pilot officer, Stan Turner, gave his opinion of the CO's views: 'Horse-shit' – adding, after a pregnant pause in which Bader looked as if he was about to explode, 'Sir.'[7]

Not a good start. Bader, to his credit, instinctively realised that he had made a tactical error, and that he would need to prove his authority in a more impressive and less rank-conscious manner. Rather than dressing down Turner he silently stumped out, climbed into a Hurricane, took off, and proceeded to demonstrate for the next half-hour his skill in Hendon-style aerobatics. By the time he landed the pilots of 242 Squadron were aware that their new commanding officer was no rulebook-bound desk-jockey.[8]

Though he was made aware that his pilots had lost much of their uniform kit in France and had not yet received replacement articles, Bader, after apologising for his remarks about their scruffy appearance the next day, insisted that they should dress like officers and gentlemen, especially in the mess. This meant borrowing ties, shirts, shoes and whatever else was missing from friends and going into Norwich to order from the local tailors whatever was needed (the CO assuring them that the necessary funds would be forthcoming). The guarantee was of course appreciated; but wearing collar and tie in the cockpit, as Bader did, was already proving difficult and was potentially dangerous. The need to constantly scan the sky meant that necks chaffed against collars, while the collar-and-tie combination could be deadly if a pilot had to ditch in the Channel and clothing swelled as it soaked up water.[9]

Smartness out of the way, Bader began to make decisions as to who should stay and who should go. The adjutant, Peter Macdonald, was a good source of information on squadron and other matters and an administrator who could keep paperwork – which Bader hated – at arm's length. The chief engineer, Warrant Officer Bernard West, was a long-service air force NCO of a kind Bader, himself a regular by training and in outlook, recognised and respected: not least, perhaps, because he knew West's sense of discipline meant that he would defer to the CO in most instances. 'I always felt that Squadron Leader Bader bullied him a bit to keep the aircraft serviceable', remembered a member of 242's groundcrew staff.[10] Executive positions in the air were another matter. Bader immediately decided that both flight commanders would have to go. 'If', as another fighter pilot put it, 'he detected any flaws, in character, in skill, in ability or in determination he was absolutely ruthless in getting rid of the individual concerned.'[11]

Whether his judgement that one of them was gun-shy is open to debate – the officer in question went on to become a DFC-winning fighter ace[12] – but it was certainly not unheard of during the war for a new CO to select his own subordinates soon after arrival. After all, as Bader himself later explained in reference to the changes he made, 'I was given the squadron and told to clean it up'.[13] He wanted his flight commanders to be reliable and experienced officers whom he would hand-pick, pilots who would recognise that their promotions were due to his intervention. Flight Lieutenant Eric Ball he knew from 19 Squadron; while the fact that Flight Lieutenant George Powell-Sheldon, recommended by 12 Group HQ, had been to Cranwell – Bader was always a bit of a snob about the college – more than made up for an unfortunate stammer.[14]

On 29 June the new CO took 242 off the normal routines of a fighter squadron on an operational station – waiting at various states of readiness, going off on patrol, and so forth – in order to concentrate on practice flying. Both as individuals and as parts of a formation, the pilots of 242 had to master the kind of aerobatic and other manoeuvres that Bader expected of them. As he later explained:

> If you have been used to controlling an aeroplane upside-down, sideways or in a vertical dive or upward zoom you have become used to being in those odd positions with the ground instead of the sky above your head and your mind remains clear. You find yourself in all these positions in combat and you don't get flustered. As a result you can shoot in whatever position you may find yourself.

Only on 1 July, after forty-two hours of intensive tutoring in the air, did the unit return to the station duty roster: and then only for an hour's readiness at dawn and dusk. The ground crews, meanwhile, were being pushed to keep every aircraft serviceable.[15]

The problem here was not the aircraft themselves, as the squadron had received no less than eighteen brand new Hurricanes, but rather the absence of parts and tools to repair them once sustained combat commenced. Mr West had put in formal requests for the necessary items to replace what had been lost in France, but when nothing had arrived within ten days of Bader's arrival, the impatient

CO decided to try and force the pace. 'Squadron Leader reported [to both 12 Group and Fighter Command HQ that] Squadron operationally trained day, so far as pilots were concerned', the 4 July 1940 entry in the 242 operations record book explained, 'but non-operational as regards equipment.' Only after the signals had been sent did Bader tell his outraged station commander what he had done. Bader did not care about having given offence. Tools and spares were vital if his squadron was to be truly combat-ready. If that meant bypassing channels and going directly to the top, so be it. Bursting to get back into action and, as always, viewing the problem in simple binary terms – right/wrong, black/white – Bader did not stop to explore the option, successfully pursued elsewhere, of asking another squadron to lend a hand. In his mind the needs of 242 –*his* needs – trumped both normal channels and the logistical requirements of other units waiting ahead in line.[16]

A response came from Fighter Command the same day. A squadron leader in charge of equipment phoned to argue that there were shortages in many units and that 242 ought to be able to borrow what it needed in the short term from other squadrons. Bader said this was not enough, and the conversation quickly degenerated into a shouting match and ended with phone receivers being slammed into their cradles. The 12 Group reaction was more sympathetic. The AOC flew in to Coltishall on 8 July to see the situation for himself, and without specifically endorsing Bader's actions said that he could see why he had done what he had done. But resolution of the crisis Bader had stirred up now rested in the hands of the Commander-in-Chief: the CO of 242 Squadron had been summoned to Bentley Priory, the Headquarters of Fighter Command, for an interview with Air Chief Marshal Sir Hugh Dowding.[17]

Bader might have been in for the high-jump, but once again luck was with him. The C-in-C did not think much of his signal, but his anger was deflected onto the unfortunate squadron leader with whom Bader had spoken on the phone when he admitted that he had predicted the C-in-C would be furious when he heard about what Bader had done. A formal and somewhat austere character, 'Stuffy' Dowding did not take kindly to anyone predicting how he would or would not react, least of all a comparatively junior officer. The offending squadron leader lost his job at Fighter Command; so too did the station equipment officer at Coltishall. 242 Squadron received the requested equipment within forty-eight hours. With everything Bader needed at hand and with the C-in-C apparently an ally, 242 Squadron became fully operational at noon on 9 July 1940.[18]

Two days later Bader scored a second official kill. The weather that day was poor, and when the call came to scramble a section for an interception of a probable enemy aircraft picked up by RDF (radar), he argued that low cloud made a section scramble too hazardous: instead he would do the job himself. Once again luck was with him. Despite layers of cloud he managed to spot the intruder – a lone Dornier 17 – and send it down in flames. What was more, a member of the Observer Corps on the coast had seen the Dornier crash into the sea, allowing Bader's claim to be confirmed. Everyone was duly impressed, the Coltishall operations record book noting his 'excellent moral[e] and fine leadership' in taking on and successfully completing a job he considered too hazardous for others to undertake.[19]

Bader had proved himself in the eyes of his men, and he in turn took an almost seigneurial interest in their welfare. 'I felt they were *mine*,' he later explained to Paul Brickhill, going on to relate how he refused to brook any criticism of or outside interference in the actions of either 242 Squadron pilots or ground personnel. With the help of Peter Macdonald he even managed to persuade the Norwich police not to lay charges when some of his team grew too rowdy during a night on the town. Maintaining absolute authority was, as he frankly later admitted, 'an obsession with me'. Thus when the station commander had consigned a number of ground-crewmen to sleep in a hangar as a punishment for being sloppy about blackout precautions in their usual quarters, the CO of 242 Squadron had instantly taken offence. Bader stumped into Bike's office, and after saluting threw his cap down, seated himself on the edge of the wing commander's desk, tapped his pipe on his knee, leaned forward with a glare and told his station commander precisely what he thought of him. Beisiegel, a nominal superior who was rapidly coming to terms with chronic insubordination from this particular quarter, commented aloud that references to his ancestry were exactly what he had expected from someone like Bader. Nevertheless the station CO gave way and the 'erks' returned to their quarters.[20]

Making the squadron his own fiefdom, though, was only a means to an end: that end being to shoot down Luftwaffe aircraft, and in large numbers. Unfortunately the rest of July and the first weeks of August 1940 within 12 Group proved frustratingly free of major enemy activity. Things were so quiet, in fact, that Bader felt no compunction in muscling in on some else's prey on 21 August. That day the CO of 242 Squadron was bringing in to land a section of aircraft he had led on a practice flight when he overheard on the radio the sector controller vectoring a section of 66 Squadron in the direction of Yarmouth. Bader at once opened the throttle and sped off towards Yarmouth in the hope of finding something to shoot at. Bader spotted and fired at a Do 17, but to his immense chagrin lost it in a bank of cloud. Though he had not seen the plane go down, he was able to claim it as his third kill when the bodies of a Do 17 crew were fished out of the sea near Yarmouth. Comparison of Luftwaffe and RAF records, however, suggests it was in fact someone from 611 squadron that, subsequent to Bader's brief encounter, had shot down this particular aircraft.[21]

Such excitement, though, was the exception rather than the rule. Luftwaffe attacks on Channel convoys had started in July, to be sure, and by mid-August a full-scale air assault on the RAF fighter airfields in south-east England had begun. These raids, however, were met for the most part by the squadrons of 11 Group under Air Vice-Marshal Keith Park. 242 Squadron was part of 12 Group to the north, whose job it was to protect the industrial midlands. Convoy patrols, formation practice, and the occasional – and usually frustratingly inconclusive – scramble to intercept an enemy reconnaissance aircraft did not satisfy a restless squadron leader. 'Long hours, boring hours,' Bader remembered of waiting at readiness, 'hell on the digestion.' When in late July he noticed Brian Lane, the CO of 19 Squadron, sporting the ribbon of a newly awarded Distinguished Flying Cross, Bader pointedly commented: 'I must get one of those'. He was acutely aware that any laurels to be won would be the result of the increasingly heavy fighting going on further south. Despite the fact that some of the new pilots he was receiving were so poorly prepared that he insisted they be posted back for further training, Bader yearned for his squadron to be sent into action. When he phoned Leigh-Mallory to plead his case, however, he was told that 12 Group could only become embroiled if 11 Group asked for help. This was true enough: but, unbeknownst to Bader, who alternately raged and sulked at the injustice of it all, the AOC made sure that as the Battle of Britain unfolded 242 was not among the squadrons rotated into 11 Group to replace weary 11 Group squadrons being sent northward to recuperate from heavy fighting. It was significant, however, that the AOC *was* prepared to allow 242 Squadron to fly down from Coltishall to Duxford, nearer the border between the two groups, at the end of August when it looked as if Park would need assistance. Bader was to be allowed to fight, but only while under the command of his mentor, Leigh-Mallory.[22]

Finally, on 30 August 1940, the day 242 Squadron was moved down to Duxford, the call to major action came. With his own squadrons committed elsewhere in the afternoon, Park wanted a 12 Group squadron to protect the airfield at North Weald while the 11 Group squadrons based there were otherwise engaged. The word was passed down to the Duxford sector controller, A.B. 'Woody' Woodhall, and 242 Squadron was ordered to scramble.

As thirteen Hurricanes climbed at full throttle, Woodhall gave Bader a series of vectors that would bring him over the North Weald area within fifteen minutes. The course, though, would bring the squadron over the aerodrome with the sun to starboard. Expecting the enemy to come from this direction, Bader recalled that he swung the squadron thirty degrees westward without consulting the controller. If true, this was, as Bader well knew, contrary to the way the interception system was supposed to work. As Pat Hancock of 1 Squadron later explained:

> You were under the control of the ground people, i.e. the controllers, who'd got the information – radar etc. etc. – where the enemy were coming in, and they decided which squadron to send up. You heard the orders to steer a certain course and climb to a certain height, which the leader of course followed and you followed with him. And it wasn't until someone in the particular group [section or squadron], be it the leader or someone else, saw the enemy and said 'tally ho'... that you then took over, i.e. the leader of the group of aeroplanes... until that time you were under ground control.

Bader, however, wanted to be up-sun when he encountered the enemy; which was why, so he later claimed, he chose to override his initial instructions.[23]

As the squadron climbed past 9,000 feet Powell-Sheddon stuttered over the R/T that he had spotted three unidentified aircraft below and to the right. Bader sent him off at the head of a section of three planes to investigate. With nine aircraft still following him, Bader continued to climb towards 15,000 feet and search the sky for the enemy. 'I turned Southwest, went up in to the sun, and then I saw them', as he later summed up his actions. Just west of Enfield he spotted more than sixty bombers, Heinkels and Dorniers, flying in tight formations staggered between 12,000 and 14,000 feet, an escort of about thirty fighters at approximately the same height as the Hurricane squadron, and an even larger formation several thousand feet higher still. One section of 242 was detailed to attack the lowest escort formation – rather cumbersome twin-engine Me 110s – while Bader led the remaining aircraft in two sections in a line-astern dive from behind, towards the unsuspecting bombers: 'we got 'em', as he later put it. The enemy formations broke up as the Hurricanes flashed through them, the sky then becoming a milling mass of diving, twisting, turning, and firing aircraft for the next few minutes. The Hurricane sections themselves quickly split up in the fray, but Bader and his pilots were flying an aircraft that had both a speed and manoeuvrability advantage over its twin-engine opponents. Suddenly the sky seemed to become empty; and the planes of 242 Squadron made their way back in ones and twos to Duxford. Just what, though, had this brief but furious combat accomplished?[24]

After they made their reports to the Intelligence Officer it seemed obvious to the 242 pilots that a signal victory had been won. In all ten enemy aircraft – including two attacked by Bader himself – were claimed as destroyed, two more as probably destroyed, and four others as damaged. What was more, not a single Hurricane had even been scratched in the fight: 'no bullet holes in any aeroplane', Bader wrote in his logbook. It was an impressive performance, as higher authority was quick to acknowledge. 'Heartiest congratulations on a first class show', Leigh-Mallory signalled. 'Well done 242.' Word also speedily reached the Chief of Air Staff. 'Magnificent Fighting', Air Chief Marshal Sir Cyril Newall signalled. 'You are well on top of the enemy and obviously the fine Canadian traditions of the last war are safe in your hands.' There was also a congratulatory telegram from Lord Balfour, the Under-Secretary of State for Air.[25]

242 Squadron's first big engagement was unquestionably a success: but it is worth adding a couple of caveats to the version of

events given by Bader to various later chroniclers. The squadron did indeed attack the enemy formation up-sun and from above, but the most detailed recent study of post-action reports reveals that this was not the result of a decision by Bader to modify or disregard instructions from the controller. The squadron took up vectors and height as ordered; instructions that, as it happened, placed them in the right place at the right time. As for the kill and other claims made, while it is impossible to ascertain who did what with certainty, it is worth noting that fighters from several other RAF squadrons were also involved in this engagement. Some of the enemy aircraft hit by Bader's men, in short, may actually have been downed by pilots from other squadrons: 242, indeed, may have been responsible for as few as four kills, none attributable to the squadron leader himself.[26]

Be that as it may, 242 Squadron had done well, and Bader's not inconsiderable self-confidence was boosted further still. At Duxford he expounded at some length to Woodhall on the need for whoever was in command in the sky, rather than the sector controller on the ground, to decide on the height and direction of an attack: controllers should confine themselves to indicating where the enemy were. 'If the controller can tell us where they are in time – direction and height – we'll sort out the tactics in the air, get up-sun ourselves and beat hell out of them'. Back at Coltishall and encouraged by Leigh-Mallory, he wrote up the battle in the form of a memo to the station commander. In it, Bader recommended that the same tactics he had used should be employed in future by 11 Group if they wished to score the same kind of success and suffer lower casualties than had hitherto been the case. This was perhaps a bit presumptuous in view of the fact that 242 Squadron had met the enemy *en masse* only once while 11 Group squadrons had been tackling them day in and day out for weeks.

More significantly, Bader was also not shy about communicating his view to the AOC 12 Group when Leigh-Mallory flew over to congratulate him that a greater victory could have been won: 'If we'd had more aeroplanes we could have shot down a lot more.' With thirty-six or more planes at his disposal, three squadrons flying off together as a wing under his control, 'we would have done so much better.' At the same time RAF casualties would be lessened. As for leading them in the air, it would be 'easy'. Though he admitted to the AOC that he had not worked out all the details, it was clear that leading 242 Squadron was no longer going to be enough for Douglas Bader.[27]

Notes

[1]Paul Brickhill, *Reach for the Sky* (London: Collins, 1954), p. 191.

[2]On Bader's surprise at being promoted rather than grounded see Mermagen in *Douglas Bader: Secret Lives* (Twenty Twenty Productions, 1996); Brickhill, *Reach for the Sky*, p. 170. On the age limit see The National Archives [hereafter NA], CAB 120/294, Dowding's Dispatch on the Battle of Britain, p. 4558. Leigh-Mallory himself would later in the war judge a highly experienced fighter pilot 'too old' to command a fighter wing at the tender age of 29. See Laddie Lucas foreword in Tony Spooner, *Night Fighter Ace* (Stroud: Sutton, 1997), p. ix.

[3]Tom Neil in *Fighting the Blue: Spirits in the Wind* (ASA Productions (UK) for UKTV, 2005). On Leigh-Mallory's career see Bill Newton Dunn, *Big Wing* (Shrewsbury: Airlife, 1992). On his character and ability see also Kenneth Cross with Vincent Orange, *Straight and Level* (London: Grub Street, 1993), ch. 5; Vincent Orange, *Park* (London: Grub Street, 2000 edn), pp. 75, 143, 150; Henry Probert and Sebastian Cox (eds), *The Battle Re-Thought* (Shrewsbury: Airlife, 1991), pp. 35, 40, 70, 72, 73; Hugh Thomas, *Spirit of the Blue* (Phoenix Mill: Sutton, 2004), p. 79. In addition to their first meeting Bader had talked with Leigh-Mallory at Duxford on 12 June. See Royal Air Force Museum Information and Research Services [hereafter RAFM], B 354, Bader logbook, 12 June 1940. The AOC consulted with the Duxford station commander, Wing Commander A.B. Woodhall, by phone in order to confirm his opinion that Bader was the right man for the job. See Dilip Sarkar, *Bader's Duxford Fighters* (Worcester: Ramrod, 1997), p. 39. It is worth stressing that Leigh-Mallory, who waived the Dowding age limit in other cases as well – see Doug Stokes, *Wings Aflame* (Manchester: Crecy, 1988 edn), p. 74 – was quite willing to remove squadron commanders on the grounds of age when it suited him. See William R. Dunn, *Fighter Pilot* (Lexington, KY: University Press of Kentucky, 1982), p. 54. The role of Bader as surrogate son is supported by Leigh-Mallory's admiration for his triumph over disability (see Mermagen in Sarkar, *Duxford Fighters*, p. 39): a vivid contrast to Leigh-Mallory's real son, who had never been able to overcome problems arising from a mastoid operation and was both a worry and a disappointment to his father. See Dunn, *Big Wing*, pp. 52, 83, 139.

[4]David L. Bashow, *All the Fine Young Eagles* (Toronto: Stoddart, 1996), p. 32; Brickhill, *Reach for the Sky*, p. 177; see also St Edward's School Archive [hereafter SESA], Bader to Dingwall, 3 January 1941. For the 'remnants' comment and L-M visiting see NA, AIR 28/168, Coltishall ORB, 20 June 1940; AIR 27/1471, 242 Sqn ORB,

20–21 June 1940. On the prior history of 242 see Hugh Halliday, *No. 242 Squadron, the Canadian Years* (Stittsville, ON: Canada's Wings, 1981), pp. 1–80. Halliday questions just how much at fault the prior leadership of 242 was for its state by the time of its arrival at Coltishall. Ibid., 80–81; see also Air Historical Section (Department of National Defence), *Among the Few* (Ottawa: Department of National Defence, 1948), p. 15. Replacing good men who failed the test of command in battle would become quite common as the Battle of Britain unfolded. See John Willis, *Churchill's Few* (London: Michael Joseph, 1985), pp. 115, 124, 129, 141–2; see also Imperial War Museum Sound Archive [hereafter IWMSA] 20486/2, J.R.C. Young. It is also worth noting that a single missing leg was thought sufficient to remove an apparently quite good CO from a squadron before it saw combat. See Willis, *Churchill's Few*, pp. 72–73. Dilip Sarkar argues that the briefing by Leigh-Mallory took place on 2 July, when Bader's logbook shows he flew to Hucknall. Sarkar, *Duxford Fighters*, p. 40.

[5]Tim Vigors, *Life's Too Short to Cry* (London: Grub Street, 2006), p. 157.

[6]Brickhill, *Reach for the Sky*, p. 178; NA, AIR 27/1471, 242 Sqn ORB, 26 June 1940; see also Brickhill, *Reach for the Sky*, p. 180.

[7]Douglas Bader, *Fight for the Sky* (London: Sidgwick and Jackson, 1975 edn), p. 65; D. Bader address to Wartime Pilots and Observers Assoc., Winnipeg, September 1970, in J.E. Johnson and P.B. Lucas (eds), *Glorious Summer* (London: Stanley Paul, 1990), p. 38.

[8]Spencer Dunmore, *Above and Beyond* (Toronto: M&S, 1996), p. 53. On Stan Turner see Lloyd Hunt, *We Happy Few* (Ottawa: Canadian Fighter Pilots' Association, 1986), pp. 81–83.

[9]On Bader insisting on smartness in 242 Squadron see Brickhill, *Reach for the Sky*, pp. 182–83. On Bader wearing a collar and tie in the cockpit see Edward Sims, *The Fighter Pilots* (London: Cassell, 1967), p. 79. On the chaffing of necks and dispensing with collar and tie see Royal Canadian Air Force Museum, R.W. Norris interview; Geoffrey Page, *Shot Down in Flames* (London: Grub Street, 1999 edn), 38; Noel Monks, *Squadrons Up!* (London: Gollancz, 1940), p. 55; Bob Doe, *Fighter Pilot* (Chislehurst: CCB, 2004 edn), p. 23. On the dangers arising from wearing collar and tie in case of ditching see e. g. D. David in Norman Gelb, *Scramble* (San Diego, CA: HBJ, 1985), pp. 108–09 and in *Spitfire: Power, Grace and Glory* (DD Video, 1998).

[10]D. Evans in Sarkar, *Duxford Fighters*, p. 42; see Brickhill, *Reach for the Sky*, pp. 181, 184. On Macdonald see Laddie Lucas, *Flying Colors* (London: Wordsworth, 2001 edn), p. 107. On Bader and paperwork see D. Bader in http://members.lycos.co.uk/jadastra/Bader.html, (accessed 12 February 2004) J. Behague, *Douglas Bader: The Man behind the Legend*, p. 3. Bader was not, of course, by any means the only combat commander to dislike paperwork. See Sandy Johnstone, *Enemy in the Sky*

(London: Kimber, 1976), p. 128; H.R. Allen, *Battle for Britain* (London: Barker, 1973), p. 100; Barry Sutton, *The Way of a Pilot* (London: Macmillan, 1943), p. 36.

[11]SESA, Bader file, C. Foxley-Norris address to St Edward's School, 4 December 1982.

[12]Halliday, *242 Squadron*, p. 84, n. 2.

[13]SESA, Bader file, Bader to Dingwall, 3 January 1941.

[14]Brickhill, *Reach for the Sky*, pp. 183–84.

[15]Douglas Bader, 'Fighter Pilot', in Eric Leyland and T.E. Scott-Chard (eds), *The Boys' Book of the Air* (London: Edmund Ward, 1957), p. 62; see NA, AIR 27 / 1471, 242 Sqn ORB, 29 June, 1 July 1940; AIR 28 / 168, Coltishall ORB, 30 June 1940; Brickhill, *Reach for the Sky*, pp. 185–6.

[16]NA, AIR 27 / 1471, 242 Sqn ORB, 4 July 1940; see Brickhill, *Reach for the Sky*, p. 187. On the option of getting spares – in one fashion or another – from another squadron see Johnstone, *Enemy in the Sky*, p. 99; IWMSA 10709 TS, D. Armitage, pp. 12–13.

[17]Brickhill, *Reach for the Sky*, pp. 188–89; NA, AIR 27 / 1471, 242 Sqn ORB, 8 July 1940.

[18]NA, AIR 28 / 168, Coltishall ORB, 9 July 1940; Lucas, *Flying Colours*, pp. 110–11.

[19]NA, AIR 28 / 168, Coltishall ORB, 11 July 1940; see RAFM, B 354, Bader logbook, 11 July 1940; Brickhill, *Reach for the Sky*, p. 196.

[20]Brickhill, *Reach for the Sky*, pp. 200–201, 192–93.

[21]Sarkar, *Duxford Fighters*, pp. 66–67; Brickhill, *Reach for the Sky*, pp. 199, 201.

[22]Brickhill, *Reach for the Sky*, pp. 198, 200; British Film Institute Library, *Battle of Britain* press material, Briefing One, Douglas Bader, 'Open Page'; Michael G. Burns, *Bader* (London: Cassell, 1998 edn), pp. 55–56; NA, AIR 27 / 1471, 242 Sqn ORB, 12 June–29 August 1940. On the system whereby Park would call on Leigh-Mallory for assistance, see John Ray, *The Battle of Britain, New Perspectives* (London: Brockhampton, 1999 edn), p. 85; On the DFC incident see Dilip Sarkar, *Spitfire Squadron* (New Malden: Air Research, 1990), p. 123; Cunningham letter to Author, 1 October 2004. On Leigh-Mallory not rotating 242 south to 11 Group see Sarkar, *Duxford Fighters*, p. 70. Park accused Leigh-Mallory of hoarding his best squadrons. See Ray, *Battle of Britain*, p. 86. Bader, to be sure, was not the only 12 Group pilot waiting impatiently to get a crack at the Hun. See Monks, *Squadron's Up!*, p. 246; P. Brown in Richard C. Smith, *Hornchurch Eagles* (London, 2002), p. 21; Allen, *Battle for Britain*, p. 39; P. Brown in Gelb, *Scramble*, p. 270; W. Cunningham to Author, 1 October 2004.

[23]P. Hancock in *The Official Battle of Britain 50th Anniversary Video* (Roymark Productions, 1990); see Brickhill, *Reach for the Sky*, p. 203.

[24]http:// home.tiscali.be / ed.rgags / awshistory / awsbader.html (accessed 12 February 2004), B. Cunningham interview with D. Bader for *Code One*, p. 2. For

Bader's recounting of this action see also NA, AIR 16/281, encl. 95B, Bader to Beiseigel, 2 September 1940; Air Ministry, *We Speak from the Air* (London: HMSO, 1942), ch. 15; BBC Written Archive, marked-up script for Bader's broadcast on 'The World Goes By' programme, 12 February 1941. See Brickhill, *Reach for the Sky*, pp. 203–05; John Frayn Turner, *Douglas Bader* (Shrewsbury: Airlife, 2001 edn), pp. 32–33. On this engagement see also Edward Sims, *The Fighter Pilots* (London: Cassell, 1967), ch. 5.

[25]NA, AIR 27/1471, 242 Sqn ORB, 30 August 1940; RAFM, B 354, Bader logbook, 30 August 1940. On the claims see AIR 28/168, Coltishall ORB, 30 August 1940.

[26]Peter Brown, *Honour Restored* (Stroud: Spellmount, 2005), p. 125. Sarkar, *Duxford Fighters*, pp. 75–81. On accounts which Bader collaborated in the writing of in which he is credited with having chosen to disobey the controller see,, Brickhill, *Reach for the Sky* pp. 203–05; Lucas, *Flying Colours*, pp. 119–21; Sims, *Fighter Pilots*, ch. 5. There also appears to be some confusion as to whether or not it was Bader who spotted the enemy first. See Sims *Fighter Pilots*, p. 85; Brickhill, *Reach for the Sky*, p. 204; Sarkar, *Duxford Fighters*, p. 78. At least one observer later speculated that the decision to employ 242 rather than any of the other 12 Group squadrons immediately available to support 11 Group must have come from Leigh-Mallory. See P. Brown in Smith, *Hornchurch Eagles*, p. 21; Brown, *Honour Restored*, p. 126.

[27]IWMSA 11716/1, D. Bader; Brickhill, *Reach for the Sky*, p. 207 see NA, AIR 16/281, Bader to Beisiegel, 2 September 1940.

CHAPTER FOUR

Wing Champion

Sir, if we'd only had more fighters we could have hacked the Huns down in scores.

Douglas Bader in conversation with Air Vice-Marshal Trafford Leigh-Mallory, Hucknall, September 1940[1]

It was at this point that Bader's views began to become part of a larger debate at high level over the best way to use aircraft in defence of Great Britain. Dowding, the C-in-C, along with Keith Park, his senior staff officer in the late 1930s and now AOC 11 Group, believed that enemy bombers should be intercepted before they reached their targets, and that Fighter Command had to be prepared for multiple raids and feints. This in turn meant making the squadron of a dozen or so aircraft the largest tactical unit. Within the system built up by Dowding the country would be divided into groups and the groups into sectors, with each sector controlling the individual squadrons based at main and satellite fields. Sightings by the Observer Corps, and, by the time war broke out, the invaluable information provided through a chain of RDF – Radio Direction Finding, better known as radar – stations, would be collected and assessed at Fighter Command HQ and then forwarded to the appropriate Group operations room. A picture would be built up of the size and direction of incoming raids at Group level, and the appropriate number of sections or squadrons ordered up to meet them. Both Dowding and Park thought that any tactical unit bigger than a squadron would take too long to assemble in the air, thereby allowing the enemy to bomb the target before being intercepted. Moreover, it would leave no local reserve if drawn into meeting what turned out to be a spoof or secondary attack. There were those in the Air Ministry, however, who believed this to be an insufficiently aggressive approach to the problem of enemy air attack. In particular Air Vice-Marshal Sholto Douglas, working first as Assistant and then as Deputy Chief of the Air Staff, argued that the key to victory lay in shooting down the maximum possible number of enemy aircraft. Irrespective of whether the casualties were inflicted before or after the target had been bombed, high losses would force the enemy to cease or diminish his attacks. Large enemy bomber formations ought therefore to be met with mass RAF fighter formations, however long it took for these fighter formations to assemble. Park would fight the Battle of Britain within 11 Group with the squadron-based system Dowding had put in place with great skill. But the growing scale of the Luftwaffe assault, combined with the mounting frustration of the AOC 12 Group, would allow proponents of mass fighter formations to ultimately gain ascendancy and supersede both Dowding and Park.[2]

Leigh-Mallory was not a happy man in August 1940. Most of the fighting was occurring further south in 11 Group under the command of Park, and he felt left out of things. Late in the month requests did come for support, but these were relatively few in number and mostly involved guarding 11 Group airfields as a precaution while 11 Group squadrons engaged the enemy. 'This limited role did not suit Leigh-Mallory at all,' one of his staff later explained, 'and he would come into our Operations Room [at Hucknall, 12 Group HQ] and fret, enquiring repeatedly of the Operations Rooms at Duxford and Wittering [sector stations] whether there was any news of our squadrons being in action.'[3]

One possible means of increasing the importance of 12 Group in the battle was to employ large formations of fighters when the call for help came. This would accord with the views of important figures in the Air Ministry; and, even more importantly, if the enemy was encountered the large number of fighters involved would increase the chances of a high kill score for which Leigh-Mallory could take credit. About a week before the CO of 242 Squadron made his request for more squadrons, Leigh-Mallory had attempted to assemble a multiple-squadron wing over Duxford in response to a call from 11 Group to patrol North Weald. What Bader was proposing, therefore, was very much in accord with the thinking of his AOC. In the first week of September 1940, Leigh-Mallory gave Bader the green light to try operating, as a single tactical unit, 242, 19, and 310 squadrons from Duxford. 'He needed to be centre stage,' as a pilot in 310 Squadron later remarked, 'he was not content with being in the wings.'[4] Despite later claims to the contrary the three squadrons had only a few chances to patrol with one another before going into battle en masse. 'We never did any practice sorties as a Wing,' remembered the CO of 310 Squadron, Douglas Blackwood, 'we just went off on an operational patrol together one day with Douglas leading.'[5]

There was no question by this point about *who* should lead. Within 242 Squadron his leadership was unquestioned. 'Fear was always there, of course,' Pilot Officer Denis Crowley-Milling acknowledged many years later, 'but Bader was afraid of nothing and through example and constant encouragement he helped us all conquer our anxieties.' On the ground, meanwhile, he pushed hard for the best possible accommodation and facilities for his men. His confidence also had an effect beyond his squadron. In the early morning of 7 September 1940 the signal for imminent invasion was sent out in error, causing a good deal of confusion and anxiety everywhere, including Coltishall. A recent arrival to 616 Squadron, Pilot Officer J.E. 'Johnny' Johnson, collided with a squadron leader outside the mess. 'I say, old boy,' this officer demanded, 'what's all the flap about?' Johnson told him as best he could, and then watched fascinated as Bader ('I thought I knew who he was') stalked into the ante-room, surveyed the scene, and in a loud and obscenity-laced voice demanded to know once again what the all panic was in aid of.

> Half a dozen voices started to explain, and eventually he had some idea of the form. As he listened, his eyes swept round the room, lingered for a moment on us pilots and established a private body of fellowship between us. There was a moment's silence while he digested the news. 'So the bastards are coming. Bloody good show! Think of all those juicy targets on those nice flat beaches. What shooting!' And he made a rude sound with his lips which was meant to resemble the ripple of machine-gun fire. The effect was immediate and extraordinary. Officers went about their various tasks and the complicated machinery of the airfield began to function smoothly again.

The authority of the AOC aside, Bader was both the most senior and the most forceful of the three squadron leaders in the wing: 'people just fell in behind him, because he had the personality to run things,' Flight Lieutenant Gordon Sinclair of 310 Squadron recalled; 'we just automatically assumed that he would lead', as Blackwood explained.[6]

September 7, as it happened, turned out to be the day on which the wing would score its first and very spectacular success. The first wing patrol in the morning brought no contact. The second, however, was mounted that afternoon and met the enemy on the most favourable possible terms. One of the drawbacks of massing fighters in a wing was that both the size and height of a raid and the intended target might be unclear. Radar plotting could not always give accurate readings as to the number or height of the enemy and the Luftwaffe had become adept at mounting attacks where multiple formations changed direction en route and split up in order to confuse the defenders. There was always the danger that fighters sent to intercept would find themselves in the wrong place or at the wrong height. The odds against successful interception were higher, moreover, when 12 Group was involved. It took time for requests from 11 Group to be made, processed, and acted on. Hence the ability of German raiders to bomb North Weald and Hornchurch on 24 August and Debden on 26 August before the 12 Group squadrons that were supposed to protect these 11 Group airfields arrived on the scene. The odds were lengthened even further in the case of a wing-size formation sent by 12 Group. Even if the wing could get off the ground quickly, three squadrons being controlled as one were inherently less likely to spot the intended raid than three squadrons being directed separately. There was, after all, a lot of sky over southern England in which the enemy could operate. On the afternoon of 7 September, however, the Luftwaffe tilted the odds more in on favour of the wing by attacking a single target in great strength: London.[7]

As in the past, the initial call came in the form of a request to patrol North Weald at 10,000 feet. Bader was not the first nor the last squadron leader to add several thousand feet to this total in order not to be caught below the enemy on arrival in the combat zone. When the wing arrived over the patrol area they were at 15,000 feet and found the sky empty. Looking several miles to the east, though, the puffs of bursting anti-aircraft shells could be seen, and then about one hundred enemy aircraft flying at 20,000 feet. Bader immediately asked for and received permission from Duxford control to engage. Climbing steeply at full throttle towards what turned out to be a bomber formation of Do 215s and He 111s with an Me 110 close escort and an Me 109 upper escort flying 5,000 feet above, the Hurricanes and Spitfires began to straggle. In spite of not having the advantages of height, sun (and therefore the element of surprise), or concentration in the initial attack, the pilots of the three RAF squadrons acquitted themselves well once the inevitable series of fighter-versus-fighter and fighter-versus-bomber dogfights commenced. Twenty enemy aircraft were claimed as destroyed – ten by 242 Squadron alone – while five others were listed as probables and six more as damaged, as against one RAF pilot killed, another wounded, one Hurricane destroyed and three others damaged.[8]

Congratulations were duly forthcoming from Leigh-Mallory and Sir Archibald Sinclair, the Secretary of State for Air. Bader, however, despite the fact the he had added two more to his score ('Destroyed 2 ME 110 personally' he wrote proudly in his logbook), and was unaware that the Luftwaffe had actually lost less than one-third of the aircraft claimed by the wing, was not happy. Leading the wing into action from below and without the sun behind it went against his principles. It seemed clear to him that if the squadrons had been scrambled earlier then fewer friendly aircraft would have been lost and more enemy aircraft destroyed. 'On landing,' he later recounted, 'I rang the Operations Room in a fury to be told that we had been sent off as soon as 11 Group had called for us'. It did not take him long to conclude that he had been called up too late. When the AOC 12 Group visited Duxford the next day Bader did not hesitate to argue that the wing ought to be scrambled while the enemy formations were still assembling across the Channel. 'Look Sir,' he remembered asking Leigh-Mallory, 'why can't we get off early when they're building up, so that we can be down there [into 11 Group airspace] by the time they come up?' The AOC was a bit dubious, pointing out the risk of the enemy feinting in order to draw up the RAF and then sending in their main attack when the defenders were forced to land in order to refuel. He also reminded Bader that the call still had to come from 11 Group. Bader, though not convinced, was mollified by a promise to try and close the time gap between 11 Group asking for help and the scramble order being issued from the Duxford operations room.[9]

Bader was totally convinced that mass fighter formations, positioned up-sun and above the enemy wherever he was concentrated, would yield better results than committing squadrons piecemeal to defend particular ground targets once it was clear where the enemy was headed. Yet as even Leigh-Mallory acknowledged at this stage, there were hidden dangers in this approach. Given the limits of RDF, the problems of both ground and air visual identification in all but clear weather, and the potential for enemy deception, the wing might miss the Luftwaffe main force altogether. Then and later, critics assumed that precious time must have been wasted forming up the wing. In fact Bader did his best to minimise any delay. 'I used to go off the ground, and absolutely straight on course', he explained in an interview, with everyone else closing up behind as they all climbed. By prior agreement the Spitfire squadron at the satellite field at Fowlmere scrambled simultaneously with the squadrons at Duxford, would rendezvous above the Hurricane squadrons over the target area rather than waste time trying to link up over the sector aerodrome. But it still took a minute or too longer to get the wing airborne compared to single squadrons. There was also potential for delay in the air. The Spitfires of 19 Squadron, for one thing, had to throttle back so as to match the climbing speed set by Bader at 140 mph for the Hurricane squadrons. For another, there were communication difficulties. Unlike some other squadrons still equipped with unreliable TR9 High Frequency R/T sets, the squadrons in the Duxford Wing were all equipped with VHF radios: yet only in the later stages of the Battle of Britain were all the R/T sets in the wing tuned to the same frequency. Thus any order Bader gave would at first have to be relayed through the squadron commanders to the individual pilots. 'There wasn't a lot of radio help in those days', as one of his pilots put it.[10]

There were, furthermore, potential problems in allowing Bader the power and freedom he thought necessary to carry out a 'decisive battle' role with the wing: the right to overrule ground control and the freedom to roam the sky in search of the enemy. Though arriving back on duty without any personal experience of the command and control system that Dowding had put in place in the years after his departure from the RAF, Bader did not remain ignorant for long. In the aftermath of the dispute over the operational status of 242 Squadron the C-in-C had shown him around the Fighter Command operations room at Stanmore, which among other things contained the huge plot table on which Britain was divided into groups and those groups into sectors. When at Duxford, furthermore, Bader was known to visit the sector operations room on occasion to see for himself what was going on. The fact remains, however, that he either still did not understand the way in which the Group system worked or, more likely, understood but thought it ought to be reorganised to make proper use of his wing.[11]

Twenty-eight years later, in a typically vigorous conversation with a pilot who had flown with 11 Group, Bader argued that it was 'absolute balls' to suggest that he had been in any way 'out of line' in taking a free-range approach.

> Look, it's no good saying to you when you go up, there's that [patrol] line Maidstone–Canterbury–Maidstone and you mustn't go over that. I mean, if you're flying at twenty thousand feet you can be fifteen or twenty miles beyond that and it's still only just under your wing. After all... we were young chaps and we were trying to destroy enemy aircraft. Well, if the aircraft were over Ashford instead of Canterbury, you can't say 'Well, I can't go over there.' You go and shoot 'em down anyway.

Any other course of action was, in his view, laughable. As we shall see, there were those who completely disagreed.[12]

Delays and misunderstandings had already occurred in translating requests for assistance from 11 Group into effective action by 12 Group squadrons: and that was with the squadrons concerned being given fixed patrol areas. If the wing possessed the kind of free rein to move southward in search of the enemy, it could play havoc with a command and control system geared to orders from group and sector stations. The different R/T frequencies used for different squadrons in various sectors and groups, along with radio range problems, would make it next to impossible to keep track of the formation as it moved at will across sector and group boundaries. Bader himself remembered how he had seen two Hurricanes from another squadron converging on a collision course with a German bomber, but found himself unable to prevent a tragedy. 'You cannot shout a warning,' he wrote, 'because there is no common radio frequency.' He later argued that Fighter Command HQ ought to have been in operational control of the Battle of Britain. This, however, was simply not how the system was designed to work. Dowding might well have done more to exert his authority to deal with the growing feud between Park and Leigh-Mallory. The fact remains, however, that the command, control, and communication system based on the principle of operational control at group level worked well in overall terms. More importantly in reference to what Bader wanted, the system had taken years to construct and could not simply be scrapped overnight in order to accommodate a method of operation that the C-in-C in any case thought conceptually flawed. Bader, however, even before Leigh-Mallory had swung fully behind his ideas, was not going to let the system get in the way of demonstrating what his boys could do when aggressively led. 'He apparently seemed to think that we who were in command [at Fighter Command and 11 Group] didn't seem to know what we were doing or talking about,' Dowding reflected wonderingly many years later, 'and that if he disagreed with our policies he could make his own decisions.'[13]

In the late afternoon of 9 September, after Bader had pushed sector control to prod 11 Group so he could get what was coming to be called the Duxford Wing into the air, the call came once again to cover North Weald. Woody Woodhall was both a widely respected ground controller – like all the best officers in this job he always sounded calm and confident when issuing instructions – and an admirer of Bader. He was frequently reminded of the squadron leader's firm opinion that squadrons in the air ought to be given helpful information from the ground but should not be tied to precise height, patrol line, and other instructions relayed by the controller. As Bader later put it:

> I do not know where they got the idea that you can really analyse these things [that is, the movements and intentions of friend and foe in the air from the operations room on the basis of radar, ground observer, and pilot reports] and pin the whole thing down like the movement on a railway timetable. I know that when you are in the Ops room and you see figures standing so still and calm round a big [sector or group map] table, with the [pointer-stick] shovels moving [formation markers] up and down like croupiers at Monte Carlo, you think how peaceful it is, and everybody is so cool it must be possible to work the whole thing like any other organised operation.

It was very different in the air, though, especially once the enemy was in sight and dog-fighting commenced: 'How do you draw this on your table?' The controller, in short, should advise rather than command.[14]

In holding this view Bader was, it is worth stressing, far from alone. H.R. 'Dizzy' Allen described in his memoirs the sort of controllers those leading at the sharp end during the Battle of Britain liked best:

They understood the problems, they realized that they could not command a tactical battle, they appreciated that only a Squadron Commander could achieve that, and they sensed that their duty was to provide a service, not to try and act like Napoleon at Austerlitz… they wouldn't demand this and that; they would simply give the Squadron Commander all the information at their disposal and leave him to sort out the mess.

The former actor Ronald Adam at Hornchurch in 11 Group was one such paragon. Woody Woodhall at Duxford in 12 Group was another.[15]

'As I saw it,' Woodhall explained in an interview, 'my job as Sector Controller was to vector the Fighter Leader on a course and to a height which would place him above and up-sun of the enemy [something Dizzy Allen did not trust any controller to do], and keep him informed of the enemy's position, course and speed as accurately as possible from the information we had on the operations table.' On occasion Bader might go too far in disobeying instructions even for Woodhall, but on the whole his was a loose approach to controlling that Bader could accept. Thus on 9 September 1940, as three squadrons began to climb, the controller, instead of issuing an order based on what 11 Group wanted, deferred to the wing leader: would he care to patrol between North Weald and Hornchurch at 20,000 feet?[16]

Bader would not. He wanted more height than that and to make sure the wing was up-sun of an enemy whom he was certain would be heading for London again: 'it wasn't easy to manoeuvre [multiple] aircraft and be in that [up-sun] position when you don't see the enemy,' as Wallace Cunningham of 19 Squadron commented. Climbing 22,000 feet over Staines and heading south, he spotted a formation of sixty plus Dorniers with some Me 110s ahead at about the same height moving northward. Another formation – which turned out to be the main Me 109 fighter escort – could be seen 500 feet above. At first, as the higher group dived out of the sun towards him, Bader took them to be Spitfires. Once it was clear that this was in fact the Me 109 fighter escort Bader detailed the Spitfires of 19 Squadron to take them on while he swung the Hurricanes of 310 and 242 squadrons in to attack the bombers. In the resulting series of mêlées the Me 109 escort could not be stopped entirely from intervening in the main battle by 19 Squadron, and four

RAF fighters were shot down. Nevertheless the bomber formation appeared to break up under attack by the other two squadrons. Two RAF pilots successfully bailed out, and claims were made for a grand total of about twenty enemy aircraft destroyed (along with two possibly shot down and two damaged). Once again the AOC 12 Group and the Chief of the Air Staff sent their congratulations on a job well done. Leigh-Mallory was so pleased at the way things were going that on a visit to the squadron he threw away his usual reserve and danced a Highland Fling on a table in the mess while those around him celebrated with champagne.[17]

Once more, however, the level of success claimed by the Duxford Wing was greater than was actually the case. This time the level of over-claiming was as high as 5:1. Furthermore, in sweeping south of the Thames the wing had left exposed Hornchurch, North Weald, and indeed the northern half of the capital itself. Bader was lucky that the Luftwaffe had not sent another raid in to attack north of the Thames in the manner of operations on 30 August.[18]

Bader, as it happened, was himself dissatisfied with the outcome. Though he did not question the scores (he himself claimed another kill), Bader was not happy with the way in which the Me 109 escort had been able to get through to the Hurricanes. The idea, after all, was to shoot down enemy bombers rather than their escorts. When he visited the satellite field at Fowlmere to see how 19 Squadron had fared, he was not impressed to see that one of the Spitfires had crashed on landing due to damage. The pilot, Sergeant David Cox, defended himself by saying 'I got one, sir'; but an angry Bader got in the last word by replying forcefully that 'one-for-one is no bloody good.' Something would have to be done to improve the kill ratio. Bader therefore flew from Coltishall to 12 Group HQ at Hucknall the following day to argue the case with the AOC for *more* fighters to be added to the wing. Another Spitfire squadron would help block the 109s while another Hurricane squadron would add to the weight of fire brought to bear against the bombers. Leigh-Mallory was aware of the danger that concentrating forces in this way would increase the odds of the enemy slipping in to bomb targets, and in his customary manner asked certain other fighter leaders what they thought of the wing idea. Sailor Malan, for one, indicated approval: it was one possible way of getting his squadron, rotated north for a rest the previous month, back into action. The AOC therefore concluded that the advantages outweighed the risks, and two more squadrons, 611 and 74 – the latter soon replaced by 302 – were added to the Duxford Wing.[19]

There was no question that this expanded formation was to be well and truly Bader's show, with his own squadron – for whom Bader had devised a typically bullish cartoon emblem showing Hitler being kicked up the bottom by a jackboot labelled 242 – in the lead. 'Woody Woodhall, the station commander [as well as sector controller at Duxford], said that each of the squadron commanders would lead the Big Wing in turn when it was operational', the CO of 302 (Polish) Squadron, Jack Satchell, explained many years later. 'But the four others of us agreed that Douglas was such a damned good leader he should be regular wing leader.' On 14 September, the day after Bader learned that he had been awarded the DSO, the first two patrols of what was now officially dubbed the No.12 Group Wing occurred with four squadrons detailed to cover familiar territory north of the Thames. It was not a particularly auspicious debut, as despite Bader climbing to over 20,000 feet and leading the entire wing far south of the Thames on the second patrol, no contact with the enemy was made and one pilot crashed and was killed as a result of an oxygen system failure. Happily operations the following day would provide Bader with everything he could wish for in terms of bombers to engage using all five squadrons.[20]

On 15 September 1940 the Luftwaffe launched a series of major raids directed at London. The squadrons of 11 Group took the brunt of the initial waves, giving Bader time to inspire the pilots of the wing with his own confidence. 'You'll soon be back in Warsaw', he quietly – though quite erroneously – assured the Poles. Park, meanwhile, rightly decided that the scale of the attacks necessitated help from 12 Group. He telephoned Dowding, who in turn telephoned Leigh-Mallory, and at 11:30 a.m. the 12 Group Wing was scrambled.[21]

Woodhall asked Bader if he would patrol Canterbury-Gravesend. This was OK by the wing leader, who expected the enemy to approach the capital from the east. The wing climbed to past twenty thousand feet, the three Hurricane squadrons levelling off at 25,000 feet with the two Spitfire squadrons stationed two thousand feet above. To the right Bader noticed anti-aircraft fire and a formation of what turned out to be about thirty Dornier 17 bombers about five miles distant, and immediately swung the wing round at full throttle to attack. On closer inspection it became clear that the enemy was already being attacked by RAF fighters from 11 Group squadrons; so much so that even Bader had to restrain himself – 'There are the buggers,' was his initial reaction, 'come on, let's get at the bastards' – until fewer Spitfires and Hurricanes could be seen and the risk of collisions had decreased. 'There were so many aircraft in the sky', Flying Officer Peter Brown of 611 Squadron remembered, 'that we had to circle above waiting to get into battle.' Then the Big Wing waded in, Bader just having time to warn his two Spitfire squadrons to hold off the Me 109 escort fighters he could see diving down as the three Hurricane squadrons – 'everyone for himself' he radioed – made their initial head-on run at the Dorniers. '[A]t that moment,' Bobby Oxspring, flying a Spitfire for 66 Squadron in 11 Group, vividly remembered, 'we witnessed the glorious sight of five squadrons from the Duxford wing, led by Douglas Bader, come sailing into the raid. The impact of a further sixty [actually 56] Hurricanes and Spitfires charging in on the already harassed bomber fleet was too much. Bombs were jettisoned indiscriminately on south-east London, and the raiders fled for home.' Many of the Me 109 pilots apparently also decided that discretion was the better part of valour and turned away without engaging: though it is worth remembering that the 109s were at the limit of their fuel endurance over London and could not afford to dawdle. With his covering role made redundant, Squadron Leader James 'Big Jim' McComb, the CO of 611 (West Lancashire) Squadron, grew frustrated at Bader's failure to call him into the fray, and finally decided to take matters into his own hands. 'To hell with this – we're coming down!' he yelled. 'The attack', Flying Officer Julian Kowalski of 302 (Polish) Squadron of the Big Wing commented in reference to the Hurricane assault, 'must have been very effective as after just one kill I could not find another [enemy aircraft to shoot at]'. The contribution of fighters from different groups made it difficult to assess claims, but 12 Group proudly recorded a total of twenty-six enemy aircraft destroyed by the Big Wing.[22]

This, however, was only the first of two fights on what would later be labelled Battle of Britain day. At 2:30 p.m. the Duxford Wing was scrambled to patrol North Weald. This time about forty enemy bombers were spotted flying at 20,000 feet while the wing was still only at 16,000 feet. Bader led his formation into a steep climb to intercept, but the wing suddenly found itself bounced by escorting Me 109s. This time Bader ordered the Spitfires to attack the bombers as the Hurricanes were already about to come into contact with the enemy fighters and had to break formation. The sky seemed to be full of hostile aircraft. 'Ran into whole of Luftwaffe over 10/10ths [cloud] over London', the CO of 19 Squadron noted in his logbook. 'wave after wave of bombers covered by several hundred fighters'. This was of course an exaggeration, and in the ensuing dogfights, which stretched as far south as Maidstone, a further twenty-six enemy aircraft were claimed as destroyed by the 12 Group Wing, which that day lost only two of its pilots.[23]

Leigh-Mallory was quite pleased with the day's results, not knowing that Fighter Command as a whole had in fact shot down 56 enemy aircraft rather than the 185 claims that were confirmed. 'I am naturally also very interested in your leadership of the Group Wing,' he had written in a letter dated the previous day congratulating Bader on his DSO, 'which I hope is going to be a prototype for future successful fighter operations against the Germans.' A very positive report he had drawn up on the effectiveness of the first five wing patrols and that he signed only two days after the battles of 15 September merely fed his growing belief that 'we are on the right lines on this'. As Leigh-Mallory liked to say, 'Meet strength with strength' was an excellent operational principle. But when he phoned Bader on the evening of 15 September to personally offer his congratulations, the AOC found his star player far from content.[24]

In Bader's opinion, expressed with his usual forcefulness, the wing had been badly let down in the afternoon. Instead of being above the enemy when within visual range, the wing had been below it. This had forced a climbing attack that in turn meant 'we got clobbered on the way up'. And the only reason for that could be that once again the wing had been called into the air too late: 'If they'd let us off ten minutes earlier we could have been just in the right spot to cope, and probably got a lot more of them.' Furthermore, the policy whereby 11 Group squadrons fought the battle while the 12 Group Wing waited to be committed as a reserve was fundamentally flawed. As he explained to the AOC 12 Group, Bader wanted his force scrambled and heading south while the Luftwaffe was still assembling its formations on the other side of the Channel. 'We should be the ones to attack them first while 11 Group get off and get height.'[25]

The drawbacks of trying to carry out such a reversal of policy have already been outlined. It is open to debate, moreover, as to whether the Duxford Wing had been caught on the climb because 11 Group had dawdled in asking for help from 12 Group. Arriving back from the first engagement many of the planes involved had barely enough time to refuel and rearm before going up again. In other words, even if the call had come earlier the wing would not have been able to get in to the air en masse sooner than it did. In addition there was the question of how long it took the wing to get airborne once the order came. At Duxford the three Hurricane squadrons would taxi one after the other into position and then take off all together heading westward, while the two Spitfire squadrons at Fowlmere did the same when they saw the Hurricanes fly overhead. Initially, at least, there were delays in getting some of the squadrons into the air quickly enough because of a shortage of starter-carts: according to J.C. Freeborn of 74 Squadron the limited number of carts necessitated a staggered series of takeoffs and a wastage of fuel as the first wave orbited the aerodrome waiting for the second to join it. Once everyone was fully airborne the wing would not pause to form up but would swing into a ninety-degree turn and head for London. The need for haste, as Flying Officer Barry Heath recalled, matched Bader's temperament:

> Takeoffs of the wing were fairly fraught because Douglas Bader was short-tempered. He was always in a hurry. He always had a good aircraft. He'd whiz off and expect everyone to stick with him and be able to climb as fast as he could. When you're manoeuvring [in the middle of] three or four squadrons, it wasn't easy keeping in the same piece of air at the same time. You'd be going flat out one minute, throttling back the next, trying to stay in formation.

Indeed, towards the rear the Big Wing could be very ragged indeed as it climbed. 'Douglas Bader was at the front', Douglas Blackwood of 310 Squadron later remarked, 'and so he never saw the "Tail End Charlies" – it was chaos at the back with chaps being left behind and all sorts.'[26]

Bader on at least some occasions seems to have been largely oblivious to what was happening behind him. 'As you climbed away into the blue sky', he remembered of his own concerns, 'you thought about how the [recently served] coffee would be cold when you got back, [so] should you order some more or wait until teatime.' On the other hand he did everything he could to cut down on the extra time it took to get the big wing into position as compared to a single squadron. But as Bader himself admitted, 'it would take a little longer' for three squadrons to taxi out and take off in successive waves from a single field; thereafter 'time, and therefore advantage, were lost during assembly', according to Pilot Officer Frank Brinsden of 19 Squadron. Bader himself thought the wing climbed 'only marginally' less quickly than a single squadron, and reckoned that 'we were never more than six minutes off the ground.' But takeoff and climb times were still significantly longer than for individual squadrons operating independently.[27]

Even some of those who flew with Bader developed doubts about what was really bring accomplished. Dennis Armitage, who flew with a section of 266 Squadron attached to the wing, later had this to say:

> We took so long to get to the job, by the time five squadrons had got off from Duxford and got down into the battle area usually all we saw were the back end of the enemy disappearing over the Channel. And even then it was only Dougie Bader and the Poles in front or whoever he was flying with who really got stuck into them if at all. It all seemed a lot of organisation and not a lot of result.[28]

Perhaps at Bader's insistence – 'he was impatient', noted Wallace Cunningham of 19 Squadron, 'and couldn't suffer delaying tactics' – on the afternoon of 17 September the Big Wing was scrambled in what one of its squadrons labelled an 'offensive patrol' in the North Weald area. The only raid plotted was a very large enemy fighter sweep, incapable of doing much damage to anything on the ground and really there only to entice the RAF into fighter-versus-fighter combat. 11 Group in the main refused to rise to the bait, and the 12 Group Wing did not sight the enemy at all.[29]

The following day 616 Squadron, battered after heavy fighting while stationed in 11 Group, flew in to Fowlmere. This gave an opportunity for Bader to demonstrate again the positive effect his boisterous confidence could have on jittery pilots. 'Quite soon the door was thrown open', related Hugh Dundas, who had himself barely escaped from a burning Spitfire, and 'an extraordinary fig- ure in squadron leader's uniform stomped vigorously into the hut. Instantly the subdued and somewhat queasy atmosphere was dis- pelled, driven away by the hard, robust character of Douglas Bader as he called noisily for Billy Burton [the CO], an old friend, and then greeted each of us individually.' The first two wing patrols of 18

September were, however, frustratingly free from contact with the enemy. But when the Duxford Wing was called up for a third time at 16:30 the fates were definitely on its side.[30]

At about 20,000 feet flak bursts to the south-east alerted Bader to the presence of enemy aircraft over the Thames Estuary. This time conditions were ideal. The wing was already 4,000 feet above the enemy formations, which consisted of less than forty Junkers 88s and Dornier 17s operating without fighter protection and highlighted against the cloud base below. The result of the ensuing dive attack led by Bader aiming at the leading aircraft was decidedly one-sided. 'In all', the 12 Group operations record book indicated, 'at least 29 E/A were shot down', not including six counted as probables and two more as damaged. Twelve kills were claimed by 242 Squadron, and congratulations were once again forthcoming from the Chief of Air Staff and the Air Minister.[31]

As always there was a good deal of over-claiming by the wing, this time by a factor of between four and seven to one. But from the perspective of those who believed in the concept of a big wing – sometimes called a 'balbo' in reference to the impresario Italian general who had showcased large formations of flying boats in the early 1930s – the 12 Group Wing had once again translated theory into fact. Leigh-Mallory, as the forwarding of the report dated 17 September on first five wing operations to Dowding indicated, was confident that 12 Group could teach the rest of Fighter Command a thing or two about the efficacy of large and offensively oriented formations. This in turn was in tune with views being expressed within the Air Ministry by among others the Deputy Chief of the Air Staff, who thought Dowding and Park were conducting the Battle of Britain with a dangerously defensive mentality. '[T]he best way of stopping an enemy air offensive', Sholto Douglas later reiterated, 'is to shoot down such a large proportion of the enemy bomber force that they are compelled to diminish the scale of their offensive, or even call it off altogether.' Furthermore:

> The best way of causing casualties to an enemy bomber force is to meet him with large (if possible, superior) numbers of fighters operating in a cohesive formation. If, however, you are going to insist every time on trying to intercept enemy bombers before they reach their objective, you very often have not time to get up large or superior numbers to meet him, and you find that your Fighter Squadrons

go into battle singly or in pairs (i.e. in inferior numbers) and are thus liable to defeat in detail. So that while in the short run you may minimise the effects of bombing by spoiling the bombers' accuracy with fighter attacks in the vicinity of the target, in the long run the quicker way to minimise or stop the offensive may be to withhold your attacks until you have massed your large fighter formations.

The 12 Group Wing was now the test case for this line of thinking, and thereby a stick with which to beat Dowding and Park into altering their operational approach to enemy attacks or positioning them for replacement.[32]

How aware Squadron Leader D.R.S. Bader was of the high-level backroom struggle over the future of Fighter Command that was starting to get underway in September, and particularly of his place in it, is open to debate. According to a senior staff officer at 12 Group it was fairly common for Leigh-Mallory to listen to ideas, and adopt them as his own, which would potentially enhance his position; and by mid-September the CO of 242 Squadron had certainly sold the AOC on the big wing concept. Bader was now personally close to Leigh-Mallory – 'I got to know him pretty well, you know, it got past the stage of "Bader", it was "Douglas" and so on' – and openly expressed his certainty that the wing was being poorly utilised by 11 Group. It was the same with those around him and anyone else, including dignitaries, who visited his station. Bader nevertheless took strong exception when it was suggested almost thirty years later that he 'did [his] best to torpedo Park and Dowding'. He had expressed his views openly and knew of no subterfuge at the time. It was only when his first biography was being written that he learned that his adjutant, Peter Macdonald, MP, had begun to criticise the handling of the wing among politicians; but he found it inconceivable that anyone concerned had acted in bad faith. In short, Bader refused to believe that he himself, Leigh-Mallory, or indeed anyone at the Air Ministry had been involved in any intrigue to displace either Park or Dowding.[33]

That there was in fact behind-the-scenes manoeuvring that involved, among others, Leigh-Mallory and Sholto Douglas, seems indisputable: but it also appears very likely that Bader really was unaware of what was going on. He was focusing his attention on the operations of his own squadrons rather than making the case for a change in fighter strategy per se. Leigh-Mallory may have seen the

Duxford Wing as the shape of things to come, but it was optimising its chances for success in battle rather than its role as a prototype that its leader really cared about. In contrast to those like Sholto Douglas who apparently believed that wings were inherently superior to squadrons, Bader later stated that it was 'nonsense' to think wings would have worked in 11 Group. The airfields concerned were simply too close to the enemy to allow for the time necessary for a wing to form up and gain height. Moreover, though more than willing to bend the AOC's ear, Bader was not so keen to be told what to do even by his admirers. Sholto Douglas, for instance, visualised the wing harrying enemy formations after they had been attacked by 11 Group squadrons and were heading back. Bader himself, though, desired a leading rather than a supporting role: he thought the wing ought to be scrambled early enough that it could engage the enemy near the coast, thereby allowing 11 Group squadrons more time to gain height. When Leigh-Mallory tried to get his protégé to do something with which he disagreed it could become clear who controlled the wing. The CO of 302 Squadron remembered an occasion when Bader laid down the law on the question of leadership to the AOC. 'You appointed me to lead the wing, sir,' Bader said as he swayed on his tin legs. 'I'll lead it my own way or not at all.' Furthermore he was both fond of and indebted to the C-in-C, 'gruff, withdrawn, inarticulate Stuffy Dowding', the man who had, after all, taken his side in the spares dispute. As for the AOC 11 Group, Bader later expressed great admiration for this 'splendid officer' and implied that only because of fatigue under the weight of 'awesome responsibilities' had he failed to grasp the efficacy of the Big Wing. As even his friends conceded, Douglas Bader was not a particularly subtle – let alone a Machiavellian – thinker. While he was capable of changing his mind completely in relation to ideas, he was widely regarded as incapable of knowingly undermining people he admired: least of all father figures like Dowding. Bader, in short, was an unwitting tool – albeit an important one – rather than a conscious player in the unfolding battle for control of Fighter Command.[34]

Be that as it may, in the latter part of September 1940 the leader of the Duxford Wing experienced a certain amount of frustration again in making contact with the enemy. 'One thing I do remember,' commented Antoni Markiewicz of 302 Squadron, 'if we missed the Germans Bader was very displeased, and let us know in very simple language!' In the last ten days of the month the wing was sent up on ten separate patrols; but in only one case was the enemy sighted, despite the fact that on several occasions Bader led the wing far south of the Thames in search of something to engage. This was not just a matter of one large formation having less of a chance to spot something than the equivalent number of squadrons independently searching the same amount of sky in the same time, though that may have played a part. It was also a matter of a change in German tactics. The big daylight raids on London, in which Bader could make educated guesses concerning the location of the enemy, were giving way to fast tip-and-run raids on multiple targets by small formations of Me 109s acting in the fighter-bomber role. Even with help from the controller, working out how to be in the right place at the right time was much harder now. Only on one of three patrols on 27 September did the Duxford Wing spot and engage the enemy. The patrol line was supposed to cover Hornchurch, but contact was actually made over Canterbury, Dungeness, and Dover. 'Bader brought us in high, still flying in a solid wedge,' remembered Hugh 'Cocky' Dundas. 'We came together with the Messerschmitts in a monstrous explosion of planes that developed into a dogfight of exceptional size and fury.' In this fighter-versus-fighter encounter two RAF pilots and three aircraft were lost. 'We shot down 13,' 12 Group recorded, 'probably another five, and damaged another 3.' The actual number of kills, though, may have been as low as four.[35]

Contact or not, some of the men responsible for getting the wing into the air sometimes two or even three times a day felt under pressure. To make the 12 Group Wing a truly Big Wing it was necessary to keep as many aircraft serviceable as was humanly possible. Joe Roddis, a mechanic with 234 Squadron, recalled that once the wing became operational Bader 'wanted everything up that could fly.' That in turn could mean memorable displays of temper directed at ground crews who, in his opinion, failed to deliver. He was not, to be sure, the only pilot undergoing the stresses of flying and fighting in the Battle of Britain to have ever shouted or threatened a fitter, rigger, or armourer. Wing Commander Victor Beamish, for example, the volatile North Weald station commander who insisted on flying operationally, not only shouted at but also sometimes threatened to shoot anyone he caught malingering. Most of those who flew in combat, however, recognised how dependent they were on the efforts of the ground-crew 'erks' who serviced their aircraft, and kept their tempers in check. Beamish himself was not above apologising – 'sorry, corporal, not your fault; sorry I shouted' – and acknowledged the job that the ground crews were doing. 'At least twice – I was a recipient – he came to dispersal with a packet of ten cigarettes', Corporal Mick Chelmick of 56 Squadron remembered: '"For all your splendid efforts, boys".' For good or ill, though, Bader was unwilling to tolerate any delay in the repair of aircraft and there is no record of the subsequent confrontations being followed up with apologies and acts of individual generosity. David Evans, who serviced aircraft for 242 Squadron and (unlike some ground staff) respected Bader, had to admit that 'he was undoubtedly a bit of an autocrat' and even at times a bully.[36]

Meanwhile those who flew with the Duxford Wing in September 1940 were for the most part pleased to be serving under the bullish Bader. As Richard Jones of 19 Squadron put it: 'as far as I was concerned he was an inspiration.' Pilots also liked the feeling of security a truly big formation of friendly aircraft provided. 'I must say from my experience, when you look round you and see anything up to seventy Spitfires and Hurricanes round about you,' added Jones, transferred from a heavily outnumbered squadron to the south, 'it does give you an enormous fillip and increases your morale considerably realising that there are all these number of aircraft there at the same time as you.' Jones was not alone in feeling this way, especially among those who had earlier fought in 11 Group. 'It's the best thing I've seen since the war started', a 616 Squadron pilot wrote to his brother after joining the wing. 'Instead of being almost invariably practically alone among many Huns, we are a large, concentrated and formidable-looking force.' Canadian pilot R.H.W. Dignah never forgot looking around from his position within 242 Squadron at the 'incredible sight of sixty Spitfires and Hurricanes in one place at one time'. As already noted, however, by the latter part of the month the wing was finding few adversaries against which to test its weight. 'Sixty aircraft in perfect formation, fifty-nine of them under strict radio silence,' Ken Wilkinson of 616 Squadron recalled many years later, 'and Bader chatting away to all and sundry.' The wing was 'a grand sight', if nothing else: 'We never saw the enemy, but we were a grand sight.' David Cox of 19 Squadron remembered the second half of September in similar terms: 'We did lots of patrols, but never saw anything.'[37]

That last point, of course, could be a problem for those looking into, rather than out from, the Duxford Wing, especially within 11 Group, and even in the first half of September. 'All too frequently,' wrote Tom Neil of 249 Squadron, 'when returning to North Weald in a semi-exhausted condition, all we saw of 12 Group's contribution to the engagement was a vast formation of Hurricanes in neat vics of three, steaming comfortably over our heads in pursuit of an enemy who had long since disappeared in the direction of France.' Billy Drake argued that the trouble with the wing squadrons was that 'they never appeared when they were wanted'; a view with which many other frustrated 11 Group pilots concurred. 'The wing always arrived too late', Pilot Officer Wally Wallens later explained; 'it never got down [south] to where we were in time', Pilot Officer John Ellacombe agreed. Moreover, when both the 12 Group Wing and 11 Group squadrons were in the air together the impossibility of direct communication meant that on several occasions friendly aircraft were mistaken for enemy formations. There was even a rumour within 111 Squadron at Debden – totally false, as it happened, but indicative of the jaundiced opinion of some of the pilots – to the effect that the first time Bader had led the wing the only casualties were three Blenheims mistaken for Ju 88s.[38]

For higher command within 11 Group the issue of the wing not appearing where it was needed as well as when it was needed was also problematic. As early as 4 September the AOC 11 Group had complained to Fighter Command about 12 Group squadrons moving into 11 Group airspace. Because of R/T range and frequency problems they could not be co-ordinated with 11 Group operations and were causing 'confusion to Observer Corps and A.A. Gun Defences who cannot be informed of their movements.' By the end of the month, by which time requests for 12 Group help from 11 Group were being routed through Fighter Command, Park had lost all patience. In another missive to Stanmore dated 29 September he pointed out the chaos the free-ranging interventions out of Duxford had caused. Both Debden and North Weald had been bombed when they were supposed to have been covered; sector controllers could never be sure where the 12 Group squadrons were. A request to patrol North Weald or Hornchurch might well translate into the wing turning up on the south coast at Dover. That in turn had given the Observer Corps in Kent in one instance the impression that an enemy raid was in progress, causing further confusion for the controllers. On another occasion, when the Command Controller had suggested that Park call on the 12 Group Wing for help (presumably after some prompting from the Duxford sector or Hucknall), the AOC 11 Group had declined – only to find shortly thereafter that a five-squadron formation was in the air over Hornchurch.[39]

Leigh-Mallory, asked to respond to Park's complaints, did not give an inch. Wing formations lessened friendly casualties by meeting the enemy on equal terms and did much to boost the morale of the pilots involved. The problem lay with 11 Group for not allowing the Duxford Wing to be scrambled early, while the enemy was still building up across the Channel, and refusing to understand that if the enemy was spotted then it was likely that any engagement would move southward.[40]

Dowding, preoccupied with problems of night defence and, as he later admitted, finding the responsibilities of command in the Battle of Britain 'a very great strain on me,' did little to resolve the dispute between Leigh-Mallory and Park over how the 12 Group Wing ought to be used. Among the Air Staff, however, there was a developing consensus that Park was simply unwilling to accept that the wing – as the reports of Leigh-Mallory indicated – was an effective tool against mass formations that ought to be encouraged rather than disparaged. That Sholto Douglas and others were determined to get their way was reflected in the agenda and attached notes for a high-level conference called to discuss fighter formation tactics in mid-October at the Air Ministry. The agenda seemed to assume that it would be agreed that wing formations were ipso facto a good thing, and that the real question at issue was how to best use them. The accompanying Air Staff notes also worked from the premise that bigger was better: individual squadrons were simply too small to meet the enemy on equal terms.[41]

It was at this point that Bader came to play a more direct role in shaping Fighter Command policy. The Air Ministry meeting to discuss what to do in future that occurred on 17 October 1940 involved the coming together of a variety of senior-ranking players wearing Air Force blue. Among those representing the Air Staff were Charles Portal (Chief of Air Staff designate), Sholto Douglas (Deputy Chief of Air Staff); Philip Joubert (Assistant Chief of Air Staff (R)), John Slessor (Director of Plans), and Donald Stevenson (Director of Home Operations). From Fighter Command came a smaller contingent: Hugh Dowding (AOC-in-C), Trafford Leigh-Mallory (AOC 12

Group), Keith Park (AOC 11 Group), and Quintin Brand (AOC 10 Group). Also at the table, much to the surprise of many of those present, was none other than Squadron Leader D.R.S. Bader.

It was Leigh-Mallory who had brought him to this important meeting, though Sholto Douglas, who thought the AOC 12 Group 'an extremely capable man' and was very much aware of Bader's views, probably knew what was afoot. By this point Bader was not only something of a legend in the RAF but also well on his way to becoming a household name thanks to the newspapers. Initially the Directorate of Public Relations at the Air Ministry had not been keen on publicising the exploits of particular pilots. The public feting of the great aces in the First World War had caused envy among the less fortunate, as had the lionising of the first ace of the Second World War, E. J. 'Cobber' Caine, in the *Daily Mail* that spring. But in the eyes of Alexander Austin, Senior PR Officer at Fighter Command and a former *Daily Herald* journalist, the fall and rise of the legless air ace was simply too good to pass up. On 19 September an Air Ministry photographer visited Duxford and two days later Bader found his face and story splashed across the papers in connection with the award of his DSO. ('Greatest Hero of Them All' blared the *Daily Mail*.) The idea was for Bader to back up the wing concept in the meeting as the only man who had led big formations, as Leigh-Mallory explained to him. Being a public celebrity, the head of 12 Group did not bother to add, would make him even harder to ignore. The CO of 242 Squadron had not actually been invited to the meeting – 'I don't know if I can get you in', Leigh-Mallory admitted – but as the senior figure present Portal did not object when the AOC 12 Group introduced him.[42]

Sholto Douglas opened the meeting by suggesting that ways should be found to launch co-ordinated attacks against the enemy in superior numbers from above. This of course meant wings: but Park – who, Bader remembered, 'looked spent and drained and totally exhausted'[43]– stuck to his guns. The report on the 12 Group Wing on which the agenda was based, he pointed out, covered only five sorties over a few weeks as against months of combat experience using squadrons singly or in pairs within 11 Group. Park stated that the time lag involved in getting a big wing where it was needed meant that it hit the enemy on the outgoing leg, after bombs had been dropped and other fighters had softened up the bombers or drawn off the fighter escorts. 'The A.O.C. 11

Group', Park recalled shortly thereafter of his contribution to the discussion, 'then proceeded to describe the confusion that had been caused to the fighter defences, the ground defences and the A.R.W. [Air Raid Warning] system in the South-East through his Group not being informed when Duxford Wings had been unable to patrol the area requested, but had proceeded unknown to No. 11 Group to the Kentish coast between 20,000 and 25,000 feet, thus causing new raids to be originated by the Observer Corps and A.A. units.' He wanted group commanders to retain the flexibility to deploy aircraft in smaller quantities in order to intercept escorted enemy bomber formations before they struck their targets. Park gained the impression after he had spoken that Sholto Douglas, Hugh Dowding, and Peter Portal accepted that the policy he had followed had been correct.[44]

That impression, however, was illusory. After Dowding had stressed the difficulty of distinguishing between major attacks and spoof raids on the way in, conversation turned to reconnaissance aircraft and tip-and-run raids. Leigh-Mallory, however, brought the meeting back to the subject of large fighter formations. The Duxford Wing, he implied, had yet to demonstrate its full potential. 'We could get a Wing of five squadrons into the air in six minutes and it could be over Hornchurch at 20,000 feet in twenty-five minutes', he asserted. 'If this type of counter-attack intercepted a big formation only once in ten times the effort would none the less be worth it.' This threw Park and Dowding onto the defensive. Park argued that he had enough squadrons to deal with a big bomber raid, but the C-in-C Fighter Command conceded that outnumbering the enemy was a good thing and more could be done to bring the Duxford Wing into action under the right circumstances. Sholto Douglas, sensing an opening, cut in and asked Bader to state his views as to the value of large fighter formations.[45]

Typically, though a trifle intimidated by the sheer weight of rank that surrounded him, Bader hesitated only a moment before getting to his feet and holding forth. He talked about the importance of height, position, and numbers. Given sufficient warning time to get where it was needed, a wing could undoubtedly do better than a squadron against a huge enemy raid: 'surely we can manage to put sixty aircraft against a couple of hundred rather than twelve against a hundred.' Having said what he had to say, Bader abruptly stopped speaking and sat down, unsure of how his words had been received.[46]

In fact, though the rest of the discussion appeared non-commital on the issue to someone as unused to bureaucratic infighting as Bader, his words had reinforced the position of those pressing for a more wing-friendly policy. 'You are the one who has actually done it operationally', as Sholto Douglas emphasised. Since neither Park nor Brand were aware that Leigh-Mallory planned to slip in a star witness, there were no leading pilots from the other groups to offer a different view of what worked in the sky and what did not. The DCAS read the drift of discussion as now moving toward agreement that the 'employment of a large mass of fighters had great advantages', and Dowding accepted that arrangements should be made to allow wings from 12 Group to 'participate freely in suitable operations over the 11 Group area'. Further multi-squadron balbos would be formed, perhaps as many as seven once there were enough VHF radio sets available. It was also accepted that 'in the conditions which enable the enemy to operate in mass formation, the fighter leader could dispense with sector control and that if he was given information about enemy movements he should be responsible for leading his formation into battle'. This was exactly the sort of thing Bader wanted. Subsequently the amendments that Dowding and, more particularly, Park, wanted to make to the circulated draft minutes of the meeting, in order to get their objections and doubts on record, were simply ignored. 'At this meeting', Sholto Douglas later reported succinctly on what the minutes – if not the recollection of some of those present – showed, 'it was confirmed that Wings of three or more squadrons were the proper weapon to oppose large enemy formations when conditions are suitable.'[47]

This meeting was not the end of Bader's role as a spokesman for the Big Wing. In the course of the next few weeks the Duxford Wing did not do particularly well, much to the dismay of its leader. What was wrong and what to do about it were questions that would further embroil Bader, albeit unwittingly, in the decision to go forward with a new strategy and replace those associated with what was considered to be an overly defensive mentality.

Though the wing was called up a total of ten times in the course of October, it only made partial contact once, at the end of the month. This lack of success was partly due to deteriorating weather, and also to the shift in Luftwaffe attacks by day from conventional bomber raids to fighter sweeps and fighter-bomber strikes. These factors made the enemy harder to keep track of and successfully intercept, not least because the speedy Me 109s might fly very low (which made them difficult to spot on radar) or very high (to altitudes that British fighters could barely reach). The time it took to get the 12 Group Wing to operational height continued to be a problem, as did communication difficulties between the groups and with the wing itself once it was airborne. On one occasion it had taken seventeen minutes for the wing to get into the air from the time a request for help was passed from 11 Group. On another day it had proved impossible for the relevant 11 Group sector controller to tell Bader where to steer because of constant radio traffic between the wing and Duxford. Park went too far in complaining that squadrons transferred from the wing to 11 Group were frightened of flying in only squadron strength. But the situation was frustrating for all concerned, and not particularly well handled by Dowding, who vacillated over rival proposals to more fully integrate the operations of the wing.[48]

Bader, of course, was well aware of the fact that neither he nor the wing had done much lately in the way of shooting down the enemy. As already indicated there were a number of reasons for this, but Bader himself continued to think in simple terms: the only reason the wing was failing to deliver on its potential was that it was still being called too late. And, while working off some steam through aerobatics, he was not shy about sharing his opinions in the mess or in the presence of distinguished visitors.[49]

One of his listeners was Peter Macdonald, not only the 242 Squadron adjutant but also Conservative MP for the Isle of Wight. Apparently without telling his CO what he was doing, Macdonald decided to use his political influence to try and bring about the kind of changes in Fighter Command that Bader's complaints seemed to warrant. Macdonald first approached Harold Balfour, the Under-Secretary of State for Air who had long favoured 'brilliant young officers' like Sholto Douglas. 'I asked Peter not to talk to me about R.A.F. affairs,' Balfour recorded in his memoirs, 'feeling that it would be wrong for me to listen to a junior officer, even though a Member of Parliament.' Balfour, however, did not try and dissuade Macdonald from making an appointment to see the Prime Minister. Precisely what Churchill was told in the subsequent interview is unclear, though it seems to have been more to do with the perceived failings of Dowding at Fighter Command than about Bader as leader of the Big Wing.[50]

It was the Prime Minister who appears to have prodded the Secretary of State for Air into making a fact-finding visit to Duxford on 26 October 1940. 'Sinclair,' according to Balfour, 'had come away feeling that there was a conflict of operational views between the two Groups, which was felt acutely by units at Duxford.' Bader, clearly, was not reluctant to voice his dissatisfaction with how 11 Group was employing his wing, and Leigh-Mallory gave him no reason to think that he might be wrong. Two days after the Sinclair visit the AOC 12 Group called on 242 Squadron to lavish some praise on it and, by extension, its commander and wing leader. Leigh-Mallory, according to the ORB, 'said it was equal to, if not superior, to any Squadron in [the] R.A.F.'[51]

Sinclair, seeking confirmation of what he had found, asked Balfour to visit Duxford and record his findings. The visit, on 2 November, was another chance for Bader to give voice to his frustration. According to the Balfour Report, written up the same day as the visit, matters had reached a crisis point. The pilots of the wing were said to 'feel resentful against 11 Group and its A.O.C.' This was because they were 'being denied opportunities of shooting down Germans' simply because 'on every occasion when the wing has gone up it has arrived too late.' No. 11 Group was not sharing radar and other plot information with No.12 Group through Fighter Command. 'If the 12 Group representative could have the full information available to 11 Group, this would allow the wing to be on the spot in time to catch the enemy instead of always being late'. Bader argued that pilots in 11 Group as well as 12 Group were 'entirely sympathetic to the Wing Formation viewpoint' and that they agreed that the wing was being 'ignored and wasted.' With enough information and time at hand, operating against mass daylight raids (which he had no doubt would be resumed), the wing 'is absolutely certain of taking [an] enormous toll.'[52]

The Balfour Report was passed on with a supportive note to Dowding by the DCAS. While willing to concede that operating the 12 Group Wing from 11 Group involved some inherent difficulties, Sholto Douglas admitted he was 'inclined to support Leigh-Mallory's point of view.' The Big Wing concept was sound and 12 Group ought to be given the same information as 11 Group so that the Duxford formation would have enough warning time and freedom to intercept the enemy, if necessary while on his way home. Park, he suggested, was being unduly prickly about another group operating successfully inside 11 Group airspace: 'The word "poaching" has, I am told, been bandied about.' The important thing was not who intercepted the enemy, or when, but how many hostile aircraft he lost in the process. In a postscript Douglas added that Balfour 'asks me to say that he hopes Bader will not get into trouble for having been so outspoken.'[53]

Dowding, after having the various claims and counterclaims investigated by his staff, came down heavily against the report. The facts were that 11 Group had recently been bending over backwards to use the wing, sometimes calling for it before any clear threat had developed. The formation itself, the C-in-C went on, had disadvantages. The big bomber raids had given way to high-altitude fighter sweeps requiring the kind of quick scramble for which the Duxford Wing was unsuited by sheer weight of numbers. Concentrating five squadrons at Duxford and Fowlmere also weakened the defences of other parts of 12 Group, on one occasion to the extent that the group had been unable to fend off a Luftwaffe attack on airfields in East Anglia. 'I am inclined to the conclusion', wrote the head of Fighter Command, 'that for the moment in this present phase, the use of the Duxford Wing is a misemployment of our very limited strength.' Dowding also recognised the key source of the unfair criticism of 11 Group:

> There remains the question of an Under-Secretary of State [Balfour] listening to the accusations of a junior officer [Bader] against the Air Officer Commanding another Group [Park], and putting them on paper with the pious hope that the officer will not get into trouble. Balfour has been in the service and ought to know better. I think that, as a matter of fact, a good deal of the ill-feeling that has been engendered in this controversy has been directly due to young Bader, who, whatever his other merits, suffers from over-development of the critical faculty.

The C-in-C ended by arguing that while '[h]is amazing gallantry will protect him from disciplinary action if it can possibly be avoided', Bader should be moved to a station 'where he can be kept in better control.'[54]

The implication was clear: the wing should be disbanded and its former leader made to understand that he was a squadron leader rather than the architect of Fighter Command strategy. But it was the air chief marshal rather than the squadron leader who would soon be shunted aside. Leigh-Mallory vigorously disputed the assertions being made by 11 Group about the effectiveness of the 12 Group Wing, arguing that it had engaged bombers on the way to their targets and that any failures were due to the lack of timely and accurate information being received from 11 Group. In his opinion the Big Wing ought to be expanded to six squadrons, and certainly not disbanded. In any event the wing concept had become sacrosanct among the Air Staff by the time Dowding made his heretical suggestion. Meanwhile the C-in-C himself was being criticised for not taking a more aggressive stance in matters of night defence, something that had been a major talking point at the meeting on 17 October. Both at the Air Ministry and in certain political circles criticism had increased to a point where even Churchill, hitherto a supporter, accepted he would have to go. Dowding was informed by the Secretary of State for Air on 13 November 1940 that his services as AOC-in-C Fighter Command would no longer be required: he was to be sent off to America as head of a supply acquisition mission. Four days later Dowding was informed through the new Chief of Air Staff, Peter Portal, that Sinclair would not countenance any action against Bader. Yesterday's man, Dowding replied that 'no reproof has been or will be offered by me'.[55]

On 25 November 1940 Sholto Douglas officially took over as head of Fighter Command. Phoning to congratulate the new C-in-C, Leigh-Mallory was overheard to say 'I am glad that I am to be closely associated with you in my next appointment.' Within a month Park was 'banished', as he later put it, to a post in Training Command, and his rival Leigh-Mallory moved from 12 Group to become AOC 11 Group.[56]

Bader does not seem to have understood that a major change in policy would necessarily mean a changing of the guard. Nevertheless the leader of the Duxford Wing had been a factor in bringing about the new order in Fighter Command. His forcefully expressed views were used by those who wanted a more aggressive stance toward the enemy as evidence in the case against both Park and Dowding. Though the problems of night defence were quite possibly the most decisive issue in the removal of Dowding, Bader had indirectly helped in the rise to power in Fighter Command of commanders who would think along lines similar to his own. As in the past, the results of Bader being given his head would be open to interpretation.[57]

Notes

[1] Paul Brickhill, *Reach for the Sky* (London: Collins, 1954), p. 215.

[2] On the early debate see John Ray, *The Battle of Britain, New Perspectives* (London: Brockhampton, 1994 edn), pp. 78–79; Dilap Sarkar, *Bader's Duxford Fighters* (Worcester: Ramrod, 1997), pp. 15–17. On the views of Sholto Douglas and the Air Ministry position in 1940 see also Imperial War Museum Department of Documents [hereafter IWM], Lord Douglas papers, Box 2, Douglas to Collier, 14 February 1956, pp. 1–2; Philip de la Ferté Joubert, *The Fated Sky* (London: Hutchinson, 1952), p. 182. On the development of the air defence system see Peter Flint, *Dowding and Headquarters Fighter Command* (Shrewsbury: Airlife, 1996), chs. 1–5. On the development of radar see David Zimmerman, *Britain's Shield* (Stroud: Sutton, 2001). On Park and the Battle of Britain see Vincent Orange, *Park* (London: Grub Street, 2001 edn); National Archives [hereafter NA], AIR 2/7771, Report on Air Fighting in No. 11 Group Area, 30 November 1940. On Dowding's position see Liddell Hart Centre [hereafter LHC], Liddell Hart 15/15/10, Notes of an interview with Lord Dowding regarding the Battle of Britain, 22 January 1948.

[3] Kenneth Cross with Vincent Orange, *Straight and Level* (London: Grub Street, 1993), p. 118.

[4] Gordon Sinclair in *Britain's War Heroes: Douglas Bader, Fighter Ace* (Blakeway Associates, 2005); see Brickhill, *Reach for the Sky*, p. 208. On the 'wing' of 24 August see Ray, *Battle of Britain*, p. 87.

[5] Sarkar, *Duxford Fighters*, pp. 93–95. On the claim that Bader led practice sorties see Brickhill, *Reach for the Sky*, pp. 208–09; John Frayn Turner, *The Bader Wing* (Tunbridge Wells: Midas, 1981), p. 55.

[6] Dilip Sarker, *Battle of Britain: Last Look Back* (Worcester: Ramrod, 2002), p. 156; Gordon Sinclair in *Britain's War Heroes: Douglas Bader, Fighter Ace* (Blakeway Associates, 2005); J.E. Johnson, *Wing Leader* (London: Chatto and Windus, 1956), pp. 41–42; see also Crowley-Milling in Norman Gelb, *Scramble* (San Diego, CA: HBJ 1985), p. 271; Imperial War Museum Sound Archive [hereafter IWMSA] 20486/3, J.R.C. Young. On Bader pushing for the best deal for 242 Squadron personnel see IWM, 97/34/1, N.G. Neale, 4; D. Evans in Sarkar, *Duxford Fighters*, p. 42.

[7] See Michael G. Burns, *Bader* (London: Cassell, 1998 edn), p. 81. On the efficacy of shifting German tactics see IWM, A.B. Austin Papers, Dowding to Austin, 7 July 1941; NA, CAB 120/294, Dowding Dispatch, pp. 124–25. On the bombing of Debden and North Weald see Ray, *Battle of Britain*, p. 87; Colin Gray, *Spitfire Patrol* (London: Hutchinson, 1990), p. 54. In defence of 19 Squadron, which was sent to protect Debden, it should be mentioned that the raid came in at 1,000 feet while the squadron had been assigned to patrol at 10,000 feet. See David Cox in Sarkar, *Battle of Britain: Last Look Back*, p. 19. On other problems with the Big Wing see D.

Crowley-Milling and F. Brisden in Dilip Sarkar, *Johnnie Johnson* (St. Peter's, Worc.: Ramrod, 2002), p. 21.

[8]NA, AIR 27/1471, 242 Sqn ORB and D. Bader combat report, 7 September 1940; Royal Air Force Museum Department of Research and Information Services [hereafter RAFM], AC 71/24/51, encl. 1A, Report on Wing Patrols sent up by No. 12 Group, 7th, 9th, 11th, 15th September 1940, 1. On other cases of leaders disregarding height instructions see Anthony Bartley, *Smoke Trails in the Sky* (London: Kimber, 1984), p. 57.

[9]IWMSA 11716/1, D. Bader; Douglas Bader, *Fight for the Sky* (London: Sidgwick and Jackson, 1975 edn), p. 78; RAFM, B 354, Bader logbook, 7 September 1940; NA, AIR 27/1471, 242 Sqn ORB, 7 September 1940. On the argument with Leigh-Mallory see Brickhill, *Reach for the Sky*, p. 212. On the 3:1 over-claim see Sarkar, *Duxford Fighters*, p. 104. On succumbing to enemy feints see Liddell Hart Centre, B.H. Liddell Hart Papers, 15/15/10, 'Reflections of a Group Controller, 1940' by T.F.H. Lang, 1 May 1941, p. 3.

[10]B. Heath in Gelb, *Scramble*, p. 272; IWMSA 11716/1, D. Bader; see also 'The Bader Notes' summary in Ray, *Battle of Britain*, p. 180. On 19 Squadron rendezvousing with the Hurricanes over the target area see W. Cunningham to Author, 1 October 2004. The argument about a wing taking too long to assemble often came from 11 Group veterans. See Cyril Bamburger, Tom Dalton Morgan, Basil Stapleton in *Fighting the Blue: Spirits in the Wind* (ASA Productions (UK) for UKTV, 2005); Paddy Bathropp, *Paddy* (Hailsham: J&KH, 2001), 23; Alan C. Deere, *Nine Lives* (Canterbury: Wingham, 1991 edn), pp. 153–54; Gray, *Spitfire Patrol*, p. 72; J.A. Kent, *One of the Few* (London: Kimber, 1971), pp. 115–16; K.W. Mackenzie, *Hurricane Combat* (London: Grenville, 1990 edn), p. 71; G. Wellum in Martin Davidson and James Taylor, *Spitfire Ace* (London: Channel 4, 2003), p. 149. As well as disputing any delay in getting the wing into the air and arguing that arriving late was the result of being called too late, Bader later argued that he had not advocated wing formations for 11 Group (Bader, *Fight for the Sky*, pp. 78–79). On problems with radio communication see NA, AIR 20/3535, HQFC to Brooke-Popham, 1 May 1943, para 4; CAB 106/1193, Dowding Dispatch, supplement to the *London Gazette*, pp. 4457–58; see also Kent *One of the Few*, pp. 115–16; Richard Bickers, *Ginger Lacey* (London: Pan, 1969 edn), p. 15; Jeffrey Quill, *Spitfire* (London: John Murray, 1983), p. 161. Bader himself noted various problems even with VHF reception in the third week of August. See RAFM, B 354, Bader logbook, 21–24 August 1940. On the wing climbing at 140 mph, see Peter Brown, *Honour Restored* (Stroud: Spellmount, 2005), p. 139.

[11]On Bader's visit to the Stanmore operations room see Laddie Lucas, *Flying Colours* (London: Wordsworth, 2001 edn), p. 111. On visiting the Duxford operations room see IWM, R. Ambrose, 'Memoirs of an Aircraftsman', p. 13. See also http://www.bbc.co.uk/dna/ww2/A3408293 (accessed 22 January 2005), E. Pitt

on Bader visiting ops at Coltishall. Dowding himself reflected near the end of his life that in not having experienced the changes in the RAF that had occurred in the 1930s Bader did not understand that the 'freebooting' style characteristic of World War I fighter operations was antithetical to the 'highly disciplined flying' and air-ground control system in place in 1940. H. Dowding quoted in Robert Wright, *Dowding and the Battle of Britain* (London: Macdonald, 1969), pp. 170–71. It has also been suggested that if Bader did not understand the Dowding system it was because his AOC, Leigh-Mallory, certainly disliked and may possibly have misunderstood it himself. See John Terraine, *The Right of the Line* (London: Sceptre, 1988 edn), p. 198. The possibility that Bader did not really understand the wider context of operations is supported by a talk he gave to fellow prisoners at Colditz in August 1942 in which he commented that the Battle of Britain really ought to be called the Battle of London. See Margaret Duggan (ed.), *Padre in Colditz* (London: Hodder and Stoughton, 1978), p. 202.

[12]Bader in conversation with Peter Townsend, July 1968, quoted in Leonard Mosley, *The Battle of Britain: The Making of a Film* (London: Weidenfeld and Nicolson, 1969), p. 88.

[13]H. Dowding quoted in Wright, *Dowding*, p. 196; British Film Institute library [hereafter BFI], *Battle of Britain* press material, Douglas Bader, 'Open Page' *Briefing One*. On the radio frequency, ground control, and sector boundary problems see, Tom Neil, *Gun Button to 'Fire'* (London: Kimber, 1987), pp. 77–78, 80; Ian Gleed, *Arise to Conquer* (New York: Random House, 1942), pp. 120–21, 200. On Bader later arguing that Fighter Command ought to have directed the battle see IWMSA 11716/1, D. Bader. On problems with this idea see also Flint, *Dowding*, p. 168. On Dowding not controlling the feud between Park and Leigh-Mallory see Ray, *Battle of Britain*, p. 116 et al.

[14]D. Bader in R.W. Clarke, J.C. Sterne, J.E.E. Smith, *The Hundred Days that Shook the World* (Hemel Hampstead: Christopher Marlowe, 1969), p. 99. On Woodhall as an admirer of Bader see Woodhall in Sarkar, *Duxford Fighters*, pp. 39, 42.

[15]H.R. Allen, *Battle for Britain* (London: Barker, 1973), p. 49. For positive pilot opinions of Woodhall see IWMSA 12795/2, J. Johnson; Jim Bailey, *The Sky Suspended* (London: Hodder and Stoughton, 1957), p. 37; Hugh Dundas, *Flying Start* (London: Stanley Paul, 1988), pp. 47–48; Gray, *Spitfire Patrol*, p. 81; Bobby Oxspring, *Spitfire Command* (London: Kimber, 1984), p. 43; A.C.W. Holland in Laddie Lucas (ed.), *Thanks for the Memory* (London: Stanley Paul, 1989), p. 136. On Ronald Adam see his 'Blake', *Readiness at Dawn* (London: Gollancz, 1941), p. 20; see also Deere, *Nine Lives*, p. 113; W.G.G. Duncan Smith, *Spitfire into Battle* (London: John Murray, 1981), p. 57; Quill, *Spitfire*, p. 174.

[16]Brickhill, *Reach for the Sky*, pp. 212–13; Woodhall in Sarkar, *Duxford Fighters*, p. 105. On Woodhall and Bader arguing and Bader disobeying instructions, see

IWMSA 20497/2, R.L. Jones.

[17]Wallace Cunningham in *Britain's War Heroes: Douglas Bader, Fighter Ace* (Blakeway Associates, 2005); see NA, AIR 27/1471, 242 Sqn ORB, 9 September 1940; AIR 25/219, 12 Group ORB, 9 September 1940; AIR 25/224, Report on Wing Patrols of 12 Group, p. 2; RAFM, B 354, Bader logbook, 9 September 1940; Brickhill, *Reach for the Sky*, pp. 213–14; Turner, *Bader Wing*, ch. 6. On mistaking the Me 109s for Spitfires see also A.B. Austin, *Fighter Command* (London: Gollancz, 1941), pp. 181–82. On Leigh-Mallory dancing see Brickhill, *Reach for the Sky*, p. 218

[18]Sarkar, *Duxford Fighters*, pp. 107, 109; Brown, *Honour Restored*, p. 139.

[19]Brickhill, *Reach for the Sky*, pp. 215–16; Norman L.R. Franks, *Sky Tiger* (London: Kimber, 1980), p. 70. It is possible that Leigh-Mallory did not fully make up his mind until he visited Duxford on 12 September and held a conference there [NA, AIR 28/232, Duxford ORB, 13 September 1940]. As Dilip Sarkar has pointed out, though more squadrons were available on 11 September, only three were used until 14 September [Sarkar, *Duxford Fighters*, p. 113]. Moreover, the report drawn up on the first four wing patrols indicates that the decision to expand came only after the wing patrol of 11 September, the only one that Bader did not lead with 242 Squadron [See AIR 25/224, Report on Wing Patrols sent up by No. 12 Group, pp. 2–4]. See also Brickhill, *Reach for the Sky*, p. 218. Perhaps because it was recognised that Malan and Bader were both emerging as strong-willed commanders and it was thought that the big wing could have only one true leader, 74 Squadron, though based at Coltishall and flying once from Duxford, was not incorporated into the Duxford Wing. See Sarkar, *Duxford Fighters*, pp. 110–13. On the confrontation with Sgt Cox see IWMSA 11510/2, D. Cox. Cox was mollified by a quiet word from his CO, Sandy Lane: 'Look, you got back lad, don't you worry.' See also D. Cox in *Secret Lives: Douglas Bader* (Twenty Twenty Productions, 1996).

[20]J. Satchell in Gelb, *Scramble*, p. 269; see Sarkar, *Duxford Fighters*, p. 118; AIR 25/219, 12 Group ORB, 14 September 1940.

[21]Bader comment to the Poles in Richard Collier, *Eagle Day* illustrated edn (London: Dent, 1980), p. 195.

[22]NA, AIR 25/219, 12 Group ORB, 15 September 1940; J. Kowalski in Robert Gretzyngier, *Poles in Defence of Britain* (London: Grub Street, 2001), p. 89; McComb quoted in Richard Collier, *The Past is a Foreign Country* (London: Allison and Busby, 1996), p. 211; Oxspring, *Spitfire Command*, p. 66 [see also D. Cox in Sarker, *Battle of Britain: Last Look Back*, p. 21]; P. Brown in Smith, *Hornchurch Eagles*, p. 22; Bader in Collier, *Eagle Day*, p. 201; see Brickhill, *Reach for the Sky*, pp. 220–21; Turner, *Bader Wing*, ch. 8; John Frayn Turner, *The Bader Tapes* (Bourne End: Kensal, 1986), p. 87. On the 12 Group Wing having an advantage compared to 11 Group squadrons because the Me 109s could dogfight in the south-east but were operating at maximum range over London and therefore could not stay and fight see J.

Kent in Wright, *Dowding*, p. 200. On Park deciding to call in 12 Group see Winston S. Churchill, *The Second World War, Vol. 2: Their Finest Hour* (Boston: Houghton Mifflin, 1949), p. 335.

[23]NA, AIR 25/219, 12 Group ORB, 15 September 1940; AIR 25/224, Report on Wing Patrols sent up by No. 12 Group, p. 5, App. A; B. Lane in Norman L.R. Franks, *Wings of Freedom* (London: Kimber, 1980), p. 64; AIR 28/168, Coltishall ORB, 15 September 1940; Brickhill, *Reach for the Sky*, pp. 221–22; Turner, *Bader Wing*, ch. 9.

[24]L-M quoted in J.E. Johnson and P.B. Lucas, *Winged Victory* (London: Stanley Paul, 1995), p. 45; RAFM, B 3303, Leigh-Mallory to Bader, 14 September 1940; see RAFM, AC 71/24/51, encl. 1A, Report on Wing Patrols sent up by No. 12 Group Wing, 17 September 1940; Brickhill, *Reach for the Sky*, p. 223. On RAF and wing claims vs. Luftwaffe losses on 15 September see Alfred Price, *Battle of Britain Day* (London: Greenhill, 1999 edn), pp. 121, 128.

[25]Brickhill, *Reach for the Sky*, p. 223; IWMSA 11716/1, D. Bader.

[26]D. Blackwood in Sarkar, *Duxford Fighters*, p. 153; B. Heath in Gelb, *Scramble*, p. 272; BFI, *Battle of Britain* press material, *Briefing One*, D. Bader, 'Open Page'. On takeoff and climb procedure from Duxford and Fowlmere see G. Unwin in Davidson and Taylor, *Spitfire Ace*, p. 150; G. Unwin in *Aviation Heroes of World War II: The Battle of Britain* (Greenwich Workshop, 1990); IWMSA 1154 TS, G.C. Unwin, p. 17; P. Brown in Dilip Sarkar, *Bader's Tangmere Spitfires* (Sparkford: Patrick Stephens, 1996), p. 24. On the problem of the time necessary to refuel and rearm between the two wing battles on 15 September 1940 see Sarkar, *Duxford Fighters*, p. 123. Bader, among other things, got Hawkers to modify the rudder bars of is own aircraft, but apparently not those of other pilots, to compensate for torque: this may have added to the difficulty of keeping station in the air. Bader, *Fight for the Sky*, p. 18. On the starter-cart shortage see Bob Cossey, *A Tiger's Tale* (Hailsham: Airlife, 2002), p. 39.

[27]IWMSA 11716/1, D. Bader; F. Brinsden in Dilip Sarkar, *Spitfire Squadron* (New Malden: Air Research, 1990), p. 157; BFI, *Battle of Britain* pressbook (microfiche), *Briefing One*, D. Bader in 'Open Page'; see also W. Cunningham to Author, 1 October 2004.

[28]IWMSA 10709, D. Amitage TS, pp. 27–28.

[29]Sarkar, *Duxford Fighters*, p. 131; W. Cunningham to Author, 1 October 2004.

[30]Dundas, *Flying Start*, p. 47; see also *Sunday Express*, 5 February 1984, p. 9. On the first two wing patrols of 18 September see NA, AIR 25/219, 12 Group ORB, 18 September 1940.

[31]NA, AIR 27/1471, 242 Sqn ORB, 18 September 1940; AIR 25/219, 12 Group ORB, 18 September 1940. On the battle see AIR 50/92, ff. 23–24; Brickhill, *Reach for the Sky*, pp. 224–27; Burns, *Bader*, pp. 103–05; Turner, *Bader Wing*, ch. 10.

[32]IWM, Lord Douglas Papers, Box 2, Douglas to Collier, 14 February 1956. On over-claiming on 18 September see Sarkar, *Duxford Fighters*, p. 134; Brown, *Honour Restored*, p. 145.

[33]Bader notes in Ray, *Battle of Britain*, App. B; IWMSA 11716/1–2, D. Bader; Cross and Orange, *Straight and Level*, p. 121.

[34]For Bader on Park see Lucas, *Flying Colours*, p. 290; on Dowding see Ray, *Battle of Britain*, p. 182; on the confrontation with Leigh-Mallory see Alexander McKee, *Strike from the Sky* (Boston: Little Brown, 1960), p. 224; on differences in thinking between Bader and Sholto Douglas see P. Townsend in Turner, *Bader Tapes*, p. 94; on wings in 11 Group see Ray, *Battle of Britain*, p. 181. On Bader changing his mind in reference to ideas see Cuthbert Orde, *Pilots of Fighter Command* (London: Harrap, 1942), p. 18. The book to which Bader took exception was Wright's *Dowding and the Battle of Britain*. On the behind-the-scenes manoeuvring that eventually led to the replacement of Park and Dowding see, Ray, *passim*. Interestingly, both Dowding and Park later expressed the belief that Bader had been an unwitting tool of others rather than one of those determined to see them go. See RAFM, X–002–9343/004, Park to Dowding, 22 July 1968; Dowding in Wright, *Dowding*, p. 219. However, it is worth noting that a squadron commander who knew Bader recorded in his memoirs that Leigh-Mallory 'fulminated and resented his role' backing up 11 Group and that 'Douglas Bader was his protégé and stirred the pot.' A.R.D. MacDonell, *From Dogfight to Diplomacy: A Spitfire Pilot's Log, 1932–1958* (Barnsley: Pen and Sword, 2005), p. 64.

[35]NA, AIR 25/219, 12 Group ORB, 27 September 1940 [see Brown, *Honour Restored*, p. 145]; Dundas, *Flying Start*, p. 49; A. Markiewicz in Sarkar, *Duxford Fighters*, p. 187. On wing patrols in the last ten days of the months see AIR 25/219, 12 Group ORB, 20–30 September 1940. On the change in German attacks see NA, AIR 16/635, encl. 29A, HQ 11 Group to HQ Fighter Command, 7 November 1940, p. 6. On the frustrating change in German tactics see IWMSA 1254/1, C.B. Brown.

[36]D. Evans in Sarkar, *Duxford Fighters*, p. 42; M. Chelmick in Doug Stokes, *Wings Aflame* (Manchester: Crecy, 1988 edn), p. 110; J. Roddis in Davidson and Taylor, *Spitfire Ace*, 197. On Bader as confrontational see J. Strachen in Bruce Barrymore Halfpenny, *Fight for the Sky* (Wellingborough: Patrick Stephens, 1986), p. 72. Bader on occasion could turn down the heat once the reasons for some perceived lapse were explained to him and the offender was a fighter pilot of equal rank. See MacDonell, *Dogfight to Diplomacy*, p. 67. On the Beamish temper and ground crews see Stokes, *Wings Aflame*, pp. 89, 102, 105–06, 129. On pilots recognising the value of their ground crews see G. Wellum, G. Unwin, J. Roddis in Davidson and Taylor, *Spitfire Ace*, pp. 116, 117, 188.

[37]IWMSA 11510/2, D. Cox; K. Wilkinson in http://www.vulch.clara.net/aw2000. html (accessed 2 December 2004), report on Air Warrior 2000 European Convention, pp. 3–4; R. Dibnah in Lloyd Hunt, *We Happy Few* (Ottawa: Canadian Fighter Pilots' Association, 1986), p. 42; H. Dundas to J. Dundas in Ralph Barker, *That Eternal Summer* (London: Collins, 1990), p. 46; IWMSA 20497/2, R.L. Jones; see also G. Sinclair in Gelb, *Scramble*, p. 267.

[38]W. Wallens and J. Ellacombe in Gelb, *Scramble*, p. 265; B. Drake in Davidson and Taylor, *Spitfire Ace*, p. 218; Neil, *Gun Button*, p. 120. On 11 Group squadrons and the 12 Group Wing nearly coming to blows see NA, AIR 16/136, Duke-Wooley letter to Air Commodore, c. February 1951, p.3; Denis Richards, *It Might Have Been Worse* (London: Smithson Albight, 1998), p. 68; Sarkar, *Duxford Fighters*, pp. 137–38; Franks, *Wings of Freedom*, p. 64. On the Blenheim rumour see IWMSA 12173/2, B.H. Bowering.

[39]NA, AIR 16/330, encl. 37A, 11A, 11 Group HQ to Fighter Command HQ, 29 September 1940, 4 September 1940; see also Park in *New Zealand Herald*, 9 September 1952, p. 9.

[40]Ray, *Battle of Britain*, pp. 116–17.

[41]LHC, Nicholas Eadon Papers, Box 3, Dowding to Eadon, 3 April 1967; see NA, AIR 2/7281, encl. 14B, Conference to Discuss Major Day Tactics in the Fighter Force; ibid, App. I, Air Staff Note on the Operation of Fighter Wings, 14 October 1940.

[42]Brickhill, *Reach for the Sky*, pp. 237–38; *Daily Mail*, 21 September 1940. On the press and Bader see RAFM, MF 10027/1, Thelma Bader pressbook; see also the poem by H. Trevelyan-Thomson in *Royal Air Force Quarterly*, 11 (1940), p. 383. On Bader, Austin, and the Directorate of Public Relations see Doug Stokes, *Paddy Finucane* (London: Kimber, 1983), p. 81; see D. Richards in Henry Probert and Sebastian Cox (eds), *The Battle Re-Thought* (Shrewsbury: Airlife, 1991), pp. 78–79; see also NA, AIR 41/9. On Sholto Douglas viewing Bader as the prime wing advocate see IWM, Lord Douglas Papers, Box 3, Note of discussion between W/Cdr Robert Wright and Lord Douglas, Bealine House, 26 February 1964. On the DCAS's views of Leigh-Mallory see ibid. Note of discussion between Lord Douglas and W/Cdr Wright, Dorland House, 5 February 1964. On Douglas probably knowing that Bader was being brought along by Leigh-Mallory see Cross and Orange, *Straight and Level*, p. 121. Slessor later wrote that it was 'amazing, and entirely wrong', that Bader was allowed to attend and speak his mind. Slessor to Balfour, 28 October 1969 in J.E. Johnson and P.B. Lucas (eds), *Glorious Summer* (London: Stanley Paul, 1990), p. 188.

[43]Lucas, *Flying Colours*, p. 151.

[44]NA, AIR 2/7281, encl 17E, Park to Orme, 21 October 1940, attaching statement by AOC 11 Group on minutes of 17 October meeting; see ibid. encl. 17A minutes of 17 October meeting.

[45]Brickhill, *Reach for the Sky*, p. 238; NA, AIR 2/7281, encl. 19A, minutes of 17 October 1940 meeting; see Lucas, *Flying Colours*, p. 151.

[46]Brickhill, *Reach for the Sky*, p. 239; Lucas, *Flying Colours*, p. 151.

[47]Douglas quoted in Sarkar, *Duxford Fighters*, p. 168; NA, AIR 2/7281, encl. 19A, minutes of 17 October meeting; see Sarkar, *Duxford Fighters*, p. 170. On the role of Bader in this meeting see also Derek Wood and Derek Dempster, *The Narrow Margin* (London, 1961), p. 412; Desmond Scott, *One More Hour* (London, 1989), p. 66; Brown, *Honour Restored*, p. 187. On Park, for one, thinking that the minutes

skewed the argument in favour of 12 Group despite the telling points he had made see IWM, Alexander B. Austin Papers, Park to Austin, 12 September 1941; NA, AIR 2/7281, Statement by AOC 11 Group on minutes of meeting, attached encl. 17E, Park to Orme, 21 October 1940; Denis Richards, *Might Have Been Worse*, p. 68.

[48]Ray, *Battle of Britain*, pp. 150–55; NA, AIR 25/219, 12 Group ORB, 5–29 October 1940. On Park's intense dislike of the Duxford Wing see also J. Satchell in Gelb, *Scramble*, p. 269. On the problems created by the new German approach in terms of accurate tracking see T.C.G. James, *The Battle of Britain*, Sebastian Cox, ed. (London: Frank Cass, 2000), p. 324.

[49]On Bader complaining in the mess see Bader Notes in Ray, *Battle of Britain*, p. 181. On his frustration see NA, AIR 16/375, Balfour to Sinclair, 2 November 1940. On aerobatics see K. Wilkinson in Sarkar, *Battle of Britain: Last Look Back*, p. 45.

[50]Harold Balfour, *Wings Over Westminster* (London: Hutchinson, 1973), pp. 134, 101. Balfour certainly thought there was a connection between the Macdonald conversation and various queries from the PM about air defence matters (see ibid., 134). Churchill, on the other hand, apparently had no clear idea who Bader was when Macdonald was trying to arrange an interview in 1954 (see Churchill College Cambridge, Churchill Papers, CHUR 2/180, f. 14, Montague Browne to James, 15 March 1954).

[51]NA, AIR 27/1471, 28 October 1940; Balfour, *Wings*, p. 134; see Ray, *Battle of Britain*, p. 160.

[52]NA, AIR 16/375, encl. 10B, Balfour to Sinclair, 2 November 1940.

[53]NA, AIR 16/375, encl. 10B, Douglas to Dowding, 4 November 1940. On the close working relationship between Sholto Douglas and Harold Balfour see IWM, Lord Douglas Papers, Box 2, Note on discussion between Lord Douglas and W/Cdr Wright, Dorland House, 5 February 1964.

[54]NA, AIR 16/375, encl. 12A, Dowding to Douglas, 6 November 1940.

[55]NA, AIR 16/375, encl. 28A, Dowding to Portal, 17 November 1940, encl. 27A, Portal to Dowding, 17 November 1940. On Leigh-Mallory's defence of the wing's performance see AIR 16/635, encl. 36B, Leigh-Mallory to HQ Fighter Command, 17 November 1940. On the removal of Dowding see Ray, *Battle of Britain*, ch. 7, *passim*; see also IWM, Lord Douglas Papers, Box 2, Note of discussion between W/Cdr Robert Wright and Lord Douglas at Bealine House, 26 February 1964; LHC, Mauruce Dean 3/2/8, Wright to Dean, 23 November 1977, p. 4; John Laffin, *Swifter than Eagles* (Edinburgh: Blackwood, 1964), pp. 236–37; see also note 57.

[56]Park to Hunt, 23 October 1956, in Brown, *Honour Restored*, p. 204; Cross and Orange, *Straight and Level*, p. 122.

[57]On the night defence question and the removal of Dowding see E.B. Haslam, 'How Lord Dowding came to leave Fighter Command', *Journal of Strategic Studies* 4 (1981), pp. 175–86.

CHAPTER FIVE

Tangmere Leader

Why the bloody hell isn't my aircraft ready? Cocky, my bloody aeroplane's not ready. Where's that prick Hally?

Douglas Bader in conversation with Flying Officer Hugh Dundas, Tangmere, summer 1941[1]

Though Luftwaffe activity decreased as the winter closed in, Bader, ever restless, continued to hunt for ways to get at the enemy. On Guy Fawkes Day he led a two-squadron patrol from Duxford in a sweep over the Thames Estuary and had his wish granted – though not in the form he wanted. One of his pilots called out a warning just as a formation of Me 109s came out of the sun in a classic 'bounce'. Luckily only a single RAF pilot was lost as the enemy fired and dove away and another managed a quick deflection shot that sent a 109 crashing to the ground. Bader was also confident that he and the few others qualified to fly at night would be able to catch the enemy when called upon to defend Coventry in mid-November 1940. However, like virtually everyone else flying single-seat fighters in darkness with engine exhaust flames burning on either side forward of the cockpit, he found that could not see well enough to spot the enemy.[2]

This was frustrating, as was the difficulty in climbing to the height at which the Me 109s were now operating during the day. Bader asked Leigh-Mallory for his squadron to be re-equipped with the new higher-climbing and faster Hurricane Mark II, and despite the fact that 11 Group was supposed to get priority in the allocation of new equipment 242 became only the second squadron in the RAF to operate the type. The results were not spectacular, but at the end of the year, back at Coltishall, Bader took understandable pride as he reflected on his achievements as a squadron commander. 'Since

I have had 242 (June)', he noted in his logbook, 'we have destroyed 67 E/A [enemy aircraft] confirmed for the loss of 5 pilots killed in action, and 1 killed diving out of cloud.' In addition to his DSO, furthermore, Bader had been awarded what Leigh-Mallory called a 'long overdue' Distinguished Flying Cross in December, which brought the squadron DFC total to nine.[3]

Meanwhile the future of Fighter Command, and along with it the prospects of Douglas Bader for further advancement and air combat, was being decided amongst the air marshals. Lord Trenchard, though officially long retired, still had a great deal of influence in the Air Ministry as the de facto father of the RAF. In late 1940 he had paid a visit to the Chief of the Air Staff in order to argue that, with the Luftwaffe beaten by day, the time had come for Fighter Command to 'lean towards France'; that is, engage in offensive sweeps. This was the kind of aggressive mentality that had guided Royal Flying Corps operations over the Western Front in World War One and that had been part of the dominant RAF ethos in the inter-war decades. Peter Portal in turn approached Sholto Douglas who, according to his own account, was at first 'very doubtful' about such a policy because of the likely casualties that would be incurred. It did not take him long, however, to suppress such 'pretty feeble' concerns, and by the time Sholto Douglas took over at Fighter Command he was an advocate for the offensive policy being promoted by the Air Staff.[4]

The new C-in-C in turn met with his group commanders at the end of November 1940 to stress the need to 'get away from the purely defensive outlook'. 11 Group, he suggested, could start sweeps by wing formations over the Channel as far as Calais, perhaps in association with attacks by Bomber Command. After Park was given the push in mid-December it fell to Leigh-Mallory to flesh out this policy. One of his better qualities was a willingness to find out what those at the sharp end thought by visiting fighter stations and calling conferences. Leigh-Mallory listened to what was said by station commanders and squadron leaders about the new policy while drawing up directives. Given his aggressive temperament it was entirely natural that Bader should support a policy of taking the war to the enemy rather than waiting for them to attack again.[5]

Within days of taking over, the new AOC 11 Group had moved 242 Squadron southward to Martlesham Heath and issued an ambitious instruction laying out the two types of offensive activity he had in mind. On the one hand fighters flying individually or in pairs, using cloud cover to mask their movements, would harass the enemy on the ground (the origin of the so-called 'Rhubarb' operations). On the other hand, under better weather conditions, 'large fighter forces', acting either in fighter-only formations (fighter sweeps) or accompanying a limited number of bombers (eventually dubbed 'Circus' operations) would force the enemy onto the defensive.[6]

Leigh-Mallory had already developed opinions as to how these 'large fighter forces' should be organised after consulting with station commanders and, of course, the leader of the vindicated Duxford Wing: 'Bader had a lot of influence over him,' Harry Broadhurst later commented. Even before he had taken command of 11 Group, Leigh-Mallory was arguing for a super wing, consisting of three wings of three squadrons each working together to produce a formation of 108 aircraft, to defend Britain. This in turn would necessitate the establishment of fighter wings in other groups, each under the command of a designated wing commander flying 'whose business would be to train and lead the wing and his Station.' Not surprisingly, Douglas Bader was among the names he put forward as likely candidates for such a role. Certain staff officers still had doubts about the big wing concept, as did some of those who would be at the sharp end. Acting Squadron Leader Gordon Olive of 65 Squadron, which had fought with 11 Group during much of the Battle of Britain, recalled many years later how shortly after Park was removed the new group commander paid a call on Tangmere in order to sell the concept:

> Air Vice Marshal Leigh-Mallory came down one lunch time and gave us a pep talk. He explained that the Battle of Britain had been fought on a wrong principle. We should have massed our fighters into huge multiple formations then attacked the bombers in strength. To show that this was the way, he proposed to send huge formations of many wings of fighters over France to tackle the Germans on terms favourable to ourselves. This time Leigh-Mallory promised, we should have the superior numbers and the Germans would have a taste of the Battle of Britain in reverse.

Quite apart from the implied slight to the work of Park and Dowding, Olive was dubious about all this talk of big-wing offensives.

I had learned that large formations of fighters had big disadvantages and small ones big advantages. Large formations could be seen too easily and from too far away; they could be stalked and taken advantage of tactically. They were also very unwieldy and as all the pilots were busy keeping station in their formations, only the leaders had any time or opportunity for effective search. This made the big formation a liability rather than an asset.[7]

Other junior commanders also had doubts. Recalling a similar visit by Leigh-Mallory to Hornchurch at the start of 1941, Squadron Leader Aeneas MacDonell of 64 Squadron noted that the reception given to the Circus idea was rather mixed. 'What the Hell was it all about? To provoke the enemy fighters to give battle? Over their own occupied territory where they could crash-land or bail out safely? The top brass was not, I am sorry to say, very convincing.'[8]

The new chief of Fighter Command, however, had no such doubts, stating bluntly that 'I am very much in sympathy with the A.O.C. No. 12 Group's proposals.' That left Leigh-Mallory with a free hand, among other things, to give Bader what he wanted – a fully operational fighter wing and more opportunities for combat.[9]

Shortly after Sholto Douglas took over, Bader was one of a very select group of officers summoned to Uxbridge HQ in order to discuss the future armament of RAF fighters. The Hurricanes and Spitfires that had won the Battle of Britain had been armed with eight .303-inch calibre Browning machine guns. The trouble was that the Luftwaffe had started to provide its bombers with armour; which was making them harder to shoot down with smallish calibre machine-gun fire. What the C-in-C wanted to know was whether or not RAF fighters should be equipped with cannon in order to provide greater hitting power. The CO of 242 Squadron spoke up at once and unequivocally opposed any short-term change. He had witnessed the first experimental attempt to introduce cannon-equipped Spitfires to 19 Squadron earlier in the year, which had turned out to be a dismal failure due to jamming problems. 'Not the slightest doubt in my mind,' Bob Tuck of 257 Squadron remembered Bader saying.

Stick to the Browning sir. Damned fine gun. Served us well enough thus far – chaps know it outside in, pilots *and* armourers... any big change would do more harm than good... The Browning's a proven weapon. Damn sight sooner carry on with eight of them than start monkeying about with four – or six, hell, even eight – of *these* things [i.e. 20 mm cannon]. Don't trust cannon, too bloody new, probably still full of bugs. Let's wait till they've worked out a few modifications.

Bader also thought that cannon would encourage pilots to open fire at long range rather than going in close for a certain kill. Other experienced pilots, however, felt strongly that cannon were the way to go. Both Tuck and Sailor Malan argued that explosive and armour-piercing shells would increase the chances of bringing down the enemy and provide the kind of hitting power needed if fighters were to shoot up ground targets in future. 'Bobbie, for God's sake, don't talk rot!' Bader interjected. 'You too, Sailor – the pair of you think this is a bloody miracle weapon, and the damn thing hasn't even been—': at which point a furious row broke out. Only after the C-in-C intervened – 'Now now, gentlemen', he said soothingly, 'no use howling at each other, that won't help me' – did the meeting quieten down.[10]

Eventually it was decided that future Spitfires would be armed with a combination of two 20-millimetre cannon and four .303-inch machine guns, which were standard equipment on the Spitfire VB introduced in the summer of 1941. Bader, however, refused to accept a cannon-armed aircraft, sticking with a machine-gun equipped Spitfire II model and then an example of the comparatively rare machine-gun armed Spitfire VA. His dislike of cannon in late 1940, however, seems to have been viewed as a personal eccentricity by higher authority and did nothing to damage his reputation as a fighter pilot.[11]

A further sign that he was very much in favour came when he was among the first pilots to be allowed to stage a 'Rhubarb' sortie early in the second week of January 1941. He was also given a prominent place by Leigh-Mallory in the very first 'Circus' raid on France mounted the following day. These and the following operations with which 242 Squadron was involved were frustrating to Bader. The Luftwaffe often failed to react at all – 'Absolutely no activity of any sort was experienced' read the 242 Squadron operations record book entry on a two-squadron sweep on 4 February – or, in the case of certain Rhubarbs, shot down friends when Hurricane pairs were bounced by swarms of 109s. Aerobatics were one form of release, but as Pilot Officer Michael

Constable Maxwell noted in his diary after a visit to North Weald, 242 Squadron flew 'much too close to allow for errors and over-shoots' and nearly hit a dispersal hut. 242 was supposed to take part in the second Circus operation on 5 February, but when the engine of the CO's Hurricane failed to start he decided not to let the rest of the squadron proceed without him. Bader, however, did manage to work off some aggression on 13 January when he spotted a small vessel he took to be a German E-Boat off the French coast. At once abandoning his plan to cross the coast and head inland, the CO of 242 Squadron went into a dive with Stan Turner behind him and shot up the enemy craft: 'It was great fun', Bader remembered. By now he was being touted in the United States by the Air Ministry as one of the RAF's top ten aces, and a further sign that his reputation was spreading came in February when he was chosen to make a radio broadcast for the BBC on the subject of his first combat with 242 Squadron.[12]

The final proof that Bader was indeed being groomed for greater things came in mid-March 1941 when he was promoted and posted to take command of the newly established Tangmere Wing. Despite the initial enthusiasm in some quarters for an expansion in the size of wing formations, it had been recognised that anything beyond three squadrons was too unwieldy to justify the extra number of aircraft involved. Like a paper air defence exercise that Leigh-Mallory ran at the end of January using wings instead of squadrons that the enemy 'won', this admission implicitly questioned the value of the five-squadron wing Bader had established at Duxford the previous autumn. Wing enthusiasts, however, could argue that big formations were very appropriate for the kind of offensive action now being contemplated, and would brook no opposition. Sceptics like Gordon Olive, whose squadron had lost a substantial number of pilots in the initial attempts to organise cross-Channel operations, the survivors of which were in his view 'not at all in the mood to offer [themselves] at that stage as sacrificial lambs to the whims of unsound tacticians' or believe that someone like Bader could 'show us how it was done', were posted away and their units broken up. Bader himself, meanwhile, seems to have been happy enough to see the ad hoc temporary arrangements made for the Duxford Wing turned into something more official and permanent in the form of the Tangmere and similar fighter wings. It cannot have hurt either that Leigh-Mallory gave him a choice of locations

– 'Which would you prefer – Tangmere or Biggin [Hill]?' – from which to operate as wing leader.[13]

His behaviour on taking command on 19 March 1941 of the Tangmere Wing, which now consisted of three Spitfire squadrons (145, 610, and 616), was typical. Within half an hour of his arrival Bader had commandeered an aircraft and was in the air over the aerodrome, ostensibly to 'get the feel again' of a Spitfire but also in order to do aerobatics. Within two hours he had two of the squadrons in the air together over the coast doing a 'snoop' for enemy aircraft. Eventually the Tangmere operations room called up to confirm that the Luftwaffe was not about and ordered the wing commander back to base. Characteristically, Bader was reluctant to give up the hunt: 'Okay' he replied. 'Just one more minute. You never know.'[14]

This set the pattern for the remainder of the month and on into April: training, patrol flights, occasional 'snoops', and – last but not least – aerobatics. Bader explained that 'no man was master of his aircraft until he could control it in all attitudes', and while acknowledging that accomplishment in aerobatics were of no use in a dogfight the manoeuvres involved did 'give the pilot complete confidence in his Spitfire.' But in the case of the wing leader there was also probably a desire to show off. 'Bader's frequent, almost daily displays', Johnnie Johnson of 616 Squadron recalled, 'were the delight of the ground crews and we all strolled on to the tarmac to watch the wing commander.'[15]

One obvious drawback to these one-man air displays was the danger of making a mistake at low level and crashing. Through a mixture of luck and skill Bader managed to avoid another prang. He was less fortunate, however, in staking some of his credibility on the assumption that he was the most skilful aerobatic pilot on the station. A few months after his own appointment Bader witnessed the aerobatic skill of Flight Lieutenant E.P. 'Gibbo' Gibbs, a regular officer his own age posted to the squadron – No. 616 – with which he habitually flew. Bader himself had only ever managed two upward rolls, and when he saw Gibbs going for a third upward roll he was certain that he would fail. 'He'll never do it, old boy', he told Johnson. When Gibbs pulled off the third roll with apparent effortlessness Johnson thought Bader 'was bloody livid.' Thereafter such aerobatic displays ceased to be part of the programme for a time.[16]

Meanwhile the wing commander had been making choices about personnel. 'Bader at Tangmere', the Belgian pilot Jean 'Pyker'

Offenberg had noted in his diary on 19 March, adding: 'That probably means a lot of changes.' Pyker was spot on in his prediction. William Walker, an RAFVR pilot with 616 Squadron who had been wounded and forced to bail out over the Channel in late August 1940 after being bounced by 109s, was finally fit enough to return to operational flying with his old unit eight months later but found Bader less than sympathetic. 'When I reported to the Wing Leader he tore a strip off me for being so careless as to have been shot down, which I thought was a bit off, to say the least', Walker later related. 'Suffice to say that I did not take to him, and he not to me, so three weeks later I was posted to an Aircraft Delivery Flight at Hendon.' This was part of a pattern: quickly deciding that several of the existing leaders needed a rest, Bader obtained permission from Leigh-Mallory to bring in some of his favourites from 242 Squadron in the weeks and months following his arrival. Dennis Crowley-Milling, Charles Bush, and Ken Holden were brought in to be flight commanders and in the latter case CO for 610 Squadron, while Charles Arthur and Stan Turner were parachuted in as flight commander and CO respectively for 145 Squadron. It was also hardly coincidental that Bader's favourite controller, Woody Woodhall, became the station commander at Tangmere. To a degree these changes made perfect sense: Bader wanted subordinate leaders and a controller whom he knew from experience he could work with, and he was by no means the only wing leader during the war to shuffle the pack on taking command.

The changes, however, meant denuding his old squadron of some of its most experienced pilots – 'if this goes on 242 will be stationed at Norwich and all its fellows will be here', Pyker remarked to his departing CO – and caused a certain degree of disruption in the new squadrons. 'All the Tangmere pilots are used to each other, know each other and have learned to work as a team,' Offenberg reflected. 'How are they going to react when given new leaders?' The CO of 616 Squadron, for one, was slightly unnerved by Bader's habit of swearing a blue streak any time the squadron leader did anything to annoy him. 'D'you know what the Wingco called me this morning?' Billy Burton took to telling to those around him; 'he called me a [expletive deleted].'[17]

Meanwhile there were plenty of indications beyond personnel shifts that Bader was seen as one of the premier combat leaders in Fighter Command whose opinions were valuable and to whom a fair degree of latitude should be granted in carrying out his tasks. There were no repercussions, for instance, when he short-circuited the process of retrofitting Spitfire IIs with metal ailerons – thus increasing the roll and turn rate – by forcing himself, and then 616 Squadron, to the front of the queue. His simple but effective tactic was to fly first himself, and then 616 Squadron, to the Southampton factory and demand that fitting be done on the spot. This led to confusion but not censure. Bader was later able to ignore with apparent impunity orders from Group HQ to return a staff car and one of the two aircraft he kept for his personal use.[18]

Bader, in the meantime, was talking through, testing, and then adopting major changes in the basic formation tactics his pilots employed. Fighter Command had gone to war using a section of three aircraft flying in a tight 'vic' as its basic formation. While this three-plane wedge looked impressive it proved to be very dangerous in the presence of enemy fighters. The supporting pilots had to spend much of their time looking inward to keep station with the section leader, co-ordinated manoeuvring was difficult to achieve quickly, and no member of the section was really in a position to support another in the event of a hostile 'bounce' from above. Bob Norris of No. 1 Squadron, RCAF, spoke for many when he later observed 'I have no idea why they ever had three aircraft in [close] formation.' Aware of the problem, Bader experimented into May 1941 with a variety of alternatives while taking heed of suggestions made by pilots such as Cocky Dundas of 616 Squadron whom he respected. 'He was wildly enthusiastic over new ideas that seemed good and would have his way about them', the artist Cuthbert Orde had earlier observed; 'if they turned out poor – and they sometimes did – he would switch to the opposite with even greater enthusiasm.' Bader eventually settled on a pair of aircraft flying more-or-less line abreast with enough space between them (about fifty yards) to allow the pilots to scan the sky and offer each other support in the event of an attack. In the case of two pairs flying together in a section of four, the pairs would break upward right and left in tight turns if the enemy was seen coming from behind, thereby precipitating a more equal head-to-head confrontation. When first tried on 8 May 1941, Bader mishandled the timing of the break, and in other cases the Spitfires lost sight of each other whilst splitting up. 'Bader was quick to detect the flaw in our breaking procedure', remembered Johnnie Johnson, 'and new tactics were immediately devised.'

Until now the two pairs of Spitfires had broken in opposite directions and for a few precious seconds lost sight of each other. Now the wingman would fly sufficiently far back for the leader to turn steeply towards him without danger of a collision. If the wingman was on the inside of a turn he would remain low while the outside pair of Spitfires swung to the top. But should the wingman be on the outside of the turn, then he would be the highest Spitfire in the manoeuvre and the other pair of aircraft would slide inside the leader. In this way we would never lose sight of each other and should be able to keep our cross-over even in the steepest turns.

The Tangmere wing leader, in short, had discovered the 'finger four' formation that had served the Luftwaffe well since the Spanish Civil War and would prove equally helpful to fighters and fighter-bombers of the RAF for the rest of the war.[19]

The only trouble (historically) is that, contrary to the impression left by Paul Brickhill and some of the authors who followed him, Bader was by no means a pioneer in this respect: indeed he was perhaps slower than some to change. While the squadrons of the Duxford Wing had mostly stuck to the conventional tight 'vic' in 1940, other units had started to seriously modify the section and squadron formations they flew. Using the last fighter as a tail-end 'weaver' did not always work too well, as the pilot concerned was often picked off without the rest of the squadron knowing that he was gone.

Other experiments, however, were more successful. The vic might be opened up so that the pilots had to concentrate less on keeping station with the leader. Alternatively, sections, flights, or squadrons could be told by the CO to fly line astern, sometimes loosely, or weaving in a 'snake' pattern to get a better sense of what was behind them. And, most importantly, pairs might be used instead of threes. 603 Squadron, when it arrived at Hornchurch in August 1940, was 'flying in threes', according to Spitfire pilot Gerald Stapleton. 'Three aeroplanes cannot stay together', he went on to explain in an interview, 'two can; so after very bad casualties in the first week, we started flying in finger fours: two and two.' Bob Tuck, to take another example, had introduced loose pairs when he took command of 257 Squadron during the Battle of Britain, and by the autumn of 1940, 611 Squadron had adopted the two-pair 'finger four'. By the time Bader tried this out, the Air Ministry was noting that 'most squadrons are now using the "pair" as the basic Unit in their formations instead of "threes".'[20]

Bader, though, was more prominent than most other operational fighter leaders by this point. 'He was now a dominant figure in the flying hierarchy of Fighter Command', believed Laddie Lucas, 'assertive, confident and very set in his commanding ways.' Bader also enjoyed a high public profile that spring through press coverage by the likes of Henry Longhurst in the *Sunday Express* and Alexander Austin in the *Daily Herald*. Victor Gollancz, furthermore, was in the process of publishing a book on Fighter Command by Austin in which Bader was used as 'a composite portrait of a fighter pilot'. And Bader himself was not above conspiring with Longhurst to get a critical article into print that would force the Air Ministry to speed up the camouflaging of the Tangmere runways. So perhaps it is not so surprising that it was he, rather than others, whose name was eventually linked to the new tactical formations.[21]

By the spring of 1941 it was clear that there was room for improvement in terms of RAF fighter performance in the offensive role. The first half-dozen or so circus operations and fighter sweeps had not been able 'to bring about a fighter battle on our initiative and under circumstances advantageous to ourselves'. Luftwaffe fighters had refused to engage in a general mêlée, choosing instead to pick off stragglers and carry out quick diving passes when the RAF formations were low on fuel and thereby unable to properly dogfight against the improved 'F' model of the Me 109. In all, offensive operations by the second week of March had cost seventeen RAF pilots as against the (inflated) claim that thirteen enemy aircraft had been downed. Nevertheless, both the Chief of the Air Staff and C-in-C Fighter Command continued to toe the Trenchard line. When the C-in-C Bomber Command expressed the belief that attacks in future 'must be profitable to us either because we shoot down more fighters than we ourselves lose, or because we inflict material damage on the enemy', Peter Portal took exception to his reasoning. 'I regard the exercise of initiative as in itself an extremely important factor in morale,' the CAS responded, 'and I would willingly accept equal or even more [losses] in order to throw the enemy on the defensive, and give our units moral superiority by doing most of the fighting on the other side.' Sholto Douglas argued that if 'damaged' claims were factored in, then the loss ratio favoured the RAF, and that in any case it was of the utmost moral importance to attack the enemy at every opportunity. Leigh-Mallory was therefore left free to pursue and expand the fighter offensive.[22]

In the middle of April 1941 the AOC 11 Group held a conference at his Uxbridge HQ, calling together his sector station commanders and wing leaders. 'Gentlemen', Leigh-Mallory announced, 'we must stop licking our wounds. We are now going over to the offensive. Last year our fighting was desperate. Now we're entitled to be cocky.' Stepped-up offensive operations over France, he continued, would do wonders for pilot morale. Not everyone was convinced that this was a good idea, however. With uncharacteristic bluntness Sailor Malan, now heading the Biggin Hill Wing, interrupted the AOC's oration to declare: 'You're trying to achieve the impossible, sir.' Bader, of course, was already straining at the leash to get at the enemy. Johnnie Johnson remembered how the wing commander had invited him to join him on an impromptu trip over the Channel 'to see if we can bag a couple of Huns before lunch.' Bader at first did not tell sector control what he was up to, and when told the station commander wanted to know, tried to hide his true intentions. 'Tell him that Dogsbody section [Bader had the initials 'DB' painted on his Spitfire for identification purposes – an idea he had borrowed from Wing Commander 'HB' Harry Broadhurst], two aircraft, are going on a little snoop over the Channel', he radioed. 'Nothing exciting, just a little routine snoop. Out.' Woodhall, though, knew Bader well enough to guess that he was out on a free-range hunt. 'Dogsbody, you are not to proceed with your flight', Bader was told. 'You are to return immediately. Is this understood?' Bader swore a blue streak but eventually complied. Someone with this kind of aggressiveness was unlikely to think anything was impossible, and other fighter leaders were also enthusiastic at the prospect of taking the war to the enemy. Malan's pessimistic assessment was written off by the AOC as the product of fatigue: 'You're tired, Sailor... Get out; take a rest.'[23]

Weather restrictions meant that it was not until late May and on into June 1941 that the Tangmere Wing began to operate en masse, first in fighter-only sweeps and then as part of the escort in circus operations. From a material standpoint these were not very successful, mirroring the experience of the other wings. Enemy fighters refused to be drawn into serious combat during sweeps, and usually kept to the periphery of circuses, content to pick off the occasional straggler. The RAF formations could not fly very far inland due to the limited fuel capacity of the fighters, while the bomber formations remained small and therefore were unlikely to do great damage to the few important targets within range. The Luftwaffe, in short, could afford to be choosy about when, how, and even if, it engaged the RAF beyond sending up flak. A further problem was that while enemy pilots could bail out of stricken aircraft and parachute to safety, their RAF opponents were mostly captured: a reversal of the situation that had existed when the fighting had been over south-east England rather than north-east France. Though the Tangmere Wing itself was as yet suffering few casualties, nine pilots had been lost on fighter sweep operations and another twenty-five on circus operations by 13 June, as against (inevitably inflated) claims for twenty-five enemy fighters destroyed. 'We're just poking the bear in his pit, gentlemen', Leigh-Mallory assured his commanders. 'You'll get some reaction in due course.'[24]

Though glad to be notionally taking the war to the enemy, Bader found the relative absence of Luftwaffe air activity annoying. It was particularly galling when other wings seemed to have more luck. In the wake of a debriefing at Stanmore after a raid on the rail yards at Lille it became apparent to his pilots that he was far from happy. 'Malan got two to-day and his boys got a few more', he stormed. 'It's damn well time we found some.'[25]

With such slim pickings the wing commander was not above making a kill claim that did not meet the strict requirement that the enemy aircraft attacked be seen to have blown up or crashed. Having fired at close range into an Me 109 during a brief dogfight on 21 June while the wing was returning from St Omer, Bader subsequently admitted that 'I foolishly followed him down with my eyes and nearly collided with a cannon [-armed] Spitfire.' Not witnessing the crash, however, did not stop him from making a case for an additional kill. The wing commander was not, however, the only pilot to engage the 109s that attacked that morning: Flight Lieutenant Roland Lee-Knight of 610 Squadron, for instance, recorded that he had left one 'smoking violently and apparently on fire', so it remains unclear – as was so often the case with pell-mell air combats involving several aircraft – precisely who accomplished what.[26]

The offensive itself was given added impetus by the German invasion of the Soviet Union that began in the fourth week of June 1941. The goal now was not only to engage and destroy as many

enemy aircraft as possible, but also to prevent transfers and hopefully force the enemy to withdraw fighters from Russia to meet the
burgeoning air attack in the West. Circus operations grew more
complex as spring gave way to summer, with the fighter wings
operating in conjunction with small formations of bombers in the
close-support, close-escort, top-cover, and latterly the target-withdrawal role. The first two aimed to protect the bombers, the third to
pounce on enemy fighters coming in from above. With a hundred
or more fast fighters flying with and above to protect a half-dozen
or fewer slower bombers, the whole thing came to be known as 'the
beehive'. The target-withdrawal wing – which arrived on the scene
as the main force was turning for home – was to allow for engage-
ments with the Luftwaffe when the fighters of the escort wing were
low on fuel.[27]

Leigh-Mallory visited Tangmere for tactical discussions, and
the wing leader's pilots was in the thick of things from late June
through July 1941, going on circus operations or sweeps almost
every day that weather permitted. Bader, who always flew with
616 Squadron, seemed absolutely fearless. As his wingman could
attest, the wing commander was often the last to leave the scene,
tarrying in order to find something to shoot at. 'I must confess
to knowing no greater thrill than combat between fighters in a
clear blue sky at 20,000 feet', he later wrote. 'There was something
almost gay about it.' When weather scrubbed major sorties Bader
continued his habit of mounting unauthorised 'rhubarb' flights in
which under the guise of 'local flying' he led his section under the
cloud base at low level towards France in search of trouble. On the
return leg of all kinds of operation he was also observed puffing
away on his pipe, despite the obvious fire hazard. ('I pointedly
drifted off to a distance which I judged immune from the explosion
which might follow,' a pilot in his section recalled.) This carefree
aggression could serve the wing well, youthful pilots taking heart
from the wing commander's obvious confidence in himself and, by
extension, the formation he led. 'I mean he used to come into the
briefing at Tangmere', Archie Winskill fondly recalled, 'and say,
"Right, chaps, it's return tickets only today to Lille." Which was
a great boost to morale.' In the evening Bader would often hold
court at Bay House, where his wife would play hostess, and discuss
tactics as well as engage in banter with pilots who felt honoured to
be part of his extended family circle. '[J]olly good fun it was', wrote

one visitor, 'much shop [talk] and much riotous behaviour and conversation.' Those picked to fly in the section he led considered themselves particularly privileged. Sergeant Alan Smith remembered being 'thrilled to bits' to be chosen as his wingman, though Bader had added threateningly: 'God help you if I get shot down.' Numbers three and four were also happy to be working alongside such a brave and dynamic character. 'Bader showed me by example how a man should behave in war', wrote Cocky Dundas. 'To fly with Bader and have him call me by my Christian name was one of the greatest things of my life, really', Johnnie Johnson reflected half a century later. Squadron Leader Ken Holden, the Yorkshire-born CO of 610 Squadron and a near contemporary to the wing leader in age, was one of the few pilots willing to risk the inevitable wrath by occasionally being less than totally respectful. For many of the younger pilots in his circle the attitude toward Bader could verge on devoted adulation.[28]

The formation he led, after all, had accomplished a lot. Between the start of the German invasion of Russia and the end of the first week in August the wing claimed over twenty-five definite kills, Bader himself adding a bar to his DSO plus half-a-dozen enemy aircraft to his personal score. 'This officer has led his wing on a series of consistently successful sorties over enemy territory during the past three months', read the second DSO citation. 'His high qualities of leadership and courage have been an inspiration to all.'[29]

There were, however, certain problems with the way Bader led the wing. Some would, indeed, eventually contribute to the downfall of a leader whom many came to consider practically invincible. His sheer aggressiveness caused even some admirers to quail on occasion. When truly bad weather set in, Bader insisted on his circle of acolytes accompanying him to relax in one or other of the local towns, whether they wanted to or not. When the weather was anything from marginal to good the same rules applied in hunting the foe. 'We found Bader a friendly type', a 504 Squadron pilot wrote of a briefing delivered by the wing leader the night before a sweep in July 1941, 'but [also] a grim and dedicated killer of Germans.' He still liked, among other things, to blow off steam doing impromptu sorties. On 4 July, for example, in the wake of an afternoon wing patrol, four aircraft took off from Westhampnett in what for official purposes was described as 'some local flying practice' but was in reality Bader leading three other pilots on an unauthorised hunting expedition over north-east France. 'His idea of a Saturday afternoon off was to take Cocky and Alan Smith and one or two other unfortunates over the Channel to the Pas de Calais', Johnson remembered, 'in the hope that he might encounter [the Luftwaffe ace] Dolfo Galland.' But many pilots, including men who flew with him, disliked rhubarbs intensely. Flying in pairs under a low cloud base left a section vulnerable to being bounced from above if the ceiling became broken or the cloud base was high enough for enemy patrolling. Flak, however, was the real danger. Spitfires and Hurricanes both had liquid-cooled in-line engines in which the glycol tank was below the nose. The tank was totally exposed to ground fire, and if hit the liquid would quickly drain off and the engine would seize up. Rhubarbs, according to 145 Squadron pilot Raymond Munro, were considered by a number of his comrades 'to be an act of sheer madness or a dirty date with fate'. By the middle of June a total of eight Fighter Command pilots had been lost on such low-level sorties for little appreciable gain. 'I loathed those *Rhubarbs* with a deep, dark hatred', Johnnie Johnson later confessed, affirming in print that most other pilots felt the same way.[30]

The impulse to get at the enemy could also generate extra difficulties when Bader was leading the wing. 'With Bader, once he had spotted the enemy, there was a semblance of directing his squadrons and deploying them in the air for the attack', Archie Winskill of 41 Squadron later conceded, 'but on the whole when he sighted the first 109s he was after them, the Wing just breaking up and it being every man for himself.'[31]

This kind of reflex action, allied with the inevitable communication and identification problems associated with directing a formation of thirty-six Spitfires, either operating alone or in conjunction with other fighter wings and bomber formations, meant that both circuses and sweeps might be fraught with difficulty even without direct enemy intervention. Rendezvousing with other formations to form a 'beehive' could be a hair-raising experience for pilots in the wing due to the risk of collision. And while the Luftwaffe did not often contest fighter-only sweeps, these too had their hazards when Bader made or confirmed a false identification. R. A. Morton of 616 Squadron wrote a letter to his parents on 20 June 1941 describing what he judged to be a typically chaotic, if bloodless, wing sortie with Bader leading:

At zero hour umpteen squadrons take off from various aerodromes, each in three sections of four aircraft. Bader leads the first section in our squadron, the C.O. the second… Each squadron climbs to its predetermined height, upon which we proceed to Dover, then swing out across the French coast. This is usually where the R/T chatter starts. 'Hello Dogsbody (Bader) six 109s straight ahead, over.' 'I can't see them, what height?' 'About a thousand feet above… no, they're diving, they must have seen us. 'OK, Billy, you turn towards them we'll follow…No, I see them now…right-oh, chaps, break up and muck in!' After which all is pandemonium – gun sights switched on, safety-catches flicked off, the formation dissolves, the sky is filled with a mass of whirling aircraft, and you set about the job of getting on someone's tail. You normally get on about half-a-dozen, only to find each one either someone in your own squadron or one of the Hurricanes which were the original '109s'. Then Bader says, 'O.K. chaps, false alarm, form up again.' I usually manage to find the C.O., and occasionally the other two aircraft of our section join us, but it's hopeless to try and find the remainder of your squadron out of the hundred-odd aircraft which have by this time joined in the 'scrap'. So you cruize [sic] about over the Channel for about three-quarters of an hour, listening to a continuous stream of messages at various volumes. 'Hello, Dogsbody, red 4 calling, two 109s coming up behind.' 'O.K., red 4, I can't see them. Tell us when they break.' 'O.K.' 'Hello, Dogsbody, Ken calling, I think it's only my section your number 4 has seen.' 'Hello, yellow leader, Jack calling, there's something diving on you tail.' 'O.K. Jack, tell me when to break.' 'Break!' You whip round to find your sights trained on a solitary Hurricane who's lost his section. After… about 45 minutes of this, you collect as many aircraft together as you can find, and set off for home. And that's that.[32]

When the Luftwaffe chose to put in an appearance, and they more often did during circus operations in the summer of 1941, there could be brushes with disaster when the wing leader made the wrong call. 'Damned good bombing', Bader wrote in his logbook after participating in a circus raid on a power station at Lille in early August, '– blown to hell.' Bob Beardsley of 41 Squadron had a less satisfying recollection of the same operation.

On this sortie I was leading a section of four, our rear cover. We were the low squadron of the Wing, and as I looked to my rear left I saw an

Me 109 closing on my port sub-section, so close that the cannon orifice in the propeller boss was very apparent! I called 'Break port!', and we all went hard at it. The attacking aircraft had not fired, but I called the Wing Leader to tell him that we had been attacked by 109s. To my amazement, Wing Commander Bader responded: 'Only Hurricanes, old boy!' I, however, failed to see the joke! The next second the whole Wing was engaged – I saw no more 'Hurricanes'. When the lead squadron was attacked, Bader did actually say: 'Sorry old boy!'[33]

Much of this sort of confusion arose from the inevitable difficulty of one man trying to command and control three squadrons at once in hostile airspace. Yet Bader added to the burdens in ways that helped undermine his decisions in the air and cause unnecessary friction on the ground.

The wing leader always insisted on leading every wing operation personally at the head of 616 Squadron. 'Bader always flew with our squadron', Laddie Lucas explained. 'That's how I got to know him so well. Not only did he fly with 616 Squadron, but he always insisted that Dundas, Smith, and me, would fly in his section of four.' For those close to the wing leader this made no difference to the overall cohesiveness of the wing. 'There was a close bond between the Spitfire units at Tangmere that summer,' asserted Cocky Dundas. 'Bader welded the wing into a single unit and we all knew each other well, so that the losses sustained by the other squadrons were almost as painful as our own.' This was not the view of all, however. Some of the pilots from the other units in the Tangmere Wing, based at nearby Merton and Tangmere itself, felt under-appreciated if not out-right ignored. 'We rarely saw him at all', recalled Frank Twitchett. 'In fact, despite having been with 145 [Squadron] for the its entire tour at Tangmere in 1941, I can only recall having seen him twice.' The same was true after 145 Squadron was replaced by 41 Squadron in July. 'He would definitely have created more team spirit if he had not led solely with 616', argued Ron Rayner. The CO of 616, meanwhile, was himself understandably unhappy at never getting to lead his own squadron independently. In addition, and in contrast to some of his wing-leader peers, Bader did little to help novice pilots. David Cox recalled how the Tangmere Wing leader was 'very brusque' and had 'not much time for' anyone but the aces whom he tended to patron-ise. 'He wasn't terribly keen on sergeant pilots either', Cox added. So much so, in fact, that, according to Twitchett, the NCO aircrew of 145

Squadron requested postings en masse when it was rumoured that Bader wanted to create an officers-only wing.[34]

By assuming command of every wing sortie, furthermore, Bader prevented the emergence of experienced alternative wing leaders in the event he was lost in combat: he was, as at least a few officers complained *sotto voce*, too much of a 'one-man band' in this respect. (Not that his loss was something that ever seems to have crossed the minds of his devoted circle of RAF admirers.) Last, but perhaps most importantly of all, through commanding in the air so much – ten sweeps over seven days at one point, and far more often than the other wing leaders – Bader allowed fatigue to impair his judgement.[35]

One possible sign that self-imposed pressure was getting to the Tangmere Wing leader was the way in which he bullied ground crews, especially if his Spitfire developed a technical fault. 'Whilst with 616 Squadron I came into contact with him', George Reid remembered, 'and learned to both fear and dislike the fellow.'

> He was a show-off and the most pompous chap I had ever met. My last recollection of Wing Commander Bader was when his Spitfire's wheels would not lock up correctly. There was a sweep to be flown at 3 p.m. and by this time it was already 2 of the clock. He came over in his car, stomped up to the Chiefy Sergeant and myself and raged, turning on high powered filth from his mouth, and thumped his car bonnet with a stick. I actually thought he would strike Chiefy with that cane. I dived back under the Spitfire and fortunately off he went!

'He was just aggressive, nearly all the time, as far as I was concerned', David Lewis agreed, 'never "please" or "thank you".' This was in marked contrast to other pilots who recognised how important ground crews were in preventing mechanical problems from occurring in the air.[36]

Meanwhile the air offensive over France was taking its toll. The Luftwaffe still held most of the cards, and though extravagant claims were made concerning the number of enemy fighters shot down – the difference between what was pronounced and what was actually achieved reached 5:1 proportions[37]– RAF casualties continued to mount. Between 21 June and 4 July 1941, for example, a period in which operations by Fighter Command were considered to have been particularly successful, a total of forty RAF pilots had been lost. 'They weren't extremely popular with us', as New

Zealander pilot Bob Spurdle of 91 Squadron later admitted. 'We had to fight over enemy territory now, and they were fairly hairy operations.' The Tangmere Wing was by no means immune from harm. 616 Squadron, for instance, lost a dozen pilots between 20 June and 10 August.

Spitfire pilots disliked being tied to protecting the bombers. Especially in the case of the close escort wing, this put them at a speed and height disadvantage when trying to confront the in-and-out diving passes the Luftwaffe pilots favoured. Over time some began to wonder what was actually being accomplished. Dundas claimed morale in 616 Squadron remained 'sky-high' despite the losses, but even in the Tangmere Wing there were those who were feeling the strain of operations and wondering, like Archie Winskill of 41 Squadron, 'was the arithmetic right?' In point of fact it was not: overall the RAF was losing three aircraft to every one lost by the Luftwaffe. Bader, however, believed that all was going 'like clockwork' and did little to hide his belief that anyone who thought otherwise was being windy.[38]

Leigh-Mallory was in the habit of visiting sector stations and holding conferences to discuss the state of things. According to a member of the Hornchurch Wing the AOC 'was always keen to hear our views and reactions to the offensive operations', expressed concern about losses, and 'made a point of putting our suggestions into effect'. At one of the frequent meetings held at Northolt that summer, another of the wing leaders questioned whether the benefits of leaning in to France really outweighed the costs. 'Hell, old boy', Bader at once retorted, 'you can't just spend the rest of your life doing slow rolls over the aerodrome!' Harry Broadhurst, another wing leader, arrived at another Northolt conference after having had several pieces of shrapnel removed from various parts of his anatomy that he had received in a sweep earlier that day. 'When I passed Douglas Bader', Broadhurst recalled, 'he thumped me on the backside and said "ullo ullo ullo, running away from the enemy again, Broadie?" I might have guessed he would do something like that and it hurt quite a bit.' Such remarks were meant and taken as jokes but were also an accurate reflection of Bader's pugilistic attitude. When Bader had his say, Leigh-Mallory was inclined to indulge him, which in turn meant that while tactics could be argued over there was never any serious questioning of the offensive as such by the AOC 11 Group.[39]

It remained, moreover, an offensive in which Bader was determined to continue taking a leading role. There were those who thought that his prior deeds and current public stature foreshadowed a major PR disaster if he was allowed to continue on operations. 'I propose that Douglas Bader be prohibited from ever stepping into an aircraft again', the *Daily Mirror*'s 'Cassandra' had informed readers in July 1941, adding that 'Such men as he... are too valuable to England.' This was not, however, a course of action that appealed in the slightest to Bader himself. As Ken Holden of 616 Squadron recalled a few years after the war, the wing leader could talk about nothing but shooting down more enemy aircraft. Fatigue, though, was rapidly catching up with Bader by the first week of August 1941. Both Peter Macdonald (who had been posted to Tangmere in an administrative capacity) and Woody Woodhall noticed the tell-tale darkening of the skin round his eyes and urged him to take a rest. Sailor Malan of the Biggin Hill Wing was also feeling the pressure. At first he resisted suggestions that he go off ops – 'I kept thinking: "Just a few more before I go"' – but then conceded that fatigue was impairing his skills. After first making sure that a designated deputy wing leader could step into the breach, Malan told the AOC that he ought to be relieved in late July. Leigh-Mallory then wondered if the time had not come for Bader to step down for a time as well. 'You'd better have a spell off operations', he told him. 'You can't go on like this indefinitely.' Bader, though, who in early August actually pestered the AOC to get the Tangmere Wing to be assigned *more* to do, would have none of it. He was fit and wanted to 'see the season out' and, he hoped, increase his personal score from its current official total of 20 ½ kills. Leigh-Mallory acquiesced; Bader, after all, was by the summer of 1941 famous enough for total strangers to stop and ask for his autograph when he was off duty, and it would not do to cross one of the RAF's star fighter pilots if it could be avoided. Yet according to what Billy Burton, the CO of 616 Squadron, later told Kenneth Cross, by the second week in August there were those in the Tangmere Wing in a near-mutinous state because of Bader's 'reckless leading in an effort to increase his own score'.[40]

Bader, in short, was riding for a fall. On 9 August 1941, he got it. The first setback occurred before the wing took off on a Target Support run. Alan Smith, who normally flew – and very effectively in terms of covering his leader – as wingman to Bader, was grounded because of a head-cold. His replacement, though far from being a novice pilot, did not have Smith's experience working in tandem with Bader.

Things actually began to go wrong when a squadron relatively new to the Tangmere Wing failed to link up with the rest of the squadrons in the air. Then Bader discovered that his radio was functioning imperfectly and that his airspeed indicator was not working at all. By rights he should have handed over command to someone else and turned for home, since knowing the airspeed was, among other things, crucial in making sure the wing arrived over the target area on time: but as Laddie Lucas put it in an interview, Bader 'wasn't that sort of chap'.

Instead the wing leader simply had Cocky Dundas move into the lead position until the formation crossed the coast. This event having occurred on time, Bader moved back into the lead, though the problem with his airspeed indicator made it difficult for him to maintain an even flying speed and therefore harder for others in the formation to keep station with the leader. Bader himself lost his bearings at one point – 'I haven't much idea where I am,' he radioed – but luckily a radio-direction fix indicated the wing was pretty where it ought to have been at that point.[41]

As the two squadrons progressed inland, they were warned by ground control of large numbers of enemy aircraft in the vicinity, and various pilots called in sightings of Me 109s behind, above, and below. Bader's attention, though, was focussed on twelve 109s ahead of 616 Squadron that were two or three thousand feet below the Spitfires: 'a perfect situation for the classic attack from behind and above', he later explained. Dundas suspected a trap, fearing that there were more 109s waiting to pounce from above when the lower twelve 109s were attacked: but the wing leader immediately led his section, followed by four other Spitfires, into the fray. 'I signalled "attacking" and dived too fast and too steeply', Bader later admitted. 'I was tense, and my judgement had gone for some reason that I did not recognize at the time... I closed so fast on the 109 that I had no time to fire, and barely time to avoid cutting him in half with my Spitfire.' Meanwhile the trap had been sprung, enemy fighters swooping down from above and behind, turning the hunters into the hunted.[42]

As the Spitfires broke formation a general mêlée ensued, but Bader, minus a working airspeed indicator, had flashed through the enemy so fast that when he pulled up the sky at first seemed empty. With aircraft moving at 350-plus miles per hour in multiple directions this empty sky phenomenon was a common coda to the chaos of kill-or-be-killed dog-fighting manoeuvres. It was also quite dangerous. A lone aircraft in hostile skies was potentially a sitting duck, which was why Bader had ordered that anyone finding himself flying alone should drop down and head for home at once. It was one thing for Bader to tell others what to do; however, it was quite another for him to follow his own advice. As the wing leader had laughingly remarked when one of his squadron commanders pointed out that he, Bader, was doing the aerobatics he bawled out other pilots for undertaking, 'Ah, that's a very different thing.' Instead of diving for home Bader looked about for something to hunt at 24,000 feet. Almost at once he saw a formation of Me 109s flying ahead, and decided to stalk them. One against nine were not good odds; but Bader believed he could pick off one or two enemy aircraft and dive away before the remainder could react. He was wrong. Though he got one of the 109s, the others moved quickly to deal with the intruder.

There was an almighty shudder in the airframe, and suddenly Bader felt the joystick of his Spitfire no longer responding. Looking behind, he saw that the entire tail assembly of his Spitfire was gone: 'Time to leave', as he later put it. With considerable difficulty because of his legs, he was able to fight free of the cockpit, successfully open his parachute, and float to earth.[43]

Once it became apparent that Douglas Bader had been brought down there was understandably a great deal of dismay among his friends and admirers within the Tangmere Wing. The shock, however, extended much further. Bader, after all, had been widely admired and made into a leading symbol of indomitable courage and tenacity within the RAF. 'Oh God no!' was the immediate reaction of the C-in-C Fighter Command when he got the news. 'This was quite a shock to me', he later explained, 'since Douglas Bader was not only one of my best Wing Leaders, but also, by virtue of the fact that he had no legs, had attained an enormous reputation in Fighter Command and, indeed throughout Britain.' His personal assistant recorded in his diary that Sholto Douglas was more agitated than he had ever seen him before: 'I knew what a blow his loss would be to the morale of my pilots.' Moreover someone had to be found to lead the Tangmere Wing, since Bader himself had made no provision for the possibility that he would be killed or captured.

Meanwhile there were those who were secretly glad to see the back of such a harsh taskmaster. 'So far as I am concerned,' George Reid stated decades later, 'after Wing Commander Bader was shot down, a happy feeling settled on 616 [Squadron].'[44]

To the end of his life Bader remained largely convinced that he had not been shot down at all. Rather, he believed, in turning away from the enemy he had collided with an Me 109. The Germans themselves thought it possible he had been brought down by an NCO pilot, but Bader, when this was put to him after his capture, found it 'an intolerable idea'. The commander therefore engaged in a little deception while Bader was briefly a guest of JG 26. 'In order not to offend Bader we chose from among the successful pilots who had taken part in this flight a fair-haired, good-looking flying officer and introduced him to Bader as his victorious opponent', Adolf Galland later admitted. 'Bader was pleasantly surprised and shook his hand warmly.' A detailed examination of the available evidence by knowledgeable historians – crash sites, interviews, and so forth – suggests that Bader probably was shot down rather than hit in a collision, perhaps even by another Spitfire: an unfortunately not uncommon experience in the heat of battle.

Whatever the exact circumstances, the Tangmere Wing leader had contributed mightily to his own downfall: first, by refusing to go off operations; second, by leading the wing in an aircraft with an iffy radio and duff airspeed indicator; and third, by hanging about and looking for trouble rather than heading home once isolated. What remained to be seen was whether a man whose manner had inspired so many men would react to the very different challenges of being a prisoner of war.[45]

Notes

[1]Hugh Dundas, *Flying Start* (London: Stanley Paul, 1988), p. 68. 'Hally' was Flying Officer Hall, the engineering officer.

[2]See Michael G. Burns, *Bader* (London: Cassell, 1998 edn), pp. 126–27, on the operations mentioned. On the problems of night vision and engine exhaust in Hurricanes see Peter Townsend, *Duel in the Dark* (London: Harrap, 1986), p. 30.

[3]Royal Air Force Museum Department of Research and Information Services [hereafter RAFM], B 354, Bader logbook, 31 December 1940–1 January 1941 [see also St Edward's School Archive, Bader to Dingwall, 3 January 1941]. On asking

for and receiving the Hurricane II see Paul Brickhill, Reach for the Sky (London: Collins, 1954), pp. 231, 237.

[4]Sholto Douglas, Years of Command (London: Collins, 1966), p. 114; see Imperial War Museum Department of Documents [hereafter IWM], Lord Douglas Papers, Box 3, TS of dictation notes to R. Wright, p. 168; National Archives [hereafter NA], AIR 41/18, f. 71 (back); Liddell Hart Centre, Nicholas Eadon Papers, Box 3, Douglas to Eadon, 5 November 1957. On Trenchard see also Andrew Boyle, Trenchard (London: Collins, 1962), p. 720; Imperial War Museum Sound Archive [hereafter IWMSA] 12524/2, C.B. Brown.

[5]Burns, Bader, p. 128; Doug Stokes, Wings Aflame (Manchester: Crecy, 1988 edn), p. 130. On Leigh-Mallory visiting and consulting in general see Kenneth Cross with Vincent Orange, Straight and Level (London: Grub Street, 1993), pp. 64, 68; D. Crowley-Milling in Henry Probert and Sebastian Cox (eds), The Battle Re-Thought (Shrewsbury: Airlife, 1991), p. 74; H. Broadhurst in Bill Newton Dunn, Big Wing (Shrewsbury: Airlife, 1992), p. 82. Sholto Douglas also struck at least some squadron commanders as keen to listen to what men at the sharp end had to say. See Townsend, Duel in the Dark, pp. 149, 116.

[6]NA, AIR 41/18, App. (IV) A&B; Basil Collier, The Defence of the United Kingdom (London: HMSO, 1957), pp. 290–91.

[7]Gordon Olive and Dennis Newton, The Devil at 6 O'clock (Loftus, NSW: Australian Military History Publications, 2001), pp. 161–2; AIR 16/367, minute 2, GC (Ops) to SASO, 15 December 1940; AIR 16/367, encl. 1A, AOC 12 Group to AOC-in-C Fighter Command, 7 December 1940; Broadhurst in Dunn, Big Wing, p. 82; see also Townsend, Duel in the Dark, p. 116.

[8]A.R.D. MacDonell, From Dogfight to Diplomacy: A Spitfire Pilot's Log, 1932–1958 (Barnsley: Pen and Sword, 2005), p. 71.

[9]NA, AIR 16/367, minute 4, C-in-C to SASO, 16 December 1940.

[10]Larry Forrester, Fly for Your Life (Garden City, NY: Nelson Doubleday, 1978 edn), pp. 192–95. On Bader and the failed 19 Squadron experiment see Douglas Bader, Fight for the Sky (London: Sidgwick and Jackson, 1975 edn), pp. 68–69; see also NA, AIR 20/4213, Conclusions of DCAS's conference, 9 December 1940. On Bader arguing that, close enough in, machine guns would always do the job see IWMSA 11086, A.C. Bartley TS, p. 21. On other pilots very much wanting the hitting power of cannon see Anthony Bartley, Smoke Trails in the Sky (London: Kimber, 1984), p. 32; Olive and Newton, Devil at 6 O'clock, p. 160; Jeffrey Quill, Spitfire (London: John Murray, 1983), p. 176; J.A. Kent, One of the Few (London: Kimber, 1971), p. 139; see also AIR 2/5065, DHO minute to ACS(T), 15 February 1940.

[11]Burns, Bader, p. 175; J.E. Johnson, Wing Leader (London: Chatto and Windus, 1956), p. 110; Peter Caygill, Spitfire Mark V in Action (Shrewsbury: Airlife, 2001), p. 17; Brickhill, Reach for the Sky, p. 271; see RAFM, B354, Bader logbook, June–August

1941. The German ace Adolf Galland took the opposite stance in refusing to give up the dual cannon of the Me 109E in favour of the single cannon of the Me 109F. See David Baker, *Adolf Galland* (London: Windrow and Greene, 1996), p. 158.

[12]http://home.tiscali.be/ed.ragas/awshistory/awsbader.html (accessed 2 December 2004), B. Cunningham interview of D. Bader for *Code One*; NA, AIR 27/1471, 242 Sqn ORB, 4 February 1941; see ibid., 12 February 1941; BBC Written Archive, Bader script for 'The World Goes By' programme, broadcast Home Service, 12 February 1941. He was identified only as a Squadron Leader of the RAF on the air, but the fact that he was chosen to make the broadcast is significant. On the RAF and radio programmes see Sîan Nicholas, *The Echo of War* (Manchester: Manchester University Press, 1996), pp. 201 *et al.* As 'Butch' Morton of 616 Squadron put it, by the time Bader arrived at Tangmere he was 'already something of a legend.' IWM, R.A. Morton narrative, p. 37. On Bader's fame in America see *New York Times*, 10 January 1941, p. 3; *Time*, 6 January 1941, p. 19. On American news and British sources see Nicholas John Cull, *Selling War* (New York: Oxford University Press, 1995). On poor aerobatics and the engine failure at North Weald see Alex Revell, *The Vivid Air* (London: Kimber, 1978), pp. 151–52; Stokes, *Wings Aflame*, p. 7. On 242 Squadron operations and their place in air strategy during the first weeks of 1941 see Brickhill, *Reach for the Sky*, pp. 242–43; Burns, *Bader*, pp. 129–30; AIR 41/18, ff. 73 ff., 79 (back).

[13]Laddie Lucas, *Flying Colours* (London: Wordsworth, 2001 edn), p. 177; Olive and Newton, *Devil at 6 O'clock*, p. 163. On Leigh-Mallory and the paper exercise see V. Orange in Probert and Cox, *Battle Re-Thought*, p. 40. On Bader taking command of the Tangmere Wing see NA, AIR 27/1471, 242 Sqn ORB, 16 March 1941.

[14]Victor Houart (ed.), *Lonely Warrior* (London: Souvenir, 1956), p. 106; Brickhill, *Reach for the Sky*, p. 248; see RAFM, B 354, Bader logbook, 19 March 1941.

[15]Johnson, *Wing Leader*, p. 73; see RAFM, B 354, Bader logbook, 24 March–8 April 1941; NA, AIR 27/2126, 616 Sqn ORB 13 April 1941; Burns, *Bader*, pp. 146–47; IWM, R.A. Morton narrative, p. 40.

[16]J. Johnson in *Secret Lives: Douglas Bader* (Twenty Twenty Productions, 1996); see Johnson, *Wing Leader*, pp. 73–74; Burns, *Bader*, p. 156.

[17]W. Walker in Dilip Sarkar, *Battle of Britain: Last Look Back* (Worcester: Ramrod, 2002), p. 74; Brickhill, *Reach for the Sky*, p. 249; Houart, *Lonely Warrior*, pp. 115–16; see Brickhill, *Reach for the Sky*, pp. 248–9. Stan Turner was very loyal and shared Bader's aggressive streak. See Brickhill, *Reach for the Sky*, p. 246; Norman Franks, *Buck McNair* (London: Grub Street, 2001), p. 40. On other commanders bringing in their own people see Alan C. Deere, *Nine Lives* (Canterbury: Wingham, 1991 edn), p. 199.

[18]On the aircraft and car see H. Jacks in Dilap Sarkar, *Bader's Tangmere Spitfires* (Sparkford: Patrick Stephens, 1996), p. 63. On the ailerons see Johnson, *Wing Leader*, pp. 90–91; Quill, *Spitfire*, p. 183. To be fair, Bader was not the only squadron

commander to jump the queue in getting metal ailerons. See MacDonell, *Dogfight to Diplomacy*, p. 65.

[19]Johnson, *Wing Leader*, p. 83; Cuthbert Orde, *Pilots of Fighter Command* (London: Harrap, 1942), p. 18; Royal Canadian Air Force Memorial Museum [hereafter RCAFM], R.W. Norris video interview; see Brickhill, *Reach for the Sky*, pp. 254–57; Dundas, *Flying Start*, pp. 63–65; Sarkar, *Tangmere Spitfires*, pp. 97–98; IWMSA 11537/2, A.L. Winskill. On problems with the vic see IWMSA 26970 TS, I. Hutchinson, p. 9; RCAFM, P.B. Pitcher video interview; C. Bamberger in Martin Davidson and James Taylor, *Spitfire Ace* (London: Channel 4, 2003), p. 146; B. Birdie-Wilson in Norman Gelb, *Scramble* (San Diego, CA: HBJ, 1985), p. 105; F/Lt Croskell in Probert and Cox, *Battle Re-Thought*, p. 60; D. Dennis in *Spitfire: Power, Grace and Glory* (DD Video, 1998).

[20]NA, AIR 20/4393, VCAS 1486, App. E, Supplement No. 3, March 1941; W.G.G. Duncan Smith, *Spitfire into Battle* (London: John Murray, 1981), pp. 32–33; Forrester, *Fly for Your Life*, p. 151; G. Stapleton in 'Recollections of an R.A.F. Squadron Leader', G. Carson featurette with 2004 MGM Special Edition DVD of *Battle of Britain* (1969) [see also Richard Hillary, *The Last Enemy* (London: Macmillan, 1942), p. 71]; see also NA, AIR 16/1136, Duke-Wolley letter, c. February 1951, pp. 2–3; IWMSA 006663 TS, H. Broadhurst, pp. 15–16; Johnson, *Wing Leader*, p. 57; Bob Doe, *Fighter Pilot* (Chislehurst: CCB, 2004 edn), pp. 21–22; T.E. Jonsson, *Dancing in the Skies* (London: Grub Street, 1994), pp. 77–78; Olive and Newton, *Devil at 6 O'clock*, p. 61. On the various other formations tried see AIR 16/416, encl. 21A, Notes on Formations and Tactics, December1940. On spreading out in vic see IWMSA 20497/1, R.L. Jones; IWMSA 26970 TS, I. Hutchinson, p. 9; Roland Beamont, *Phoenix into Ashes* (London: Kimber, 1968), p. 29. On the danger of having a tail-end-charlie 'weaver' see Deere, *Nine Lives*, p. 106; C. Bamburger in John Willis, *Churchill's Few* (London: Michael Joseph, 1985), p. 154; see also RCAFM, J.E. Johnson video interview. On the Tangmere Wing using vic and line-astern formations as late as April 1941 see IWM, R.A. Morton narrative, p. 45. Bader later quoted Laddie Lucas to the effect that he, Bader, 'never claimed to have pioneered the [pair and finger four] technique' (Bader, *Fight for the Sky*, p. 111), but this was certainly the impression left in *Reach for the Sky*: see also J. Johnson in John Frayn Turner, *The Bader Wing* (Tunbridge Wells: Midas, 1981), p. 139; Mike Spick, *Allied Fighter Aces* (London: Greenhill, 1997), p. 82; Sarkar, *Tangmere Spitfires*, p. 97.

[21]Lucas, *Flying Colours*, p. 178; see Brickhill, *Reach for the Sky*, pp. 226, 251; A.B. Austin, *Fighter Command* (London: Gollancz, 1941), pp. 92–93; *Sunday Express*, 17 August 1941; RAFM, MF 10027/1, Henry Longhurst, 'Stories of Bader – Leader of Men' press cutting, n/d; ibid., A.B. Austin, 'The Bader Bus Service', press cutting, n/d; see also David Masters, *'So Few'* (London: Eyre and Spottiswoode, 1941), ch. 5.

[22]NA, AIR 8/546, Portal to Peirse, 15 February 1941, Peirse to Portal, 12 February

1941; see AIR 41/18, f. 89 (and back). On German tactics see also IWM, R.A. Morton narrative, p. 52.

[23]Oliver Walker, *Sailor Malan* (London: Cassell, 1953), p. 110; Johnson, *Flying Colours*, p. 77; see Brickhill, *Reach for the Sky*, p. 253. On Bader borrowing the idea of painting initials on the fuselage of his aircraft from Broadhurst see J.E. Johnson and P.B. Lucas, *Winged Victory* (London: Stanley Paul, 1995), pp. 39, 41 On other fighter leaders being keen to go over the Channel see Forrester, *Fly for Your Life*, pp. 207–08; Norman L.R. Franks, *Fighter Leader* (London: Kimber, 1978), p. 82; Richard Townshend Bickers, *Ginger Lacey* (London: Pan, 1969 edn), p. 116.

[24]Brickhill, *Reach for the Sky*, p. 253; NA, AIR 41/18, f. 93 (back); see Sarkar, *Tangmere Spitfires*, pp. 94–102. The Luftwaffe, when it did engage, also had the advantage of being able to come down out of the sun. See IWMSA 26959, N. Rose TS, p. 19.

[25]Brickhill, *Reach for the Sky*, p. 258.

[26]Brickhill, *Reach for the Sky*, p. 259; Burns, *Bader*, p. 163; see Sarkar, *Bader's Tangmere Spitfires*, p. 102; RAFM, Bader logbook, 21 June 1941.

[27]See Bader, *Fight for the Sky*, p. 110. On Russia and the aims of the offensive see NA, AIR 41/18, f. 96 (back); AIR 16/639, encl. 5B, Notes of a Conference at Headquarters Fighter Command, 19 June 1941; AIR 14/706, encl. 61A, HQFC to HQ 10, 11, 12 Groups, 11 July 1941.

[28]IWMSA 12795/3, J. Johnson [see also J. Johnson in Dilip Sarkar, *Johnnie Johnson* (St. Peter's: Ramrod, 2002), p. 26; Johnson and Lucas, *Winged Victory*, pp. 62–65, 238]; B. Morton in *Secret Lives: Douglas Bader* (Twenty Twenty Productions, 1996)]; H. Dundas in *Sunday Express*, 5 February 1984 [see also Dundas, *Flying Start*, p. 47; IWMSA 10159, H. Dundas TS, p. 11]; A. Smith in *Secret Lives: Douglas Bader* (Twenty Twenty Productions, 1996) [see also A. Smith in *Britain's War Heroes: Douglas Bader, Fighter Ace* (Blakeway Associates, 2005)]; Orde, *Pilots of Fighter Command*, p. 18 [see also L. H. Casson in Sarkar, *Tangmere Spitfires*, pp. 45–46]; IWMSA 11573/2, A.L. Winskill; D. Bader, 'Fighter Pilot', in E. Leyland and T.E. Scott-Chard (eds) *Boys' Book of the Air* (London: Edmund Ward, 1957) p. 63. On Bader as the last to leave and smoking see A. Smith in Sarkar, *Tangmere Spitfires*, p. 47; Dundas, *Flying Start*, p. 76. On unofficial 'rhubarbs' see Burns, *Bader*, p. 159. On Holden teasing Bader see Dundas, *Flying Start*, p. 71. On adulation see Brickhill, *Reach for the Sky*, p. 270.

[29]*Times*, 18 July 1941.On the scores see Sarkar, *Bader's Tangmere Spitfires*, pp. 105–25.

[30]Johnson, *Wing Leader*, p. 80; Johnson and Lucas, *Winged Victory*, p. 48 [see also IWMSA 12795/1, J. Johnson; RCAFM, J.E. Johnson video interview]; J. Johnson quoted in Robert Jackson, *Douglas Bader* (London: Barker, 1983), p. 95; Raymond Z. Munro, *The Sky's No Limit* (Toronto: Key Porter, 1985), p. 57; Burns, *Bader*, p. 168; Ray Holmes, *Sky Spy* (Shrewsbury: Airlife, 1989), p. 143; see NA, AIR 41/18, 93 (back). On considering Bader invincible see Brickhill, *Reach for the Sky*, p. 273.

On insisting that his friends go with him to relax see ibid., p. 272. On disliking rhubarbs see also RCAFM, P.B. Pitcher video interview; Duncan Smith, *Spitfire into Battle*, p. 78; P. Brown in Richard C. Smith, *Hornchurch Eagles* (London: Grub Street, 2002), p. 28. By 1941–42, while junior pilots still liked the idea of rhubarbs as a way of testing themselves or letting off steam, squadron commanders 'felt the damage done did not warrant the risks involved'. Arthur Sager, *Line Shoot* (St Catherine's, ON: Vanwell, 2002), p. 65; see also Munro, *Sky's No Limit*, p. 57.

[31]A. Winskill in Sarkar, *Tangmere Spitfires*, p. 122. Even those in his own section sometimes found it hard to keep tabs on Bader once combat started. See,, NA, AIR 50/176, combat reports for H. Dundas and A. Smith, July 1941. Individual squadrons and sections might be just as hard to keep tabs on once combat began. See RCAFM, R.W. Norris video interview.

[32]RAFM, B4000, R.A. Morton letter, 20 June 1941. On the hazards of rendezvous see Johnson, *Wing Leader*, p. 87.

[33]B. Beardsley in Sarkar, *Tangmere Spitfires*, p. 125; RAFM, B354, Bader logbook, 7 August 1941.

[34]IWMSA 11510/2, D.G.S.R. Cox [see also Cox in Gelb, *Scramble*, p. 52]; J. Johnson, D. Crowley-Milling, R. Rayner, F. Twitchett in Sarkar, *Tangmere Spitfires*, pp. 69–70, 162; Dundas, *Flying Start*, p. 66; RCAFM, J.E. Johnson video interview. Bader also never flew with the other Tangmere squadrons unattached to him. See Colin Gray, *Spitfire Patrol* (London: Hutchinson, 1990), p. 81. On other wing leaders helping new pilots see Patrick Barthropp, *Paddy* (Hailsham: J&KH, 2001), pp. 27–28. On the value of sergeant pilots see Desmond Scott, *One More Hour* (London: Hutchinson, 1989), p. 31.

[35]See Burns, *Bader*, pp. 181–82, 191. On the 'one-man band' complaints see Brickhill, *Reach for the Sky*, p. 270.

[36]D. Lewis and G. Reid in *Secret Lives: Douglas Bader* (Twenty Twenty Productions, 1996); G. Reid in Sarkar, *Tangmere Spitfires*, p. 51; see also Dundas, *Flying Start*, pp. 67–68. On recognition of the work of ground crews see Hillary, *Last Enemy*, p. 71; Geoffrey Wellum, *First Light* (London: Penguin, 2003 edn), p. 139; I. Hutchinson in Smith, *Hornchurch Eagles*, pp. 85–86; Alymer Aldwingle, Bob Doe, Peter Brothers in *Fighting the Blue: The Fighting Few* (ASA Productions (UK) for UKTV, 2005). It might be argued, though, that sometimes ground-crew work in Fighter Command was not up to standard and that a tough line needed to be taken. See André Dezarrois (ed.), *The Mouchotte Diaries* (London: Staples, 1956), p. 79.

[37]Between June and December 1941, Fighter Command claimed to have shot down 731 enemy aircraft, while the Luftwaffe had in fact lost only 135 fighters from all causes in the West. Sebastian Cox, 'The Sources and Organisation of RAF Intelligence and Its Influence on Operations', in Horst Boog (ed.), *The Conduct of the Air War in the Second World War* (Oxford: Berg, 1992), p. 566.

[38]Bader, *Fight for the Sky*, p. 111; IWMSA 11537/ 2, A.L. Winskill; Dundas, *Flying*

Start, p. 70; Robert Spurdle in *Hunters in the Sky: The Great Defenders* (Anthony Potter Productions, 1991); see NA, AIR 41/18, f. 100. On wondering what was actually being accomplished by sweeps and circuses see IWMSA 11623, J.A. Goodson TS, p. 15; IWMSA 10709 TS, D. Armitage, p. 30; IWMSA 1254/2, C.B. Brown; Christopher Foxley-Norris, *A Lighter Shade of Blue* (London: Ian Allan, 1978), p. 28; Desmond Scott, *One More Hour* (London: Hutchinson, 1989), p. 34; see also Terence Kelly, *Hurricane and Spitfire Pilots at War* (London: Kimber, 1986), p. 75; Spencer Dunmore, *Above and Beyond* (Toronto: M&S, 1996), p. 128. On the dislike for escort duties see Deere, *Nine Lives*, p. 185; Johnson, *Wing Leader*, p. 88; Kent, *One of the Few*, p. 164. On feeling the strain of ongoing operations over France see Roger Hall, *Clouds of Fear* (Folkestone: Bailey and Swinfen, 1975), p. 148; Doug Stokes, *Paddy Finucane* (London: Kimber, 1983), p. 72; Wellum, *First Light*, pp. 254–55. Many pilots continued to argue that operations were worthwhile in that they took the war to the enemy, kept him from transferring units eastward, and gave pilots combat experience. See IWMSA 10202, W. Ash TS, p. 10; IWMSA 11510/3, D. Cox (see also D. Cox in Dilap Sarkar, *A Few of the Many* (Worcester: Ramrod, 1995), p. 103); Deere, *Nine Lives*, p. 185; Duncan Smith, *Spitfire into Battle*, p. 68; Foxley-Norris, *Lighter Shade*, p. 28; Kelly, *Hurricane and Spitfire*, p. 77. On German 'one pass' tactics see also Donald L. Caldwell, *JG26* (New York: Orion, 1991), pp. 87–89. On the overall failure of the campaign see John Terraine, *The Right of the Line* (London: Sceptre, 1988 edn), pp. 283–88.

[39]Stokes, *Wings Aflame*, p. 153; Lucas, *Flying Colours*, pp. 182–83; Duncan Smith, *Spitfire into Battle*, p. 67 [see also Kent, *One of the Few*, p. 165]; see also Burns, *Bader*, p. 182; RAFM, B354, Bader logbook 16, 17, 18, 20, 24, 26 June, 4, 11, 12, 24, 25 July 1941 for visits to Northolt. On Leigh-Mallory indulging Bader's aggressive views see Johnson, *Wing Leader*, p. 111.

[40]Cross and Orange, *Straight and Level*, pp. 123–24; Bader in Lucas, *Flying Colours*, p. 184; Leigh-Mallory in Brickhill, *Reach for the Sky*, p. 274; Malan in Walker, *Sailor*, p. 118; Holden in Brickhill, *Reach for the Sky*, p. 273; Cassandra *Daily Mirror* comment repeated in *Time*, 25 August 1941, p. 20. On Malan and preparing a replacement see also Norman L.R. Franks, *Sky Tiger* (London: Kimber, 1980), pp. 143, 143, 151; Neville Duke, *Test Pilot* (London: Grub Street, 1992), p. 53. On pilots making mistakes through fatigue and going off ops see IWMSA 20497/3, R.L. Jones; Dezarrois, *Mouchotte Diaries*, p. 85; Kent, *One of the Few*, p. 170; Peter Townsend, *Time and Chance* (London: Collins, 1978), p. 115; Wellum, *First Light*, p. 291. On Bader pressing for more action see Johnson, *Wing Leader*, p. 111 [see also J. Johnson in Sarkar, *Johnnie Johnson*, p. 28]. On Bader and autographs see Brickhill, *Reach for the Sky*, p. 272. Leigh-Mallory also allowed a tired Peter Townsend to extend his operational time in command of 85 Squadron; but Townsend, unlike Bader, did heed his chief's advice to take it easy. See Townsend, *Duel in the Dark*, pp. 189, 206–07.

[41]RCAFM, J.E. Johnson video interview; RAFM, AC 96/55/1, Beachy Head forward relay station logbook, 9 August 1941; see Sarkar, Tangmere Spitfires, pp. 126–9. On the fighter goals for Circus 70 see NA, AIR 16/212, Operational Order No. 77, 8 August 1941.

[42]Bader, Fight for the Sky, p. 31; Sarkar, Tangmere Spitfires, pp. 130–31.

[43]Bader, Fight for the Sky, pp. 31–33; RAFM, B354, Bader logbook, 9 August 1941 entry; Bader quoted in Brickhill, Reach for the Sky, p. 269; see Bader account in Sunday Express, 21 October 1945, p. 2. On the dangers of being in combat without a wingman see R.V. Ashman, Spitfire Against the Odds (Wellingborough: Patrick Stephens, 1989), pp. 89–90. On the 'empty sky' phenomenon see Gray, Spitfire Patrol, p. 26; Tom Neil, Gun-Button to 'Fire' (London: Kimber, 1987), pp. 87, 110; C. Bamburger in Spitfire: Power Grace and Glory (DD Video, 1998).

[44]G. Reid in Sarkar, Tangmere Spitfires, p. 161 [see also Cross and Orange, Straight and Level, pp. 123–24]; Douglas, Years of Command, pp. 138–39; IWM, Lord Douglas Papers, Box 3, DCAS Fighter Command file, TS of Douglas dictation notes to Wright, p. 175. On Bader not leaving a successor see Burns, Bader, pp. 191–92. On dismay at his disappearance see D. Crowley-Milling in Sarkar, Tangmere Spitfires, p. 139; Duncan Smith, Spitfire into Battle, p. 78; Dundas, Flying Start, p. 76; Johnson, Wing Leader, p. 117; Forrester, Fly for Your Life, p. 242; IWMSA 11537/2, A.L. Winskill. In reference to 616 Squadron it should be noted that the Operations Record Book entry indicates that Bader was 'much admired' and 'very popular with everyone'. NA, AIR 27/2126, 616 Sqn ORB, 9 August 1941. On the Daily Mail piece see Brickhill, Reach for the Sky, p. 274. On press coverage of the loss see Daily Express, 13 August 1941; The Times, 13 August 1941; see also Brickhill, Reach for the Sky, p. 283. On Bader's general public profile see L.E.O. Charlton, Britain at War: The Royal Air Force: From September 1939 to December 1940 (London: Hutchinson, 1941), p. 266. On Bader being specifically identified in the public mind with the fighter offensive see Basil Cardew in Daily Express, 7 July 1941; A.J. Wilson, Sky Sweepers (London: Jarrolds, 1942), pp. 14–15, 33. On admiration within Fighter Command see also Keith Ayling, They Fly for Victory (New York: Nelson, 1943), p. 88.

[45]Adolf Galland, The First and the Last (New York: Henry Holt, 1954), p. 88; see Lucas, Flying Colours, pp. 189–91; Burns, Bader, pp. 190–91; and especially Sarkar, Tangmere Spitfires, ch. 7; Andy Saunders, Bader's Last Flight London: Grub Street, 2007). On blue-on-blue incidents and near misses see Deere, Nine Lives, pp. 136–7; Duke, Test Pilot, p. 51; David Guthrie (ed.), Spitfire Squadron (London: Hale, 1978 edn), pp. 83, 143; Ernie Burton, Go Straight Ahead (Evensham: Square One, 1996), p. 57; see also Neil, Gun Button, p. 106; Dezarrois, Mouchotte Diaries, p. 85. Bader himself eventually acknowledged the possibility that he was shot down

by a hostile or a friendly aircraft (see http://home.tiscali.be/ed.ragas/awshistory/aswsbader.html (accessed 2 December 2004) B. Cunningham interview of Douglas Bader for *Code One*), though still thinking it was probably a collision (see IWMSA 6630/6, J. Cox).

CHAPTER SIX

Prisoner of War

Do you realise that the Government at home would rather have me back than all the rest of you put together?

Douglas Bader in conversation with Lt. Col. W.M. Broomhall, Colditz Castle, 1943[1]

By the time he fell into enemy hands Douglas Bader had become something of a celebrity not only in the RAF but also within the Luftwaffe. Having sustained a concussion and some scrapes and bruise injuries while bailing out, Bader was taken to hospital in nearby St Omer for treatment. News quickly spread that the famous legless British air ace had been captured, and in the following days as he recovered he was visited by a succession of curious but respectful German officers. Bader, being Bader, did not hesitate to try and turn this unexpected fame to his advantage. 'I've lost my right leg,' he told a Luftwaffe engineer who spoke English. 'Will you telephone England and have them send me my spare.' And while that was being decided, could a search be made near the wreckage of his Spitfire for the tin limb he had lost while bailing out? When the missing leg was found it was, not surprisingly, damaged. Undaunted, the famous wing commander asked: 'D'you think your chaps at the aerodrome could repair this for me?' They could and they did, allowing Bader to, among other things, accept an invitation to tea from *Major* Adolf Galland on behalf of the pilots of nearby JG 26.[2]

The spur-of-the-moment suggestion that England be contacted to send over a new leg, meanwhile, had the potential to cause the RAF a certain amount of embarrassment and allow the enemy to score propaganda points. When Hermann Goering heard through Galland of Bader's wish, he quickly agreed that a radio message should be sent on the frequency both sides used to monitor the location of downed pilots spotted in the Channel. The Luftwaffe offered to allow a British plane free passage to and from St Omer in order to deliver the leg. To accept would give the impression to the loved ones of other POWs that Bader was being afforded special treatment by not having to wait the many months it took for the Red Cross to deliver medical and related supplies sent from Britain to Germany. As it was the offer made Nazi Germany look chivalrous – that of course was the intention – and promoted the impression that the enemy was fighting a 'clean' war. To decline the offer, however, would leave Britain looking as if it cared less than Germany for the wellbeing of prisoners of war in the eyes of the foreign press, and disappoint Bader's wife and many friends within the RAF, including Sholto Douglas and Leigh-Mallory. It was the C-in-C Fighter Command, by his own account, who eventually hit upon a possible solution to this dilemma. 'I at once rang up Leigh-Mallory, the AOC 11 Group', Sholto Douglas later explained, 'and he agreed that it was cheek for the Germans to offer us free passage for Douglas Bader's leg this way, and we agreed that we should send the leg over in a Blenheim with an escort of 300 Spitfires.' The spare limb was duly dropped by parachute with a thank-you note on 19 August over the Longuenesse aerodrome while a bombing raid was carried out, and a press release issued by Fighter Command indicating that the RAF did not require Luftwaffe permission to fly 'where and when it pleases'. Churchill was not happy to hear about the affair – 'You are fraternising with the enemy, Douglas', the C-in-C remembered him growling over the telephone, 'I won't have it' – but was apparently mollified by the news that several enemy aircraft had been shot down in the process.[3]

Bader had also stored up difficulties for the future when first examined by a doctor – and still in a state of concussion – as he admitted in a newspaper article written after returning home in 1945:

> When the artificial leg came off in my aeroplane I had badly bruised my own bit of leg, which had in a very limited area produced a large swelling like a tennis ball. The German doctor, as far as I could understand (which was not at all) seemed to want to operate on me. This caused me to become very excited, as the last thing I wanted was anybody, particularly a German doctor, playing around with what was left of my legs... I suppose I was not exactly normal, because I demanded a [Red Cross] letter form and wrote to my wife asking her to have me repatriated quickly, since I feared for my legs, or what remained of them.

The swelling disappeared in a day or two, but the request for repatriation eventually reached London where it was acted on. By the time diplomatic pressure was brought to bear on the Germans, however, Bader was refusing to be repatriated on medical grounds, which caused 'people in responsible positions a lot of trouble'. His leg was no longer in danger, he had lost his lower limbs before the war rather than in it, and even if that had been overlooked he would have had to forego operational flying for the duration of the war. Repatriation, which was what the authorities thought he wanted, was therefore out of the question. Only if he escaped successfully from enemy hands would he be allowed to fight again.[4]

Escape, indeed, was already very much on Bader's mind once the Luftwaffe had kindly repaired his damaged limb. During his visit to JG 26 he tried to get Galland to allow him to test-fly an Me 109 – sitting in the cockpit with armed officers standing on the wings was as far as he got – and then tried to make a break for it on foot. 'On his capture a great party was held in his honour,' the son-in-law of the Luftwaffe officer assigned to watch over Bader remembered his father-in-law, Helmut Swantje, relating, 'Bader promptly escaped by throwing his artificial legs through a washroom window.' His two tin legs were of course an enormous impediment – he could not trek for miles on end and his stiff gait was a dead give-away in terms of disguise – and the famous wing commander was recaptured at once.[5]

Bader, though, was determined to try and make a break while still in Occupied France. In the same guarded hospital ward as the wing commander there were three other injured pilots from the RAF of lesser rank. The doctor was German but some of the orderlies were French. Bader had one of his ward-mates, who spoke better French than he did, quietly ask one of the young Frenchwomen on his behalf 'if she can help me get out or put me in touch with friends outside.' This was asking a lot, since for anyone in Occupied Europe to be caught aiding downed Allied flyers meant a one-way ticket to a concentration camp. By an extraordinary stroke of luck the young woman, Lucille de Becker, not only admired his courage but also knew whom to contact. The next day she passed on a message to the effect that a young man would wait outside the hospital gates each night from 12 p.m. to 2 a.m. to help shepherd him to a safe house. Having persuaded the guards that it was beneath the dignity of such a distinguished officer to be seen stumping about in only a night-shirt – twenty-four hour garb for prisoners in the hospital – Bader had reacquired his uniform. Learning that he was to be transported to Germany the next day, Bader made his move. Knotting together various bed-sheets, including those of two bed-ridden patients, he made a rope after midnight with which to ease himself from a ward window to the ground many feet below. With great difficulty he was able to let himself down from the upper storey at about 1:45 a.m. on 19 August 1941 and make his way outside the hospital gate for his rendezvous. The man was there as promised, and with Bader enduring considerable pain the two men walked for an hour until they reached the house of the elderly but brave Hiècque couple. The plan was for Bader to hide there until arrangements could be made through their son-in-law, a British soldier named Hollingdale from World War I who had settled in St Omer, to pass him on to representatives of one of the escape lines run by the Resistance. Unfortunately the plan had been betrayed by another of the young women working at the hospital, Hélèn Lefèvre, and the following afternoon the Germans, conducting house-to-house searches in St Omer, discovered Bader hidden beneath a pile of straw in the garden shed.[6]

Later rumours that Bader had elbowed his way into, and then messed up, an escape being planned by other RAF patients at the St Omer hospital were more a reflection of the friction generated by the Bader ego than of the truth. All the other pilots were, after all, truly bed-ridden, and knew that it was an officer's duty to escape if he could. On the other hand the means of escape from the hospital could not really be hidden, and the others would have been treated as accessories to a *Verboten* activity. Bader himself, furthermore, though regarding help from junior officers as his right, recognised the unacceptable danger he was placing the Hiècque family in through taking refuge in their house: if caught he would merely be sent to a POW cage; they would go to a very different sort of camp. It was a great irony, however, that in making his own failed escape attempt Bader threw into disarray a plan being formulated by one of the escape-line organisations to spring him from hospital using a fake ambulance.[7]

After his recapture Bader found the Germans were taking no chances. 'They wouldn't give me my legs', he later explained to an American journalist. 'Two goons carried me while another carried my legs and an officer marched along in front.' He was sent by train, via Brussels and under close escort, to the Luftwaffe interrogation centre for shot-down Allied flyers known as Dulag Luft outside Frankfurt-am-Main. Through sheer belligerence as much as guile he quickly dissuaded the staff of any hopes they may have had of getting useful information from this famous wing commander. As he later put it he was asked some 'rather stupid questions' by the commandant, who after five minutes of receiving no satisfactory answers gave up. Bader even managed to intimidate the enemy into providing him with soap, a towel, and afternoon tea. Unlike many other RAF prisoners Bader spent only a day in solitary before being sent on into the adjacent transit camp, where he at once began to exert himself. Sergeant Richard Pape, who was there at the time, admiringly recalled how 'he kept the R.A.F. personnel on tip-toe the whole time. A dynamic leader, he would not tolerate any flagging or weakening. "Escape... escape... escape... by God!" was his constant exhortation. "Never mind hunger pains, discomfort, or any other agony. Let escape become your passion, your one and only obsession until you finally reach home."' To his great disgust, Bader discovered that not all aircrew were that keen to risk life and limb when they could sit out the war in a prison camp. 'Blast you and your kind!', Pape remembered the wing commander exploding at one of the more vocal proponents of this school of thought. 'You're getting paid while you're in captivity. Earn the money! If you get recaptured twenty times you're helping the war effort by making the Germans spend time, money and manpower in organised manhunts.' There were, however, enough enthusiasts to help with the digging of an escape tunnel. Whatever prospect Bader himself may have had of getting out by this means was, however, ruined by his utter refusal to salute German officers of inferior rank: within the hour, despite his protests, he was transferred from Dulag Luft to an officer POW camp at Lübeck.[8]

This camp, which was mostly inhabited by army officers captured earlier that year in Greece, was a bad one: the rations were poor and the guards dangerously unpredictable. Bader was only in residence for about a month before the officer prisoner population was transferred to a camp at Warburg; but it was at Lübeck that he had his first taste of what it meant to be a celebrity POW. 'The Germans had a very high opinion of Douglas Bader and obviously tried to exploit to the full any propaganda situation they could think of,' a British Army lieutenant later recorded. 'They included him in numerous photographs and gave him V.I.P. treatment. This he invariably scorned.' This refusal to be anything but bloody-minded towards his captors won the affection of many other prisoners – 'he was that sort of man, the very best of British' – but would eventually escalate elsewhere to the point where his presence seemed more a physical liability than a psychological boon.[9]

In October everyone, including Bader, was transferred to Oflag VIB, another hut-and-wire affair where the German High Command seemed intent on concentrating as many captured British officers as possible. This camp at Warburg was if anything even worse than the camp at Lübeck. It was seriously overcrowded, the hut roofs leaked, there never seemed to be enough light or fuel, the ground outside turned into a sea of mud when it rained, and, as always, food was in short supply even with the delivery of Red Cross parcels. Five-star hotel accommodation would not have satisfied Bader if it meant remaining a POW; but the poor living conditions certainly did nothing to ease his restlessness. 'Douglas Bader hadn't changed', Wallace Cunningham recalled of meeting his former wing commander in captivity: he was still 'seeking the limelight'. Luckily Bader had two outlets available for his increasingly pent-up energy: scheming to escape and indulging a penchant for being difficult about anything and everything if it involved dealing with the enemy.[10]

In order to make a successful break it was usually necessary for someone wanting to get out to consult the camp escape committee, presided over by a nominated escape officer. The committee could evaluate the potential of specific ideas, provide technical assistance in the form of civilian clothing, counterfeit papers, and money, and for big schemes decide on a priority list for those wanting to get out. Bader was not happy to learn that in the opinion of the escape officer his tin legs prevented him from being nominated for or participating in certain types of escape scheme. 'How he imagined he would either be able to walk any distance on his aluminium legs, or avoid immediate recognition if seen by any German over five years old', Roger Mortimer, an army officer heavily involved in escape efforts from Warburg, later reflected, 'has remained a mystery.' Bader's sailor-roll gait would be spotted if he tried to get out through the gates in disguise, while his inability to climb or run would make it impossible for him to go over or through the wire. Tunnels were still an option, and Bader was put down for a number that were being dug. The trouble with tunnels were that they took a long time to complete, were often discovered before they could be finished, and were endeavours in which Bader himself could not easily lend a direct hand. He could stooge – that is, keep a lookout for guards roaming inside the wire – but he could not easily dig. If it became necessary to close down the tunnel digging in a hurry he would need extra time to strap his legs back on, and descent ladders were virtually impossible for him to negotiate alone in any case. It was all very frustrating to a man quite unwilling to sit out the war.[11]

There were those, however, who were willing to help him. Lieutenant David Lubbock (Fleet Air Arm) and Pilot Officer Pete Gardner (RAF), had developed an escape plan and approached Bader about joining the team. 'What, in winter?' was his startled initial reaction, but Bader being Bader it did not take him more than a moment to recover and declare 'I'm in.' There was a clothing store hut just beyond the main wire fence to which prisoners would occasionally be taken under guards to draw kit. Gardner had worked out how to pick the lock of an off-limits room in this hut. The idea was as follows: the three pilots, along with a Commando officer, would go out with a clothing party, hide in the locked room, and then climb out through a window under cover of darkness and a staged diversion that would focus searchlights on another area of the camp. Everything went well until the quartet began to climb out the window. The first man out slipped away unobserved, but the other three, who planned to travel together and could only move as fast as Bader, were spotted by a guard.[12]

While the three would-be escapers – soon joined by the fourth in the party after his recapture – were serving their inevitable sentence in the camp cooler, Lubbock managed to pick the lock of his cell one night and free the others. The Germans had left for the night and only two doors separated the prisoners from freedom. Bader, typically, was all for making a break at once. The others, though, wisely argued that they had no food or winter clothing. Now that it was known the locks to the cell doors could be picked, it seemed prudent to wait until spring, stage an offence that would land them in the cooler again, and then make a break when the weather was good and supplies had been smuggled in. Even Bader had to recognise the logic in this: but though he gave way in this instance he did not stop searching for another way out.[13]

He next got involved in a tunnel scheme. A group of RAF officers had been digging a tunnel that was about to be completed in late April 1942, and he made it clear he wanted to be among the escape party after having helped transport and scatter soil from the dig using his hollow legs. Lubbock at first protested – 'You'll never get through, Douglas. There's a right-angled turn at the bottom of the shaft and its very small' – but acquiesced when Bader suggested that his legs be carried by the man behind him through the tunnel. Lubbock agreed to act as the wing commander's Sherpa, but on the night of the escape the hastily dug exit turned out to be short of the intended mark and within view of two sentries. Five men got out by dashing off when the sentries' backs were turned, but Bader for obvious reasons was not among them. There was no getting round the fact that the tin legs made Bader a potential liability. Wallace Cunningham recalled that in the aftermath of a 'moler' tunnel exit coming up too close to the wire he and Bader were forced to crawl from the tunnel mouth back to their huts with 'Douglas making a noise like a knight in armour'. Such miscarriages were frustrating for all concerned.[14]

'His imperious manner, unreasoned and frequently unreasonable efforts to escape, without thought for the consequences for others,' an RAF prisoner wrote retrospectively, 'did not endear him to those who had spent a couple of years in careful planning.' Bader, to be fair, did not insist on taking a leading role in escape schemes for which his disability made him unsuitable even in his own eyes. When he learned that a quartet of officers needed a diversion while they made an attempt on the wire at dusk a month or so after the tunnel débâcle, Bader guaranteed that he could distract the attention of the relevant sentry at a specified time. Captain Terence Prittie observed how he delivered on his promise:

Wing Commander Bader suddenly appeared, coming across the Rugby football ground, with his usual limp and cheery smile. He was always a tremendous 'draw' with the sentries, who were mostly filled with a curiosity about his doings that was tinged with genuine admiration. The attention of the sentry in the nearest box was at once focused on him. [When signalled] Bader proceeded to address the sentry. He pointed to his wooden [sic] legs, lifted one slightly as if to test the other, and then fell over heavily. Two of his friends were coming along the path at this moment, and he shouted at them, 'For God's sake, come along and help me, you chaps! Can't you see I've damaged myself?' There was a lot of back-chat, while Bader fumbled with one leg. Then suddenly he detached and held up an artificial foot and calf, which he waved in front of the eyes of the fascinated sentry, shouting 'What do you think of this, eh?' followed by a few words of German learned for the occasion. There was still plenty of by-play to come, with the other two lifting him clumsily, dropping him and finally carrying him off, grinning wildly and still shouting at the sentry, 'These are a couple of clumsy asses, aren't they? No way to treat a legless man,' and so on.

The diversion was a complete success, the three escapers getting through the wire and a hundred yards beyond before the sentry ceased concentrating on the legless wonder.[15]

Similarly, when some distraction was needed to prevent a sentry in one of the towers from observing the transfer of a ladder from one hut to another in the run-up to a mass escape, Bader was ready to play his part. Officially known as Operation Olympia, and more commonly as the Warburg Wire Job, this particular scheme involved dozens of men climbing the perimeter fences at night using makeshift ladders after the lights had been fused. Bader, for obvious reasons, could not be among those rushing up-and-over, but he certainly did his bit in getting the home-made ladders to the huts nearest the fences, as Captain Robert Loder, the officer in charge of this diversion, later related:

> We staged an act, and we pretended to have a row immediately under the sentry box, and as you know he has two false legs one of which he unscrewed [sic], and, shouting wildly, threw over the perimeter fence, much to the amusement of the goon in the box upstairs, but of course for the vital four minutes while they were taking the ladders out from one hut to another, his attention was drawn down to us.

Thanks to Bader as well as the efforts of scores of others, the Wire Job became feasible and was put into action that night with considerable success.[16]

Furthermore, whatever limits there may have been on his escape prospects were compensated for to some degree in the form of ragging the enemy. Making the Germans look foolish, known as 'goon-baiting', was a fairly common sport, but Bader was among the most persistent, if not always judicious, players among British officers held here and elsewhere. 'He was a natural goon-baiter,' Pilot Officer Maurice Butt explained, 'as a prisoner he provoked mischief and fun at every opportunity.' One winter morning he refused to leave his room to attend roll-call. When a German officer came in and demanded that he do so, Bader refused to oblige. 'My feet would get cold in the snow', he artlessly protested. 'If you want to count me, come to my room and do it.' Only when the enraged officer drew his pistol and levelled it did the wing commander acquiesce. On parade during counts he would stand on his pins swaying slightly to maintain stability and when a German officer or NCO came within range he would manage to fall all over him, much to the glee of all except the Germans. After two successful pull-downs the Germans insisted on his having a chair to sit out the count and whenever they spotted him about the camp they would hurriedly steer clear.[17]

Such antics, in combination with his generally upbeat pugnacity regarding the war, made Bader a boon to someone like Captain Earle Edwards, captured in 1940, who later commented on how 'his unshakeable optimism was a pleasant tonic to those of us who found little excuse for laughter in prisoner-of-war existence.' Major Jack Poole, a prisoner in both world wars, agreed: in his view Bader was definitely good for camp morale, a dynamo of a man who 'with his unbounded optimism and personal vitality roused many from their winter hibernations.' Not everyone, though, was happy with the consequences of the wing commander's behaviour. An officer in the Royal Marines remembered an occasion in the winter of 1941–42 when it was snowing on parade. Bader made a snowball, threw it, and managed to knock off a German officer's cap. A guard opened fire, forcing everyone to sprawl to the ground, and a very touch-and-go situation had to be diffused through the intervention of some of the more responsible British Army officers. Captain Roger Mortimer of the Royal Sussex Regiment remembered how on roll-call parade Bader 'carried his teasing so far that had he not been physically restrained by his fellow prisoners, I am sure that he would have got himself and the rest of us shot.' In fact as a star prisoner Bader usually got off lightly, and no blood was spilt on his account. German retaliation for some of his activities might, nevertheless, easily extend to the whole camp in the form of mail stoppages and the withholding of Red Cross parcels. Not that he paid any attention to this. Colonel Gerald Sharpe, while an admirer, commented in a letter that Bader 'doesn't care a damn for anybody'. Consequently his continued presence in the camp 'did not receive an unalloyed welcome from all', as another RAF prisoner later put it diplomatically.[18]

In early May 1942, before the plan to break out of cells could be put into operation, most of the RAF prisoners at Oflag VIB were suddenly transferred under guard to a new camp run by the Luftwaffe: Stalag Luft III at Sagan. Bader himself was briefly held in the NCOs' compound there. 'Apparently,' Sergeant Leslie Frith later wrote, 'he had been virtually thrown out of his last camp as being too much of a disruptive influence and frog-marched to Stalag Luft 3 to start all over again.' Though he arrived quietly, Bader quickly took to urging the sergeants to take a more defiant stance toward the enemy. 'Very bumptious, of course,' Sergeant William Stevens recalled, 'throwing his weight about, "we must do this, we must do the other".' Though admired for his own courage, Bader's goon-baiting and other antics drew more mixed reviews when the Germans retaliated by extending count parades and withholding privileges. 'We were pleased to get rid of him', an admirer admitted when the wing commander was sent into the officers' compound.[19]

His fellow RAF officers viewed Bader at Stalag Luft III with a mixture of awe and exasperation. Sometimes, to be sure, his fearless goon-baiting – 'Bader was anti-German to the *n*th degree', as Oliver Philpot recalled – served to boost morale. Roger Boulding, a fighter pilot shot down some weeks before Bader, fondly remembered an episode from the winter of 1942–43:

It was snowing hard, and we were playing snowballs. Wing Commander Bader was enthusiastically joining in the fun. A young German Leutnant then came rushing over with a note from the Kommandant for the 'Ving Commander'. Bader, quick as a flash, said: 'Be a good chap and just hold that for me will you?', holding out his snowball for the German. Instinctively the young officer took the snowball, and then, not knowing what to do and realising that he had made a complete fool of himself, just stood there holding it whilst several hundred prisoners had hysterics!

The RAF contingent from Warburg in particular also appreciated his efforts to break the step of squads of singing German troops marching by through catcalling and whistling tunes out-of-sync. His humour could also inspire affection. The impromptu choirs he organised to serenade the guards sent in to dig up newly discovered tunnels with 'heigh-ho, heigh-ho, it's off to work we go' from *Snow White and the Seven Dwarfs* were well received. So too was his reaction to a harangue from the commandant directed at the assembled inmates. When he had finished speaking Bader broke ranks, stumped over to the still-simmering *offizier*, threw his arms around him and announced: 'You're the most lovely boy!'[20]

The trouble once more was that although the Germans 'respected him very highly,' as one of his hut-mates put it, 'and they put up with a lot more from him than they would from any other prisoner', Bader sometimes went too far and brought about collective retribution in carrying on what another prisoner described as 'his own private war against the Germans behind the wire.' Incoming or outgoing mail might be held up, and even more important the supply of Red Cross parcels – which provided a vital supplement to the inadequate camp rations – would be interrupted because Bader, say, refused to stand to attention in front of the commandant or insulted another German officer. This won him few friends among prisoners who were unwilling to risk their few comforts and necessities in order to allow one particularly restless soul to let off steam. More than a decade after the war was over there were RAF officers who could not bear to hear his name mentioned because of the privations they had undergone as a result of his behaviour, and even some of those who admired Bader admitted he could be rather insensitive. Paddy Barthropp, for instance, remembered how Bader simply laughed when he and another officer were caught messing up the count on parade and got twenty-eight days in the cooler while Bader, who had organised the affair, got away clean. 'I mean he was all right,' Barthropp added on another occasion, 'they wouldn't shoot him, he was a fairly well known figure, but they might have shot us.'[21]

Aeneas MacDonell, though quite fond of his fellow fighter pilot, recalled in his memoirs the kind of potentially dangerous incident that Bader tended to generate at Stalag Luft III.

The Germans called an unscheduled Appell. Bader, then a Wing Commander, assembled the senior officers of each barrack block and proposed a 'sit-in'. No one was to go out on Appell. The meeting broke up in disarray. Only two representatives decided to follow Bader. The rest said he was talking balls. The German guard came into the camp. No one knew what to do and I'm not sure whether the SBO gave instructions. Bader and his followers went from block to block shouting to the inmates to stay put. Quite a lot did. Bader had a commanding personality. But others drifted out to the parade ground in dribs and drabs. The main gate was opened and a troop of heavily armed tin-helmeted Germans marched in, their tommy guns at the ready. Orders were shouted in English and German. Then tommy guns were opened up at the base of the the the barracks. Within minutes the 'sit-in' was over...[22]

The escape committee, for its part, while glad enough to receive the contraband material Bader smuggled into Sagan from Warburg concealed inside his artificial legs, believed that the guards ought to be lulled into complacency rather than put on a state of high alert because of Bader's antics. To them he became, as one friend put it, 'a bloody nuisance'.[23]

Bader himself remained determined to escape. Once again his artificial limbs made him an unlikely candidate (his legless protégé Colin Hodgkinson, captured the following year, rapidly concluded that for a legless man to escape alone was impossible while 'to propose to others that they should take me with them was idiotic') but by now Bader had developed what he regarded as a highly promising plan to get out of Germany once clear of the camp. Instead of trying to hike or train-hop to neutral territory, for which he was clearly not well equipped physically, he would simply steal an aeroplane from a nearby airfield. He had obtained starting instructions for the Me 110 that he required through code-letter cor-respondence with England, and was consequently keener than ever to find a way out of Sagan. Little wonder, therefore, that he should become known as '"Dig Me a Tunnel" Bader' to some of his fellow prisoners. Within the escaping fraternity, however, there were secu-rity worries – 'he was always talking at the top of his voice', one officer remembered – and ongoing concerns about his tin legs. He was far from pleased when the escape committee turned down his participation in a scheme developed with his friends Lubbock and Gardner to do a 'mole job' overnight under the wire from a trench the Germans had dug round the perimeter to deter tunnelling from under the huts. They simply did not believe that Bader would be able to get away from the tunnel exit without slowing down the others. 'They say I'm no good for that scheme', he growled to Harry 'Wings' Day, his former mentor in the Hendon air pageant and now de facto camp leader at Sagan. 'It's a lot of balls.'[24]

Aside from the artificial legs as such, the problem here, as else-where in Germany, was twofold. Bader was a fearless but also an unimaginative officer, who had difficulty understanding the need in a prisoner-of-war camp, where the inmates were quite literally at the mercy of the enemy, to practise the art of compromise and gain advantage indirectly. This in turn was related to the second problem, which was that for the first time in a long while Bader was not himself running the show. Higher-ranking officers or wing commanders such as Day with greater seniority were already occupying the key post of Senior British Officer when he arrived, and it was they who appointed and supported the more junior officers on the escape committee with whom Bader came into conflict. That junior officers were saying 'no' to a man who had got his way pretty much continuously in the two years prior to his capture bred enormous frustration. So much so, indeed, that after war he was said to have lodged an official complaint against one of the survivors of the Great Escape for alleged insubordination: that is, for not letting Bader do what he wanted.[25]

Eventually he wore out his welcome. Von Lindeiner-Waldau, the commandant and a decent man, asked Day why Bader was making life so difficult. ('We lost track of the number of times we heard a commotion coming from that direction', Leslie Firth observed with respect to wherever Bader was, 'and there seemed to be a continual to-ing and fro-ing of heavily armed guards in the officers' compound.') Day replied that Bader was an energetic man with no means of dissipating his energy and vitality through sport because of his artificial legs. The commandant then decided that Bader ought to be sent to Lamsdorf, a huge camp for British Army soldiers that, among other things, contained a significant number of British medical officers. Whether Von Lindeiner really believed that Bader would be happier at Lamsdorf or simply wanted an excuse to get rid of an *enfant terrible* is not clear, but he was determined that Bader should leave Stalag Luft III. As might have been predicted, Bader, as much for the hell of it as anything else, balked at the idea and refused to co-operate. On 10 July 1942 over fifty heavily armed guards were sent into the camp to fetch him. According to some accounts Bader had immersed himself in the compound fire-pool, and forced the Germans to fetch his legs from his hut and escort him back there in the buff. All accounts agree that once in his hut Bader refused to budge. Day, sensing that if the guards were forced to manhandle Bader a scuffle would break out which in turn could lead to bloodshed, finally persuaded him to go by pointing out that it would be easier for him to escape from Lamsdorf than from Sagan. Thus mollified, Bader got to his feet and stumped off, giving his escort a mock-inspection in the process. 'The remainder of the camp annoyed the Germans exceedingly by turning out to say Cheerio to Doug,' Squadron Leader C.N.S. Campbell noted in his diary, 'and to offer free advice on how to manage a cripple.' Some of those observing were secretly glad to see the back of such a disruptive influence. 'To tell the truth,' Leslie Frith confided in his unpublished memoirs, 'it was a relief to everybody, friend and foe, to see him go.' Aeneas MacDonell was more ambivalent in his published memoirs. 'In a strange way I missed him,' he admitted; adding, though, that 'Our guards relaxed and we settled down to our undercover activities without the constant risk of their being blown by the Germans reacting to Bader-provoked nonsense.'[26]

As soon as Bader arrived in the sick quarters at Lamsdorf he began to assert himself and think about escape. One of the compounds at Stalag VIIIB contained captured NCO fliers from the RAF, but relations between the sergeants and the wing commander were mixed. Summoned by Bader to chat with him along with another sergeant, Brian Treloar of the RAAF was pleasantly surprised. 'We found Bader sitting in a room of his own', Treloar later related. 'He had his "legs" under the bed. He was, we found, a very pleasant man who did not pull rank. We talked about all sorts of things – progress of the war, his prior escape, his never being without the "legs" dropped to him after he was shot down.' Others, however, recalled that Bader did in fact soon throw his weight about by demanding to know why more was not being done to annoy the enemy and stage breakouts. He evidently did not understand the curious democracy that had developed among captured NCO aircrew here and elsewhere, and made the assumption that he could simply order the sergeants to act more aggressively. Bader won no friends by arguing that the swap-over system carefully developed by the RAF contingent in association with the far larger British Army population at Lamsdorf had to be revamped. Under the existing scheme soldiers agreed to exchange identities with airmen in order to allow the latter to go out to the more lightly guarded working camps to which the former were sent on a fairly regular basis and, hopefully, stage a successful break. The only proviso was that if they were caught the RAF types should admit to their true identity so that their double, back in camp, could return from the RAF compound to his mates in the army compounds. Bader argued that, whatever assurances might have been given in the past, if a disguised flier was caught making a break from a working party – an *Arbeitskommando* – then he should continue to pretend to be a soldier until he was able to get away again. To his mind the need to get highly trained aircrew home took absolute precedence over the wishes of mere private soldiers. To many of the RAF sergeants this was both an arrogant and a foolish view. The RAF at Lamsdorf, after all, were absolutely dependent on the boys in khaki who controlled the manning of work parties to arrange any swap-over, and if ordinary soldiers wanted the chance to get back to their mates then so be it. To Bader, on the other hand, the RAF contingent was simply failing to pursue escape with sufficient aggression. Friction ensued: when Bader interrogated a sergeant-pilot as to why he, unlike Bader, had not made an escape bid, the NCO gamely replied: 'There is less chance of a well known person like Wing Commander Bader being shot than unknown Sergeant Smith.'[27]

Not surprisingly, Bader was as interested in getting himself out as in pushing his fellow RAF prisoners to do more. On one occasion he apparently hid himself away in the rafters of a hut in an empty compound while the inhabitants of the RAF compound were kept on parade for several hours, the Germans demanding to know where he was, getting no answer, but finally tracking him down. On another day Bader joined up with a local working party as it was leaving the camp, trading places with a dummy that had been counted during the head count on previous days so that there was nobody extra to count on the day of the escape. 'Bader wanted to get to Lamsdorf airfield,' Sapper John Andrew remembered, 'where he would take a German plane.' In return Bader promised to take six men with him. All went well until Bader proved unable to keep up the pace of the others, and though held up by those on either side he was then recognised. He ducked into the surrounding trees, but was soon re-caught. Such abortive attempts, however, were only the lead-up to his major – and last, as it turned out – effort to stage an escape from Lamsdorf.[28]

Bader and his roommate, Flight Lieutenant John Palmer, who had an injured foot, wanted the escape committee to help them do a swap-over and get out to an *Arbeitskommando* from which they could escape. 'You'll excuse me saying so, sir,' RSM Sidney Sherriff noted in reference to Bader's legs, 'but you might look a bit obvious going out.' The wing commander was adamant, however, wanting not any working party but one that was going to be near an aerodrome: like many other escaping pilots he was thinking about stealing a plane. Sherriff acquiesced, and arranged for Bader and Palmer to switch identities with two soldiers due to go out to work near an aerodrome at Gleiwitz. The exit went like clockwork, with Bader and Palmer, disguised in army battledress, unobtrusively joining the middle of the column near the gate while the guards' attention was diverted. The other members of the working party helped shield his distinctive gait on the journey to and from the train station, and once at the camp did so again by making him the caretaker while the others went off to do heavy labour. Plans were made to break through the single fence around the camp at night, but before they could be carried out Bader and Palmer were caught. While still at Lamsdorf the wing commander had sent a letter – presumably a complaint of some sort – to a Luftwaffe general. News that the famous legless air ace was at Stalag VIIIB spread to the local air stations, and as Bader was arriving at the Gleiwitz work camp a Luftwaffe officer came to visit Lamsdorf specifically in order to meet him. For obvious reasons it proved impossible for the army corporal lying in his bed to pretend for long that he was indeed Bader. A search revealed that the man occupying Palmer's bed was an impostor too. All the working parties administered through Lamsdorf were told to assemble every prisoner on parade and then have them lower their trousers. Rather than endure this indignity Bader gave himself up, the party sent from Lamsdorf to collect him rightly presuming that Palmer would be there too.[29]

Thwarted yet again, Bader took out his frustrations on the Germans. When the furious Lamsdorf commandant informed Bader that he had caused him a great deal of trouble, the wing commander told the interpreter to reply that 'it was my job to cause him trouble.' Thrown into cells, he made a nuisance of himself by demanding accommodation suitable for an officer rather than a mere soldier – 'I demand a spring bed, not that damned plank' – and brushing off a threat to take away his legs. Bader was still a celebrity prisoner, and, somewhat to his surprise, he got his way, receiving a spring mattress and also a table, chair, food, and even a servant. It was clear, however, that Bader was not going to settle down, and after ten days in solitary-but-comfortable confinement he was informed that he was being transferred again, this time to Colditz Castle.[30]

Officially designated Oflag IVC, this was the special fortress-camp to which the Germans sent persistent escapers and other troublemakers for safekeeping. Any doubts that Douglas Bader belonged among the 'bad boys' were instantly dispelled when, after his arrival on 17 August 1942, a thousand Reichsmarks, three compasses, and seven maps were found concealed in the chess set he had brought with him. He now found himself among old friends such as Geoffrey Stephenson and many officers just as determined to goon-bait and escape as he was. 'Colditz was a good camp where everybody was united in dislike of the enemy,' he later recalled, 'though naturally we all felt great frustration at being out of the fight.' Yet in contrast to assertions made by his brother-in-law, Bader was not always loved by his fellow prisoners at Colditz.[31]

He was, to be sure, widely admired within the castle. 'Wing Commander Bader – the legless air ace – has arrived', Padre Ellison Platt wrote excitedly in his diary. 'He is as vital as a naked electric wire... All nationalities [there were at this stage Belgian, British, French, Dutch and Polish contingents at Colditz] are thrilled by his presence, and doubly so when they have felt the pep of his conversation.' Prisoners did indeed marvel at his refusal to behave like a cripple – unless, that is, it caused inconvenience to the Germans – and were impressed by his general verve. To Alois Siska, a Czech pilot who had developed frostbite on his feet after crash-landing a bomber in the North Sea, Douglas Bader was a 'very good man, very brave man.' Ion Ferguson, one of the physicians at Colditz, was equally impressed. 'His was the most magnetic personality in the prison', the doctor later wrote, 'and indeed such was his dynamic energy that it made some of us tired even to watch him.' Others had similarly positive reactions. Army engineer Jim Rogers described Bader as 'an inspiring figure' while Jack Pringle of the 8th Hussars recalled him as 'a person of great morale, very amusing, [a] very nice man.' A former commando officer described Bader as a 'great chap' in an interview. 'He was a tonic,' Corran Purdon went on to explain in his memoirs, 'ever cheerful and friendly and I admired him immensely.'[32]

Bader was of course still restless. 'With a driving personality Douglas found it hard, even with his artificial legs, to sit still', Earl Haig recalled. 'His whole being was hungry for action.' The wing commander was able to work off some of his superabundant energy in the prisoners' courtyard by participating in team sports. 'The British game was cricket, of which Douglas Bader was particularly fond', wrote Jim Rogers. 'I can see him now when I think of the courtyard, with one of his tin legs locked, which made it easier for him to play. Certainly with his wonderful eye he would lash the ball all over the yard.' There was also 'stoolball', a notoriously rough contact sport in which Bader excelled as a keeper. One of the doctors wonderingly recalled how the legless Bader 'was constantly coming to grief at the stool-ball game'.

> He always played goalkeeper and he guarded his stool by sitting firmly on it, and warding off his opponents with his powerful arms. This goalkeeper, who would have been most offended if anybody had suggested that he make any concessions on account of his having no legs, very often finished below a pile of struggling humanity on the cobbled ground.

As one player put it, 'if you got near him you wouldn't come out alive.' The consequent inflammation of Bader's stumps was, from his perspective, a low price to pay for a chance to fight. 'I was not in the least surprised to see him, two days later [after being told he should allow his legs time to heal] playing a storming game as I watched from the window,' Ion Ferguson related. 'When he spotted me, as he sat on the stool with his back firmly against the wall, he gave me a rude "V" sign and burst into happy laughter.'[33]

The greatest sport of all, however, was still annoying the Germans as much as possible. Goon-baiting was well established at Colditz by the time Bader arrived, but he pitched right in and, if anything, helped push it to a dangerously high state of intensity. The wing commander, for example, made a point of refusing to salute a particular major, the second-in-command on the commandant's staff, on the grounds that he was inferior in rank, and added insult to injury by carefully blowing pipe smoke towards his face. His loud voice was also well to the fore when prisoners greeted visiting dignitaries with choruses such as 'Deutschland, Deutschland, UNTER alles', and he also wrote insulting messages on pieces of toilet paper that he threw towards the town below when the winds were favourable. It was at his urging that another RAF officer dropped a bucket of water on the head of the security officer from an upper window. 'Douglas Bader provided the fun', messmate Jack Pringle remembered. 'He was fanatically anti-German, and baited them at every possible opportunity.'[34]

As in other camps both the Germans and the British were willing to tolerate more from the legless one than they did from other prisoners. But even at Colditz there were officers, particularly older ones in positions of authority, who began to think that constantly rubbing the guards the wrong way in the manner encouraged by Bader might eventually produce a bloody confrontation. 'Bader was the sort of man you would follow into the jaws of hell, especially in a Spitfire,' Walter Morison observed retrospectively, 'but possibly not someone you would have looked to for calm and sober judgement.' Others, including some admirers, found him to be rather too much of a loose cannon. He was not at all hesitant about bullying anyone whose views on a problem did not accord with his own. That could mean that while being admired as 'a marvellous chap', the legless wonder might also be seen as 'a bit of a pain in the neck, you know' (Haig) or even 'a real bastard' (Pringle). There were also some doubts about constantly courting the withdrawal of privileges seemingly just for the hell of it. 'He was a perennial nuisance to his captors,' David Walker explained, 'and in being a nuisance to them was often a nuisance to us.' Others were more trenchant in their summations. 'Douglas Bader,' Hugo Ironside observed, 'for all the wrong reasons, was a real shit.'[35]

A disturbing sign of just how self-centred Bader could be at Colditz arose during 1943 in connection with his medical orderly. Bader had first met Alec Ross when this bandsman from the Seaforth Highlanders had been assigned to be his batman while he was in cells at Lamsdorf. Tired of the dreariness of life in Stalag VIIIB, Ross had requested that he be allowed to accompany Bader to Oflag IVC, a request that the wing commander eventually supported. 'When I first got to Colditz,' Ross remembered, 'I thought "this is going to be a good place".' The wing commander, to be sure, though dependent on him to provide piggy-back rides up and down the castle stairs, treated him very much as a below-stairs servant: 'I don't think all the time I knew him he said "please" or thank you" to me', Ross recalled, 'I was only a little squirt compared to him, weren't I?' Bader was like this with everyone of lower rank. 'He was very, very regimental [i.e. demanding]', Ross also remembered. 'He was the boss. Wherever he was, he liked to be the head one. When he shouted, you ran to do whatever he wanted.' Despite all this, or perhaps because of a need to follow a dynamic leader, Ross had volunteered to attach himself to Bader during his transfer because 'I liked him.' Such devotion ought to have been rewarded in some form, but *noblesse oblige* was apparently not part of the wing commander's makeup at Colditz. As a medical orderly Ross was eligible to be repatriated in one of the few exchanges of seriously sick, severely wounded, and non-combatant personnel that took place between Germany and Britain during the war. A year or so after he had arrived at Oflag IVC Ross was buttonholed by one of the more respected German officers. 'Good news, Ross', he was told. 'You're going home.' A happy Ross told Bader of his good fortune – 'I'm going home!' – to which Bader angrily retorted: 'No you're bloody not. You came here as my skivvy and that's what you'll stay.' Even for a man as notoriously rude as Bader this was breathtakingly insensitive. It was one thing for Bader to refuse repatriation himself, but quite another to deliberately prevent someone else from returning just because he happened to be useful fetching and carrying around the castle. 'I had to stay another two bloody years when I could have gone home with the rest of my mates', Ross bitterly reflected many years later.[36]

Bader, to be sure, was not a happy man at the time. He still desperately wanted to get back to the war – within days of his arrival at Oflag IVC he was organising tutorials on fighter tactics – and pushed hard to be included in escape bids in the hope of being able to steal an aeroplane. The best way out in his case was unquestionably through the gate, but when Bader tried to disguise himself as a laundry worker he was disconcerted to discover the guards checking the party as it left to see if anyone had tin legs. Getting out from the maximum-security *Schloss* was hard enough for those without artificial limbs to worry about, and once again Bader soon found himself coming into conflict with a camp escape committee. Collaborating with Geoffrey Stephenson and another officer, the wing commander made a pitch to the committee for a scheme that was almost laughably unsuitable for someone with two tin legs, as Paul Brickhill later related.

> They would crawl out of an attic window on to the steep roof high over the courtyard and away from the searchlights, scramble somehow up on to the ridge and crawl from there till they could drop into the German part of the castle. Then, skulking through the shadows and climbing over more roofs they would reach a point where the cable of a lightning conductor stretched to the ground a hundred

feet below. After sliding down this they would drop by rope forty feet into the dry bed of the moat, climb over a couple of barbed-wire fences and terraces sown with anti-personnel mines and then make for Switzerland. Would the escape committee be good enough to cough up some German marks, forged papers and other details?

The escape committee would not. 'I'm sorry,' Dick Howe, the escape officer, firmly replied, 'but with your legs you just couldn't make it.' Bader, of course, thought he could, and continued to hunt for ways out of the castle, including through the sewers. Either the potential escape routes turned out to be dead ends or the escape committee poured cold water on the plans. Frustrated in 1943 by yet another refusal to include him in an escape bid, Bader told the Senior British Officer with total conviction that his contribution to the war effort would be greater than that of anyone else in Colditz.[37]

Bader was not always utterly selfish while at Colditz. He was willing to 'stooge' for other officers' escape bids – though his exuberance could sometimes get the better of him – and as the most senior-ranking airman in the castle he served as a 'consultant' during the making of the famous Colditz glider – though, typically, there are indications that he expected to act as pilot when it was completed. By the last years of the war, though, he had more or less admitted that he would have to sit things out and listen to his favourite Bing Crosby records.

His most important role during his time in the castle was as a smuggler late in the war. Bader was one of the very few prisoners at Oflag IVC eventually granted – in his case for reasons of health – the privilege of occasional walks, on parole and under guard, in the town and countryside around the castle. Aside from trying to chat up any young women he met, Bader was able to engage in surreptitious trade with the locals. Soap, tobacco, cigarettes and other items the prisoners had received earlier in Red Cross parcels could be exchanged for foodstuffs the prisoners desperately needed in the last months of the war when rations had dwindled to almost nothing. Bribing the escorting sentry to look the other way, Bader was able, in collaboration with his walking companion Peter Dollar, to hide about his person (under his cap, in special bags hidden inside his trousers) and bring in up to fifty pounds of grain. 'Believe me,' commented Phil Pardoe, 'it made a big difference to our starvation rations at the time.'[38]

Colditz was finally liberated in the middle of April 1945 by advancing American forces, though Bader was nearly killed in the process. When US tanks had first driven into view he, like others, had crowded the upper windows to catch a glimpse. A battle was raging in the town below the castle, though, and a shell burst against a nearby wall. The concussion was strong enough to knock the wing commander off his feet, and for once he decided that discretion was the better part of valour. 'I retreated into what seemed a safe place under some stairs, feeling somewhat ashamed,' Walter Morison remembered, 'only to find that I shared it with Douglas Bader and Tommy Catlow.' That changed things for Morison: 'If it was OK for a legless fighter ace and a submarine commander [to take shelter] I reckoned it was OK for me and I felt a little better.'[39]

In a move that was considered 'typical Bader' by his fellow prisoners, the wing commander immediately spotted a female American reporter by the name of Lee Carson and promptly presented himself for an interview once the US Army had actually entered the castle. Through her intervention Bader was able to fly home within twenty-four hours and was back in England, fellow ex-prisoner John Wilson recalled, 'well ahead of us'. So abrupt was his departure that Bader forgot to bring his spare pair of tin legs with him. When he phoned up Alec Ross and discovered that his former servant had left them in Colditz, Bader swore, hung up, and never spoke to Ross again. Like many other newly liberated prisoners of war, to be sure, he was having a certain amount of psychological difficulty adjusting to the outside world. Bader was by no means the only man to find himself losing his temper, not being able to relate easily to other people, and being forced to think again about what to do with his life. Things were made worse in his case by the fact that he was still very much in the public eye. Douglas Bader, indeed, was about to begin his transformation from war ace into what a future leader of the Conservative Party would describe as 'an archetype of his generation.'[40]

Notes

[1]Henry Chancellor, *Colditz* (London: Hodder and Stoughton, 2001), p. 252.
[2]Paul Brickhill, *Reach for the Sky* (London: Collins, 1954), pp. 283–87, 291; http://home.tiscali.be/ed.ragas/awshistory/awsbader.html (accessed 12 February 2004),

B. Cunningham interview of Douglas Bader for *Code One*, p. 4.

[3]Sholto Douglas, *Years of Command* (London: Collins, 1966), pp. 139–41; Imperial War Museum Department of Documents [hereafter IWM], Lord Douglas Papers, Box 3, DCAS – Fighter Command File, TS Dictation Notes to Wright, n/d, p. 175; see Royal Air Force Museum [hereafter RAFM], MF 10027/4, 'Delivery of a new leg for Wing Commander Bader' memo; The National Archives [hereafter NA], AIR 4/210, R.L. Knight logbook, 19 August 1941; Imperial War Museum Sound Archive [hereafter IWMSA] 11623, J.A. Goodson TS, p. 32; Bill Newton Dunn, *Big Wing* (Shrewsbury: Airlife, 1992), p. 84.

[4]*Sunday Express*, 31 October 1945, p. 2. On Bader later refusing repatriation see Brickhill, *Reach for the Sky*, pp. 347–48. On Bader in fact being a pretty good shape with the help of massage therapy after being shipped to Germany see NA, PIN 38/526, encl. 91A, Extract from Col. Lavack letter, 11 May 1942. The bruise, but not the request for repatriation, was reported in the first semi-official biography. See Brickhill, *Reach for the Sky*, p. 284.

[5]St Edward's School Archive, Bill Mascott to Katie Rudaz, 14 November 2003. On the Me 109 incident see Brickhill, *Reach for the Sky*, p. 293; Adolf Galland, *The First and the Last* (New York: Orion, 1954), p. 91.

[6]Brickhill, *Reach for the Sky*, pp. 292–302; Robert Jackson, *Douglas Bader* (London: Barker, 1983), pp. 113–15; see also IWM, L.M.E. Hollingdale Papers, Bader to Harrison, 3 January 1980.

[7]On the ambulance scheme see Jackson, *Douglas Bader*, p. 116. On the rumours see IWMSA 17156/2, E.F. Chapman. On Bader knowing the danger his presence spelled for the Hiècques see Brickhill, *Reach for the Sky*, p. 300. The family were indeed sentenced to death and sent to a German concentration camp, but still managed to survive the war. Some of the German hospital staff were court-martialled but, after Bader gave evidence of their innocence, they were let go. See Brickhill, *Reach for the Sky*, pp. 312–15.

[8]Richard Pape, *Boldness be my Friend* (London: Elek, 1953), pp. 108–09; Brickhill, *Reach for the Sky*, pp. 306–10, 315; NA, WO 344/13, Bader Liberation Questionnaire; Don Whitehead, *"Beachhead Don": Reporting the War from the European Theater, 1942–1945* (New York: Fordham University Press, 2004), p. 148. On Bader protesting the move see M. Booker in *Colditz Society Newsletter*, vol. 2, no. 19, January 1999, p. 4.

[9]R.G.M. Quarrie, *Oflag* (Durham: Pentland, 1995), p. 25. On the camp see Brickhill, *Reach for the Sky*, pp. 316–17.

[10]W. Cunningham to Author, 1 October 2004; see Jane Torday (ed.), *The Coldstreamer and the Canary* (Hexam: Black Cat, 1995), pp. 75–76. On conditions at Warburg see Charles Rollings, *Wire and Worse* (Hersham: Ian Allan, 2004), chs. 4–5.

[11]Mortimer in Torday, *Coldstreamer*, p. 76; see Brickhill, *Reach for the Sky*, pp. 318–19.

[12]Rollings, *Wire and Worse*, pp. 194, 202; Brickhill, *Reach for the Sky*, pp. 320–21; T.C.F. Prittie and W. Earle Edwards, *Escape to Freedom* (London: Hutchinson, 1953), p. 129; IWMSA 17156/2, E.F. Chapman.

[13]Rollings, *Wire and Worse*, pp. 210–11.

[14]W. Cunningham, 'Memoirs of a British Veteran', in Paul Addison and Jeremy A. Crang (eds), *The Burning Blue* (London: Pimlico, 2000), p. 134 [also W. Cunningham to Author, 1 October 2004]; Brickhill, *Reach for the Sky*, pp. 322–23; see D. Lubbock in Dilap Sarkar, *Douglas Bader* (Worcester: Ramrod, 2001), p. 43; Rollings, *Wire and Worse*, pp. 212–13.

[15]Prittie and Edwards, *Escape to Freedom*, pp. 136–37; Victor F. Gammon, *Not All Glory!* (London: Arms and Armour, 1996), p. 72. On the removal of the leg see also IWMSA 18735/8, E.L.C. Edlemann.

[16]IWMSA 4827/2, R. Loder. On the Warburg Wire Job see S.P. MacKenzie, *The Colditz Myth* (Oxford: Oxford University Press, 1994), p. 332.

[17]Rollings, *Wire and Worse*, 180–81; Butt and Gammon in Gammon, *Not All Glory*, pp. 71–72.

[18]Sharpe quoted in *Daily Mail*, 2 June 1942; Prittie and Edwards, *Escape to Freedom*, pp. 231–32; J.S. Poole, *Undiscovered Ends* (London: Cassell, 1957), p. 145; Mortimer in Torday, *Coldstreamer*, p. 76. On the snowball incident see IWMSA 17156/2, E.F. Chapman.

[19]IWMSA 15608/2, W. Stevens; IWM, Leslie Frith, 'What a Way to Win a War', p. 71.

[20]John Frayn Turner, *Douglas Bader* (Shrewsbury: Airlife, 2001 edn), p. 208; Brickhill, *Reach for the Sky*, p. 324; R. Boulding in Dilip Sarkar, *Bader's Tangmere Spitfires* (Sparkford: Patrick Stephens, 1996), p. 159; Oliver Philpot, *Stolen Journey* (London: Hodder and Stoughton, 1950), p. 138.

[21]P. Barthropp in *Britain's War Heroes: Douglas Bader, Fighter Ace* (Blakeway Associates, 2005); see P. Bathropp in *Secret Lives: Douglas Bader* (Twenty Twenty Productions, 1996); B.A. James, *Moonless Night* (London: Kimber, 1983), p. 63.

[22]A.R.D. MacDonell, *From Dogfight to Diplomacy: A Spitfire Pilot's Log, 1932–1958* (Barnsley: Pen and Sword, 2005), p. 102.

[23]Ibid. On the escape committee and Bader see L. Ray Silver, *Last of the Gladiators* (Shrewsbury: Airlife, 1995), p. 154; Jackson, *Douglas Bader*, p. 126. On the contraband hidden in the legs see Gammon, *Not All Glory*, p. 73. On the Germans respecting Bader and giving him a lot of slack see IWMSA 11337/4, H. Bracken; Sydney Smith, *Wings Day* (London: Collins, 1968), p. 103. On resentment long after the war because of stoppages see Laddie Lucas, *Flying Colours* (London: Wordsworth, 2001 edn), pp. 204–05; see also IWMSA 6630/6, J. Cox. On the counter-argument that it was a POW's job to make life difficult for the enemy even if it meant reprisals see IWMSA 10202, W. Ash TS, p. 26. See also Brickhill, *Reach for the Sky*, p. 325.

[24]Brickhill, *Reach for the Sky*, pp. 324–25; Colin Hodgkinson, *Best Foot Forward* (London: Odams, 1957), p. 232. On Bader talking too loudly about escape see IWMSA 11337/4, H. Bracken. On gate-crashing other people's schemes see IWMSA 6630/6, J. Cox. On the 'Dig Me a Tunnel' label see IWMSA 1154, G.C. Unwin TS, p. 30. On obtaining the Me 110 starting instructions see M.R.D. Foot and J.M. Langley, *MI9* (London: Bodley Head, 1979), p. 101.

[25]On lodging an official complaint against a survivor of the X organisation see Silver, *Last of the Gladiators*, pp. 160–61. On Bader having difficulty coming to terms with no longer being in command see Lucas, *Flying Colours*, p. 203. On Bader's unsuitableness to lead a POW camp see John Nicholl and Tony Rennell, *The Last Escape* (London: Viking, 2002), p. 9.

[26]MacDonell, *Dogfight to Diplomacy*, p. 103; IWM, Leslie Frith, 'What a Way to Win a War', p. 72 [see also William James Hunter, *From Coastal Command to Captivity* (Barnsley: Leo Cooper, 2003), p. 25]; IWM, C.N.S. Campbell diary, 10 July 1942; see Philpot, *Stolen Journey*, p. 139; F. Ash in Richard C. Smith, *Hornchurch Eagles* (London: Grub Street, 2002), p. 51; R. Stanford Tuck in Sarkar, *Douglas Bader*, p. 43. On Day persuading Bader to go, see Smith, *Wings Day*, p. 103. This was apparently not the first time that Bader had clashed with higher authority within the wire. According to Canadian pilot Arthur Deacon, Bader had at least once before been called on the carpet by the SBO for assuming that he, rather than the wing commander, was in charge inside the wire (Wayne Ralph communication to author, 10 July 2005). On the story that Bader was first found in the fire-pool see IWMSA 15336/4, J.C. Wilson; Ron Mackenzie, *An Ordinary War* (Wangaratta: Shoestring, 1995), pp. 54–55; see also IWM, Frith, 'What a Way to Win a War', p. 71. Another prisoner was told that Bader had been talked out of settling in the fire-pool. See Arthur A. Durand, *Stalag Luft III* (Baton Rouge, LA: Louisiana State University Press, 1988), p. 101.On Day himself apparently being glad to see the back of Bader see Silver, *Last of the Gladiators*, p. 155.

[27]Gammon, *Not All Glory*, p. 74; B. Treloar in J.E. Holliday (ed.), *Stories of the RAAF POWs in Lamsdorf* (Holland Park, Queensland: Lamsdorf POWs' Association, 1992), p. 113. See Frank Taylor, *Barbed Wire and Footlights* (Braunton: Merlin, 1988), pp. 50–51.

[28]http://www.bbc.co.uk/dna/ww2/A2312731 (accessed 22 January 2005), J. Andrew account. On the local working party attempt see also Albert Paice and Alwyn Ward, *For the Love of Elizabeth* (privately published, 1984), pp. 28–29. On the rafter attempt see Gammon, *Not All Glory*, pp. 74–75. Neither of these efforts is mentioned in other sources, and it may be that the descriptions actually refer to other events in other places.

[29]NA, WO 208/3322, MI9/S/PG(G)2245, p. 3; Brickhill, *Reach for the Sky*, pp. 328–44; IWM, W.L. Stephens, 39–40; IWMSA 4816/4, J.M. Moran. Three other

swap-overs from the RAF compound remained undetected and were able to stage an escape. See Brickhill, *Reach for the Sky*, 333, n. 1.

[30]Brickhill, *Reach for the Sky*, pp. 334–36; Jackson, *Douglas Bader*, pp. 129–30. On the way RAF NCO compounds were run see MacKenzie, *Colditz Myth*, p. 127. Bader was also reputed to have cut down the Wehrmacht flag at some point. See IWMSA 2268/9, R. Bateson.

[31]Liddell Hart Centre, Nicholas Eadon papers, box 3, Conway to Eadon, 8 November 1979. On Colditz see Chancellor, *Colditz, passim*. On the assertion that there was no criticism of Bader among the inmates of this special camp see Lucas, *Flying Colours*, p. 201. On the chess set discovery see Reinhold Eggers, *Colditz* (London: Hale, 1991 edn), p. 83.

[32]Corran Purdon, *List the Bugle* (Antrim: Greystone, 1993), p. 54; IWMSA 17896/3, C. Purdon; IWMSA 17585/3, J.C. Pringle; Jim Rogers, *Tunnelling into Colditz* (London: Hale, 1986), p. 135; Ion Ferguson, *Doctor at War* (London: Christopher Johnson, 1955), p. 141; Liddle Collection, University of Leeds [hereafter LC], Tape 1527, A. Siska; Margaret Duggan (ed.), *Padre in Colditz* (London: Hodder and Stoughton, 1978), p. 200.

[33]Ferguson, *Doctor at War*, pp. 140–41; J. Chrisp in Chancellor, *Colditz*, p. 296; Rogers, *Tunnelling*, p. 94; Earl Haig, *My Father's Son* (London: Leo Cooper, 2000), p. 131.

[34]Jack Pringle, *Colditz Last Stop* (Lewes: Temple House, 1988), p. 140; see Brickhill, *Reach for the Sky*, p. 340; Chancellor, *Colditz*, p. 118; P.R. Reid, *The Colditz Story* (London: Hodder and Stoughton, 1952), p. 212.

[35]Colditz Society Video Archive 11, H. Ironside; David Walker, *Lean, Wind Lean* (London: Collins, 1984), p. 152; IWMSA 17583/3, J. Pringle; LC, 1995 D. Haig interview TS, p. 7; Walter Morison, *Flak and Ferrets* (London: Sentinel, 1995), p. 156. On senior-officer worries about Bader and goon-baiting see Chancellor, *Colditz*, p. 118; see also MacKenzie, *Colditz Myth*, pp. 144–48, 218–20. On Bader getting away with more than would be tolerated from other POWs see Pringle, *Colditz Last Stop*, p. 140. On the risk that goon-baiting might lead to bloodshed see NA, WO 208/3288, pp. 16–17.

[36]A. Ross in *Secret Lives: Douglas Bader* (Twenty Twenty Productions, 1996); A. Ross in Chancellor, *Colditz*, pp. 251–52; A. Ross obituary, *Telegraph*, filed 23 September 2003; A. Ross in Richard Garrett, *Sky High* (London: Weidenfeld and Nicolson, 1991), p. 173; see Brickhill, *Reach for the Sky*, pp. 335–37. On Bader refusing repatriation see ibid., pp. 347–8. On the upstairs-downstairs attitude of Bader (among others) at Colditz see also J. Hedley in Hillary Kingsley and Geoff Tibbits, *Box of Delights* (London: Macmillan, 1989), p. 130.

[37]Brickhill, *Reach for the Sky*, p. 343; see Bromhall in Chancellor, *Colditz*, p. 252; see also IWMSA 15336/4, J.C. Wilson; LC, Haig interview TS, p. 7; Reid, *Colditz Story*, p. 212. On the laundry worker bid see C. Linlithgow in Sarkar, *Douglas Bader*, p. 44.

Supporting the hypothesis that Bader still hoping to steal a plane is the fact that the Colditz security officer intercepted cockpit instructions for the Me 109 in mail destined for the wing commander. See M. Booker in *Colditz Society Newsletter*, vol. 2, no. 19, January 1999, p. 4. Bader was, in should be noted, still being celebrated at home. See the account by Arthur Bryant of the Battle of Britain written for the *Daily Sketch* for the fourth anniversary reproduced in Arthur Bryant, *The Battle of Britain* (Manchester: Grove, 1948), pp. 23–24. On Bader holding fighter-pilot tutorials at Colditz see IWM, H.N. Fowler letter, 23 August 1942.

[38]P. Pardoe in Jackson, *Douglas Bader*, p. 133; see Pringle, *Colditz Last Stop*, p. 140; Walker, *Lean, Wind Lean*, p. 141; Brickhill, *Reach for the Sky*, pp. 346, 349–50. On the Bing Crosby records see http://www.awm.gov.au (accessed 1 September 2003), D. Crawford interview TS. (Bader had picked up a liking for the crooner from Willie McKnight, one of the Canadians in 242 Squadron. See Brickhill, *Reach for the Sky*, p. 194.) On Bader deciding to sit things out see ibid., 343–44. On Bader and the glider see Whitehead, *"Beachhead Don"*, p. 148; Brickhill, *Reach for the Sky*, p. 350; IWMSA 4816/7, J.M. Moran. On Bader helping others escape, though sometimes not without difficulty, see K. Lockwood on Pat Reid escape in *Escape from Colditz* (Windfall Films, 2000); Reid, *Colditz Story*, pp. 249–51; NA, WO 208/3311, MI9/S/PG(G)995–998, p. 5; see also P.R. Reid, *The Latter Days* (London: Hodder and Stoughton, 1953), p. 47.

[39]http://www.bbc.co.uk/dna/ww2/A1119837 (accessed 22 January 2005), W. Morison.

[40]I. Duncan Smith in *Telegraph*, 4 August 2001; IWMSA 15336/4, J.C. Wilson. On Lee Carson see Nancy Caldwell Sorel, *The Women Who Wrote the War* (New York: Arcade, 1999), pp. 213–14. Her report on the liberation of the castle is contained in the *New York Journal-American*, late edition, 17 April 1945, p. 1. On Bader having trouble adjusting see Brickhill, *Reach for the Sky*, pp. 356–7. On adjustment difficulties in general see MacKenzie, *Colditz Myth*, pp. 395–96. On the missing legs see Alec Ross obituary, *Daily Telegraph*, 23 September 2003. On getting back with Carson's help see Chancellor, *Colditz*, pp. 381–2.

CHAPTER SEVEN

National Hero

All I can say is that you are leaving behind an example which as the years roll by will become a legend.

Letter from Air Chief Marshal Sir James Robb to Douglas Bader, February 1946[1]

It was entirely in character for Douglas Bader to be determined to get back into action as World War II drew to a close. Even before he left Colditz he told an Associated Press correspondent that he wanted to 'get another squirt at the bloody Hun', adding in high good humour 'I'll never be satisfied until I do.' Put through to his wife on the telephone by a well-meaning American general after he was flown to Versailles, he announced that he would not be coming home just yet as he was hunting for a Spitfire: 'I want to have a last fling before it packs up.' Thelma was understandably distraught, asking rhetorically if he had not already done enough for his country. Bader evidently thought he needed to prove himself again after years in captivity, but the Royal Air Force did not want to lose one of its heroes at such a time. Disregarding the changes in design that had occurred over the past four years, he contacted Tubby Mermagen, now an air commodore based at Rheims, and asked if there was a spare Spit he could use because 'I want another crack.' A message from the C-in-C Fighter Command had already been circulated to the effect that under no circumstances was he to be allowed back into combat: instead Bader was to be flown straight back to London. Sent on leave, he managed to wangle flights, first in a Magister and then a late-model Spitfire courtesy of Rupert Leigh. This was not for old times' sake: within days Bader began lobbying the Air Ministry hard for a posting to Burma. Thelma was horrified, but told that this was absolutely impossible because his stumps would sweat and chaff too much in a tropical climate, Bader reluctantly had to abandon his plan to fly against the Japanese.[2]

Instead, he was offered and accepted a posting to head the Day Fighter Wing of the Central Fighter Establishment at the rank of group captain starting on 1 June 1945. This must have seemed like picking up where he had left off, commanding a wing of fighters based at Tangmere. Unfortunately it turned out to be a mistake for all concerned. Though still a natural fighter pilot, Bader had no previous experience of contemporary aircraft such as the pis-ton-engined Hawker Tempest or the jet-powered Gloster Meteor, and for the most part chose to fly the Spitfire IX and Hurricane IV instead. Just as problematic were the changes that had taken place in tactics over the previous four years, especially with respect to ground attack. All this might have mattered less if the students had been novice pilots willing to submit themselves to a legendary commander. The officers flying under Bader, however, were now all veterans, more familiar with contemporary tactics and machines than he was and often with impressive kill scores to their name. With the war in Europe over they did not share their leader's sense of urgency and soon came to resent his overbearing presence. Johnny Checketts, for example, who met Bader for the first time at Tangmere, found him 'brusque and opinionated', someone who rarely listened to what others had to say. The friction soon became such that it reached the ears of the C-in-C Fighter Command. Air Chief Marshal Sir James Robb decided to move Bader out of harm's way, posting him to take command of the North Weald sector on 20 July 1945.[3]

Though it was winding down as an operational station, North Weald was more to Bader's taste. It came under the command of Air Vice-Marshal George Dermot, AOC 11 Group, who remembered Bader well from his days as an instructor at Cranwell. Their rela-tions were close enough to enable Bader to arrange for his future brother-in-law, Laddie Lucas, to avoid a posting to the Far East – 'Bloody ridiculous, old boy! Get that stopped tomorrow!' – and instead take up residence at nearby RAF Bentwaters. Bader, mean-while, had plenty of opportunity to perfect his flying technique on a Spitfire IX. Whatever doubts Fighter Command HQ may have had about his contemporary relevance, moreover, there was apparently no hesitation in nominating Bader when it came time to decide on someone to lead the flypast to commemorate the Battle of Britain.

The weather was not too good, but the pilot that the public was already automatically thinking of in reference to 'The Few' took off at the head of the formation due to fly over London to great acclaim on 15 September 1945.[4]

Leading the flypast, however, proved to be something of a swan song; at least as far as Bader in the Royal Air Force was concerned. Barely six months later the press was reporting that the famous legless air-ace Group Captain Douglas Bader, OBE and Bar, DFC and Bar, was being 'released from the R.A.F.' In light of how he had fought to get back into the Air Force, as well as what he had accomplished subsequently, why was he now packing it all in?[5]

There is indirect evidence to suggest that Bader, as the time he spent in Germany stretched from months into years, grew concerned that being a POW would blight his chances for a place in the post-war RAF. Moreover Leigh-Mallory, his great patron within Fighter Command, had been killed in an air crash late in the war. It did not escape Bader's attention that the current AOC had not let him fly operationally in the last days of the war with Germany. Nor was he unconscious of what the Air Ministry refusal to let him transfer to the tropics in order to fight the Japanese (on the grounds that his legs would not be able to stand the heat and humidity) might mean for the future. The RAF would still have extensive responsibilities in the Middle East and Far East, and if Bader found himself barred from serving in such places his prospects for future promotion would be severely limited. Last but not least, Bader probably knew that being an officer in the post–1945 Air Force was going to be something very different and rather unwelcome compared to life as a swashbuckling fighter leader in war. 'If a man is a prick he calls him a prick,' as one of his friends explained. 'In the peacetime Air Force you daren't do that, especially if he's a senior chap. You've got to say yes, sir, no sir, three bags full.' As this friend rightly observed, Bader 'would never have done it'.[6]

That left open the question of what an ex-fighter pilot in his mid-thirties with two artificial limbs was going to do by way of earning a living. Friends in the Conservative Party were keen to have such a famous figure stand for parliament. Bader, though, recognised that as an MP he would not always be free to speak his mind and turned them down, explaining on later occasions – and perhaps only half facetiously – that the only post he would be suited to in politics

The First Eleven, St. Edward's School, 1928. Bader, captain of the team, is in the centre. © Archives, St. Edward's School, Oxford.

An Avro 504, the aircraft type in which Douglas Bader learned to fly in the late 1920s. © Royal Air Force Museum.

Bristol Bulldogs in a display of formation flying. Bader would test his luck once too often on this interwar fighter. © Royal Air Force Museum.

The increasingly famous CO of 242 Squadron leans on the cockpit of his Hurricane for a publicity photo, summer 1940. © Imperial War Museum.

242 (Canadian) Squadron in tight formation over southern England, summer 1940. © Imperial War Museum.

Bader, along with Eric Ball and Willie McKnight, examines the nose art adopted by 242 Squadron. © Imperial War Museum.

Bader, again flanked by McKnight and Ball, stares directly at the camera in a typically pugnacious pose outside the Officers' Mess at Duxford. © Imperial War Museum.

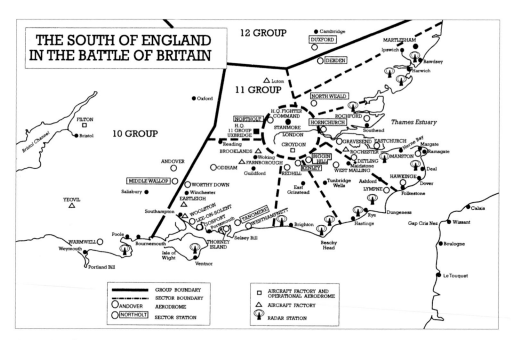

Sector Operations Room, Duxford. Bader would not always heed instructions from the Controller. ©
Imperial War Museum.

Gun camera still of He-111s under attack during the Battle of Britain. © Imperial War Museum.

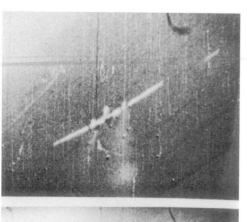

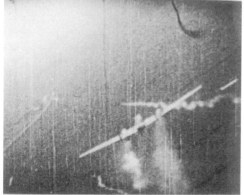

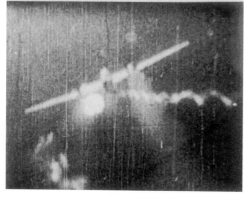

Gun camera footage of an Me-110 under attack during the Battle of Britain. © Imperial War Museum.

Messerschmitt 109Es over England, 9 September 1940. © TopFoto.

He-111s in formation above Southeast England, 1 September 1940. © TopFoto.

Messerschmitt 110s flying along the Channel coast, 20 August 1940. © TopFoto.

Trafford Leigh-Mallory, AOC 12 Group and a big supporter of Bader in 1940, outside the Air Ministry, 1943. ©
Imperial War Museum.

Claims such as this were in fact considerably greater than the number of enemy aircraft actually shot down during the Battle of Britain.

Keith Park, commander of 11 Group during the Battle of Britain. © Imperial War Museum.

Hugh Dowding, C-in-C Fighter Command, 1940. © Imperial War Museum.

Sholto Douglas, successor to Dowding at Fighter Command and one of the architects of fighter sweeps over France in 1941.
© Imperial War Museum.

S/LDR. DOUGLAS BADER. D.S.O. D.F.C.   (CANADIAN) SQUADRON

242

ORDE
15 March 1941

Portrait of Douglas Bader by Cuthbert Order, March 1941.

The cannon-equipped Spitfire VB. Bader was dismissive of cannon-armed fighters and hung on to a machine-gun armed Spitfire VA. © Imperial War Museum.

Free at last! Bader after being liberated from Colditz, 18 April 1945. © TopFoto.

Group Captain D.R.S. Bader, after being formally presented with the bars to his DSO and DFC at Buckingham Palace, 27 November 1945. Thelma, his first wife, is to his left. © TopFoto.

Ambassador for Shell: Bader, now a civilian, at the controls of his Miles Gemini. © TopFoto.

Arise, Sir Douglas … Bader with his second wife, Joan, after being knighted on 28 July 1976. © TopFoto.

The statue of Douglas Bader unveiled at Goodwood Aerodrome, 9 August 2000. © TopFoto.

Douglas Bader as drawn by J. F. Watton, Colditz Castle, September 1942.

was that of prime minister. Fortunately the heads of Shell Oil were happy to have him rejoin the company in July 1946.[7]

For the next twenty-three years Bader worked as an executive for the aviation department at Shell. On the whole the relationship between the ex-fighter pilot and the oil giant was mutually beneficial. Quite apart from his sheer energy and willingness to take on any challenge, having a famous war hero on the salary roll was a great asset to the company in terms of publicity. Looking after aviation fuel supplies and the mixed fleet of company planes sent Bader on trips all over the world, commonly in the pilot's seat of a twin-engine light aircraft. 'At Shell he was virtually his own boss and his own master and he could come and go as he pleased', a friend recalled, allowing among other things time for appeals and visits on behalf of the disabled; charity work for which Bader would be eventually awarded a knighthood. Little wonder that, in conversation with another ex-fighter pilot he met one day in El Aden, he should have been 'full of praise' for his post-war employer.[8]

This is not to suggest that no friction occurred. As always Bader demanded that his needs – everything from secretaries to air transport – take priority over everyone else's; and on the days when he was in the office, rather than flying, things would usually be in a state of uproar. Along with the positive publicity, moreover, there was sometimes embarrassment at the way in which Bader might sound off in public on potentially sensitive topics.

There was the matter of contributing a foreword in early 1952 to the English-language edition of the memoirs of a German pilot, Hans Ulrich Rudel, who had lost a leg during the war but refused to be grounded. The parallel was obvious, and Bader was approached by Euphorion Distribution Ltd of Dublin to see if he would be willing to write something. Bader had admired this tank-buster ace when he was interrogated at Tangmere just after the war, and agreed. 'I am happy to write this short foreword to Rudel's book,' he explained, 'since although I only met him for a couple of days he is, by any standards, a gallant chap and I wish him luck.' Soon after *Stuka Pilot* appeared in English, however, it emerged that Rudel had been a dedicated member of the Nazi Party – something that could have been surmised from the manuscript – and that his English-language publishing house had connections with the pre-war British Union of Fascists. Made aware of this by the English newspaper press after publication, Bader refused to admit that prior knowledge would have altered his decision to help. 'You know, I really think it wouldn't have made any difference', he was reported as saying. 'I didn't know who they [the publishers] were. But I was delighted to do it for Rudel, just for Rudel.' This was said out of simple admiration for the skill of a fellow flier, Bader apparently missing the point that his name, and potentially that of his employer, now might be linked with the extreme right in politics.[9]

Four years later, while on a visit to New Zealand during the Suez Crisis, when some of the more recent members of the Commonwealth were critical of British military action, Bader was reported as saying that such ungrateful former colonial subjects could 'bloody well climb back up their trees'. Perhaps not surprisingly he was later a vehement and vocal opponent of sanctions against white-ruled Rhodesia. During a visit to South Africa in November 1965 he went so far as to say that if he had been in Rhodesia when Ian Smith made his unilateral declaration of independence, 'I would have had serious thoughts about changing my own citizenship papers.' This sort of thing did not go down well at Shell, where there was justifiable concern that such public remarks, widely reported in the press, would have a negative impact on company relations with Third World governments. Though he badly wanted the job, Bader was turned down flat when he applied for a senior personnel manager appointment at Shell.[10]

A large part of this concern had to do with the fact that Douglas Bader was a name that everybody recognised; even more so, in fact, than when he had been in the RAF. Instead of fading from public consciousness as the war receded into the past, Bader had become more famous than ever, thanks largely to a hand-picked biographer and above all the film production team that transformed the subsequent book into a celluloid triumph. Association with such a recognised name might, in short, turn into a double-edged sword for Shell if fame ever turned into notoriety.

After the war Bader was asked by several people to write up his own story, but declined. 'No', he tended to say, 'the question of me writing the story is simply not on.' Firstly, he believed he did not possess the necessary writing skills; and secondly, nobody with any 'sense of proportion' would do an autobiography while still in his early forties. Yet while Bader claimed to be indifferent or hostile to fame he often seemed to enjoy it, and was quite prepared to ask someone else to tell the tale. He was particularly impressed with

Paul Brickhill, an Australian journalist who had flown with the RAAF, been a POW at Stalag Luft III, and subsequently written two best-selling volumes on particular wartime events involving the Air Force: both crammed with heroes and heroism. The first book, published in 1949 under the title *The Great Escape*, narrated the mass tunnel break from Sagan five years earlier that had ended in tragedy. Three years later a second book came out, *The Dam Busters*, which chronicled the 'bouncing bomb' raid by 617 Squadron on the German dams. Bader was particularly impressed with the way in which the author seemed able to bring back to life men he had not known personally and events in which he had taken no part in the pages of *The Dam Busters*. 'If anyone writes our story,' he declared to his wife, 'it must be Paul Brickhill.'[11]

The author was happy to oblige, talking at length to the wife, friends, and of course his subject about the latter's life and personality. The collaborative process was not always without its creative tensions, especially on those occasions when Bader thought Brickhill was indulging in a bit of creative licence. But there was no doubt among family members when the story was finished that the author had correctly narrated the essential facts and caught the authentic atmosphere of the times and places, as well as the personalities of the people, about which and whom he was writing. Bader himself thought Brickhill was wrong in suggesting that he was constantly trying to prove himself, but in general was happy enough with the portrait that the author produced. He was subsequently not shy about allowing his friends in parliament to help arrange a meeting with Winston Churchill so he could present him with a copy of his biography. The £10,000 lump sum he was paid for the rights to his life story also doubtless came in handy.[12]

Reach for the Sky, as the narrative came to be titled, was by no means a hagiography. The author was quite aware that his subject could be terribly impatient, was often simplistic in his outlook, and was thoroughly disliked by some of his former comrades. Nevertheless the book had been authorised by Bader, and Brickhill tended to downplay, excuse, or put a positive gloss on some of his less laudable character traits and actions. This was not, it is worth noting, simply a matter of calculation. Brickhill was most definitely an admirer, deeply impressed by the way in which Bader had overcome his disability and at one with him on subjects such as the Big Wing and its centrality in the Battle of Britain. 'I agree with all those who class him as the best fighter leader and tactician of World War II', as he straightforwardly explained in the book's conclusion.[13]

When *Reach for the Sky* first appeared under the Collins imprint in the spring of 1954, it was a major success with book critics and the reading public alike. 'As a story of war adventures this is an excellent book,' *The Times* declared, 'but it goes further in revealing what the body can stand if only the spirit will put it under fierce compulsion.' According to the *Daily Mail* the story was sure to 'stir a glow of pride in British hearts', and the *Sunday Express* predicted that it was 'certain to sweep to startling success'. The more left-leaning press was equally enthralled. According to the *New Statesman*, for instance, the book was 'a brilliant piece' of reportage, both 'vivid and compelling'. A total of 100,000 copies were sold upon publication and another 72,000 by early June. *Reach for the Sky*, in short, became an instant – and, as it turned out, very much an ongoing – book trade sensation.[14]

Success often breeds further success. Within the year an episodic radio adaptation, featuring Rod Taylor in the lead role, was being broadcast by a Sydney radio station, and there was keen competition for the film rights to the book. The winner was producer Daniel Angel, who paid out £15,000 and engaged Lewis Gilbert to direct the subsequent picture. Backed by the Rank Organisation, the screen version of *Reach for the Sky*, with Kenneth More playing Douglas Bader, was a huge success when it premiered in July 1956. 'This film, like the story of the legless flyer's life, is courageous, vividly exciting and deeply moving', argued the *Daily Herald* critic. 'This is not just a "war picture", nor a "flying picture"', the reviewer for the *News Chronicle* explained, 'it is a great human document, presenting in simple unheroic terms the true meaning of courage.' According to the *Daily Mirror* the film version of *Reach for the Sky* was 'one of the greatest British films ever made and one of the most inspiring.' It was, explained the film critic for the *Sunday Express*, 'a film you must see.' People did so in large numbers, making *Reach for the Sky* the number one box office attraction of the year.[15]

Apparently the one person not particularly happy with the film was Douglas Bader himself, even though it had among other things confirmed the picture Brickhill had painted of his importance in the Battle of Britain. The main reason seems to have been that, in turning the book into a screenplay, the filmmakers had been forced to leave out or merge characters and incidents. This was necessary in order to prevent confusion on the part of the audience and keep down the running time, but the film's subject was incensed enough at not getting his way when he protested during the production process that he refused to double for long-shots. He was also conspicuous by his absence from the premiere. Story modifications aside, Bader was worried about how his former RAF comrades would react to seeing him portrayed in an unabashedly heroic light. 'No man should look at himself on the screen as a hero in his lifetime', was what Angel told the press Bader had said to him. 'I don't think I could stand it.'[16]

He would have to, since for millions of Britons his life and character were defined by the film version of *Reach for the Sky*. Whether they had seen it during the initial run in 1956, on re-release in 1959, or subsequently and perhaps multiple times on their television screens, either broadcast or from the 1980s on video, people often assumed that Douglas Bader was just as Kenneth More had portrayed him. 'Some of you', as the chairman of the British Limbless Ex-Service Men's Association stated mischievously but not entirely inaccurately when introducing Bader as a guest speaker, 'may remember him as the man who played the part of Kenneth More in the film *Reach for the Sky*.' Even those who knew the man could think this way. The film 'is a pretty good evocation of not only Bader but how he behaved and everything else', former Spitfire pilot John Young recalled in an interview. Joseph Cox agreed: 'that was him', he argued in reference to Kenneth More. Bader himself commented several decades after *Reach for the Sky* was first released that in real life people 'still think [I'm] the dashing chap that Kenneth More was.'[17]

Bader seems to have come to accept over the passing years the way in which the film defined him for the general public. But as a few of the more acute observers recognised even at the time, the version of Douglas Bader presented on screen was in certain ways different from the more-or-less accurate (though still heavily positive) portrait developed in the book. Given the censorship rules of the day there was an obvious need to avoid having Kenneth More swear and curse as Douglas Bader often did with great abandon, a habit that was at least mentioned by Brickhill. The trouble was that in presenting 'a story of courage', and employing the amiably bluff Kenneth More to play the lead role, the filmmakers managed to downplay or more commonly simply ignore all of their subject's more controversial traits that Brickhill had touched on. 'Bader's irascibility is converted into a sort of dogged pipe-smoking stubbornness', John Gillett wrote perceptively in *Sight and Sound*, 'many of the living, revealing rough-edges are smoothed away, leaving only a likeable, headstrong R.A.F. ace.' Bader had been converted into the kind of unblemished champion once seen in the *Boy's Own Paper*: little wonder that he subsequently ended up number one in a schoolboy poll of favourite heroes.[18]

Douglas Bader had been transformed into a mythical figure, a living legend who had overcome a cruel fate and gone on to become a leader of The Few. It was a story that fitted so well into the wider mythology of the Battle of Britain that it proved impervious to anything critics or indeed he himself might say. And however uncomfortable the legend might make him feel at times, Bader was not averse to using it when it might be to his advantage. When he applied for an instrument flying rating a few years after the film first appeared, the civil aviation authorities quickly agreed to his request to forego the usual air test. They also gave him extra time when re-sitting the written examination after lack of preparation led to him failing at his first attempt.[19]

As Bader grew older he mellowed somewhat as he continued to work for and inspire the disabled, particularly children. He began to take a more inclusive stance on the Commonwealth, stressed the contribution of the British people – not just the officer pilots of the RAF – to victory in the Battle of Britain, and expressed enormous admiration for Keith Park as well as Hugh Dowding. He could, however, still be alarmingly rude and make potentially embarrassing remarks in public. After being persuaded to attend a reunion of Luftwaffe pilots, for example, Bader looked down on a beer cellar in Munich filled with his former foes and commented in the presence of Dolfo Galland; 'My God, I had no idea we left so many of the bastards alive.' He used similar invective in reference to the Trade Union movement ('bastards') in the 1970s, having earlier argued that the leading figures in the Campaign for Nuclear Disarmament should be expelled from the country ('deport the rabble'). For the most part this sort of thing was tolerated without comment or dismissed as typically blunt and forthright observations from a larger-than-life, if somewhat unsophisticated, old-fashioned patriot.[20]

The same attitude applied when efforts were made to send up the legend or expose the darker side of the real man. Despite the great popularity in the early Sixties of the satiric revue *Beyond the Fringe*, on those occasions when Alan Bennett chose to imitate Bader's stiff-legged gait in the 'Aftermyth of War' sketch he ran the risk of being hissed at by the audience. To the public at large he remained 'one of the most inspirational figures to emerge from the Second World War', as an admiring American observer put it a few years later. Early in the 1970s his status as a fighter leader in the Battle of Britain remained sufficiently strong for him to be approached about collaborating on a new biography and also to be the author of a book on the history of the Spitfire and Hurricane. Though also in fact a collaborative effort, the latter volume was to a significant degree a first-person narrative of Bader's own experiences as a wartime flier, as its title, *Fight for the Sky*, was doubtless meant to suggest. The passage of time only seemed to add new elements to the legend, as another biographer noted at the start of the 1980s. 'From being a wartime fighter hero he has developed into a world figure,' Laddie Lucas asserted, 'a force in his own right, a champion of the disabled and the handicapped, known and recognized wherever he goes and sought after as keenly overseas as he is here in Britain.'[21]

The subject of all this admiration died quite suddenly of a heart attack in 1982 at the age of seventy-two, an event which offered observers a chance to take stock of a man who had been 'a legend in his own lifetime'. The result was a series of laudatory obituaries. *The Times*, for example, while acknowledging that Douglas Bader had had his faults, hailed the deceased as someone who was both 'the personification of RAF heroism and determination' in war and 'a shining example of that defiant courage that overcomes disablement and refuses to accept that anything is impossible.'[22]

Bader was dead, but his legend – appropriately enough for a man who said he believed in reincarnation – only seemed to grow stronger over the next couple of decades, with comedians once again getting into trouble for sending him up. There have been several biographies and books dealing with Douglas Bader published in the twenty-five years since his death, and though some of the authors have been critical of various aspects of their subject's career, their works have tended not to have done much to alter the established heroic image. The same is true of television documentaries and video histories. Even a 1996 TV programme in the *Secret Lives* series which focussed at length on some of Bader's less admirable traits, for instance, could be rejected as a 'hatchet job' or absorbed without too much difficulty into the legend. Despite everything, as Tony Purnell put it in a review of the episode for the *Daily Mirror*, Douglas Bader 'was still the bravest man on tin legs'. In August 2001 a statue by Kenneth Potts that had been commissioned by the Duke of Richmond was unveiled at what had once been RAF Westhampnett. 'Douglas Bader was a very British hero,' the Duke explained. 'He was defiant, single-minded and fought for the things in which we believed.' From time to time since the war there had been suggestions that such as old-fashioned hero was an anachronism. But when the BBC conducted a public poll at the end of 2001 to determine the hundred greatest ever Britons, Douglas Bader was still being voted for enthusiastically alongside everyone from Princess Diana to Michael Crawford. 'Legend of Douglas Bader is set in stone', as the headline to a *Telegraph* piece on the statue aptly put it.[23]

Notes

[1]Paul Brickhill, *Reach for the Sky* (London: Collins, 1954), p. 363.

[2]Ibid., pp. 355–58; *Sunday Express*, 19 April 1970; Don Whitehead, *"Beachhead Don": Reporting the War from the European Theater, 1942–1945* (New York: Fordham University Press, 2004), p. 148. Colin Hodgkinson, who had been repatriated from Germany on medical grounds some months before, also tried without success to get 'another bash at the Hun', but realised that 'with my tin legs I never could, or would never be allowed to, fly in the Far East.' Colin Hodgkinson, *Best Foot Forward* (London: Odams, 1957), pp. 247, 246.

[3]The National Archives [hereafter NA], AIR 28/603, North Weald ORB, 20 July 1945; AIR 29/927, Central Fighter Establishment ORB, 1 June 1945; Robert Jackson, *Douglas Bader* (London: Barker, 1983), pp. 137–38; Laddie Lucas, *Flying Colours* (London: Wordsworth, 2001 edn), pp. 211–12; Brickhill, *Reach for the Sky*, p. 359; RAFM, B354, Bader logbook, June-July 1945. On the Central Fighter Establishment see NA, AIR 20/1792; AIR 2/5644.

[4]Vincent Orange, *The Road to Biggin Hill* (Shrewsbury: Airlife, 1986), pp. 143–44; J.E. Jonson and P.B. Lucas, *Winged Victory* (London: Stanley Paul, 1995), p. 231. See,, *Evening News*, late extra, 15 September 1945; see also Brickhill, *Reach for the Sky*, pp. 360–61. On Lucas, flying ability, and Boyle see Lucas, *Flying Colours*, pp. 14–15; Laddie Lucas *Five Up* (Canterbury: Wingham, 1991), p. 155. On North Weald winding down see NA, AIR 28/603, North Weald ORB, August –September 1945.

[5]*Daily Mail*, 26 March 1946. Bader did, however, maintain an association with the RAF as the guest of honour at various parades and other ceremonies. See

Rutherford M. Hancock, *Flight Cadet* (Durham: Edinburgh: Pentland, 1996), p. 164; *The Times*, 2 April 1977. He also used his connection with the *News of the World* to take issue with current policies and certain conclusions of an official history of the RAF in the Second World War. See Noble Frankland, *History at War* (London: DLM, 1998), p. 121.

[6]Non-attributed quote in John Frayn Turner, *Douglas Bader* (Shrewsbury: Airlife, 2001 edn), p. 207. On the other reasons for leaving the RAF see Brickhill, *Reach for the Sky*, p. 362; Lucas, *Flying Colours*, p. 209; Jackson, *Douglas Bader*, p. 136. Colin Hodgkinson took the same decision for similar reasons. 'I knew' he later wrote, 'that the dead-end discipline of a career in the post-war R.A.F. would be an anti-climax I couldn't endure.' Hodgkinson, *Best Foot*, p. 247. It is perhaps significant that Peter Macdonald, MP, who had served as adjutant to 242 Squadron and with Bader at Tangmere in 1941, should have asked in parliament on 6 March 1945 about the status of captured volunteer aircrew in relation to service in the post-war regular RAF. See 408 HC Deb. 5s. col. 1882. (Bader, on the other hand, already *was* a regular.)

[7]On not standing for parliament see Brickhill, *Reach for the Sky*, p. 358; Turner, *Douglas Bader*, pp. 133–34, 136.

[8]Dennis David, *My Autobiography* (London: Grub Street, 2000), p. 91; non-attributed quote in Turner, *Douglas Bader*, p. 207; see Lucas, *Flying Colours*, chs. 23–25, 28. On appeals and work on behalf of the disabled see *The Times*, 12 December 1947, 3 November 1954, 6 September 1958, 22 August 1969; Turner, *Douglas Bader*, pp. 135, 172, 188, 226–27. On the knighthood see *The Times*, 12 June 1976.

[9]Jackson, *Douglas Bader*, p. 144; Bader foreword to Hans Ulrich Rudel, *Stuka Pilot* (Dublin: Euphorion, 1953).

[10]On Bader being turned down for personnel manager see Lucas, *Flying Colours*, pp. 241–42. On the Rhodesia remark and the Shell reaction see Jackson, *Douglas Bader*, pp. 153–54. On the 'trees' remark and the Shell reaction see Turner, *Douglas Bader*, p. 174. On the office being in an uproar when Bader was around see John Frayn Turner, *The Bader Tapes* (Bourne End: Kensal, 1986), pp. 123.

[11]Turner, *Douglas Bader*, pp. 154–55. It is worth noting that prior to the appearance of *Reach for the Sky* there were signs that Bader, like other wartime heroes, was in the process of being replaced in the public imagination – or at least in the minds of the nation's young – by more contemporary figures. See Bob Doe, *Fighter Pilot* (Chislehurst: CCB, 2004 edn), p. 95.

[12]Turner, *Douglas Bader*, pp. 155–56; Lucas, *Flying Colours*, p. 229. On the meeting with Churchill see Churchill College Archives, Cambridge, CHUR 2/180, Macdonald to Soames, 16 March 1954, Soames to Churchill, 17 March 1954, Soames to Macdonald, 25 March 1954, Dodge to Churchill, 11 March 1954, Churchill to Dodge, 6 April 1954.

[13]Brickhill, *Reach for the Sky*, p. 371. On Brickhill at least acknowledging Bader's rudeness, snobbery, and impatience see pp. 78, 186, 198, 200, 272–3.

[14]*New Statesman*, 24 April 1954, p. 542; *The Times*, 17 March 1954. For the *Mail* and *Express* review extracts and sales figures see ads in *The Times*, 18 March 1954, 13 May 1954, 9 June 1954. *Reach for the Sky* has remained more-or-less permanently in print down to the present day.

[15]*Kinematograph Weekly*, 13 December 1956, p. 6. For the review extracts see British Film Institute Library [hereafter BFI], *Reach for the Sky* pressbook; see also BFI, microfiche press cuttings on *Reach for the Sky*. On the cost of obtaining the film rights see Kenneth More, *More or Less* (London: Hodder and Stoughton, 1978), p. 168. On the making of the film itself see Lewis Gilbert in *Film and Filming*, vol. 2, no. 2, September 1956, p. 9; Trevor Popple, 'Reach for the Sky', *After the Battle*, no. 35, pp. 38–53; More, *More or Less*, pp. 167–70. On the Australian radio adaptation see Richard Lane, *The Golden Age of Australian Radio Drama, 1923–1960* (Melbourne: Melbourne University Press, 1994), pp. 322, 360.

[16]L. Mosley reporting in the *Daily Express*, 5 July 1956; see also W. Hickey in *Daily Express*, 6 July 1956. On the differences between the book and the film compare Brickhill, *Reach for the Sky* with BFI, S14922, *Reach for the Sky* shooting script. On Bader being angry at the way in which his friends were either written out of or fictionalised in the screenplay see L. Gilbert in Brian McFarlane, *An Autobiography of British Cinema* (London: Metheun, 1997), pp. 221–22; Turner, *Douglas Bader*, pp. 157–58; Turner, *Bader Tapes*, pp. 68–69.

[17]D. Bader in Turner, *Bader Tapes*, p. 69; Imperial War Museum Sound Archive [hereafter IWMSA] 6630/6, J. Cox; IWMSA 20486/3, J.R.C. Young; Peter Ryde, *Out on a Limb* (Norwich: British Limbless Ex-Service Men's Association, 1982), p. 79. On Kenneth More defining Douglas Bader for the public see Turner, *Bader Tapes*, p. 70; Alan Bennett, *Writing Home* (London: Faber, 1994), p. 200; see also Clive James, *Visions Before Midnight* (London: Cape, 1977), pp. 29–30; Robert Murphy, *British Cinema and the Second World War* (London: Continuum, 2000), p. 208. On the longevity of the film version of *Reach for the Sky* see Malcolm Smith, *Britain and 1940* (London: Routledge, 2000), p. 121. Perhaps because of their similar wavy hair as much as mannerisms, another pilot thought that the way More portrayed Bader was in fact more applicable to Al Deere. See R.W. Needham in Richard C. Smith, *Al Deere* (London: Grub Street, 2003), p. 122. A thinly disguised version of Bader also appears in the script of the 1969 film *Battle of Britain*, though in the film itself the part was cut back to the point where he became unrecognisable. See BFI, S1127, *Battle of Britain* script, reel 11 (6a), scene 36.

[18]*Sight and Sound*, vol. 26, no. 2, Autumn 1956, 97; BFI, S14922, *Reach for the Sky* shooting script, reel 14, scene 46, p. 10; see also Mark Connelly, *We Can Take It!* (London: Longman, 2004), p. 105; Andrew Spicer, *Typical Men* (London: Tauris,

2001), p. 40. On the schoolboy poll see Turner, *Douglas Bader*, p. 188. On the unblemished Bader story as suitable for children see Charles Wyndham, *Douglas Bader* (London: Blackie, 1966); Michael Hervey, 'A Study in Heroism – Douglas Bader', *Silver Jacket*, 24 (1955), pp. 10–11.

[19]NA, DR 4/212, encl. 88, 86, 85, 64, 57.

[20]On 'deport the rabble' see Turner, *Douglas Bader*, p. 214. On the unions see Jackson, *Douglas Bader*, p. 161. On the 'bastards alive' remark see IWMSA 11623, J.A. Goodson TS, pp. 32–33. On Bader being rude see L. Ray Silver, *Last of the Gladiators* (Shrewsbury: Airlife, 1995), p. 161. On ongoing egotism see the prize-giving story in IWMSA 15336/4, J.C. Wilson. On making allowances for Bader see the non-attributed quotes in Turner, *Douglas Bader*, pp. 206–10; Leonard Mosley, *The Battle of Britain* (London: Weidenfeld and Nicolson, 1969), pp. 142–43. On the older Bader and Keith Park see Lucas, *Flying Colours*, App. C. On the older Bader and Dowding, see Mosley, *Battle of Britain*, p. 140. On stressing how much of a combined effort the Battle of Britain was see IWMSA 16180/1, T. Fleming programme, D. Bader comments; National Sound Archive [hereafter NSA], T3252 BWC1, D. Bader comments in *Battle of Britain* programme; Turner, *Douglas Bader*, p. 246. On Bader mellowing in general see J. Bader in *Secret Lives: Douglas Bader* (Twenty Twenty Productions, 1996). He could still nevertheless be rude [see Robert Chesshyre, 'We Can Be Heroes', *Saga Magazine*, August 2004, p. 93] and continued to swear vividly when roused [see IWMSA 11716/1, D. Bader; see also the entirely apocryphal story in Alan Clark, *Diaries* (London: Weidenfeld and Nicolson, 1993), p. 224]. On taking a more racially inclusive view of the Commonwealth see *News of the World*, 19 September 1965. On helping disabled children see Lucas, *Flying Start*, pp. 248, 277–78; Turner, *Douglas Bader*, pp. 186–87. Bader was, by all accounts, good with boys whether or not they were disabled – see Richard Branson, *Losing My Virginity* (London: Virgin, 1998), p. 22 – perhaps because he maintained a boyish outlook throughout his life.

[21]Lucas, *Flying Start*, p. 15; Edward Sims, *The Fighter Pilots* (London: Cassell, 1967), p. 6; Bennett, *Writing Home*, pp. 125, 201 [see also Humphrey Carpenter, *That Was Satire That Was* (London: Gollancz, 2000), p. 113]. See Douglas Bader, *Fight for the Sky* (London: Sidgwick and Jackson, 1975 edn), p. 4. On the collaborative nature of this book see Turner, *Douglas Bader*, p. 246. Bader's talks with John Frayn Turner (see ibid., 245) eventually resulted in a series of books published prior to and after his death (see bibliography).

[22]*The Times*, 6 September 1982; see also *Daily Mail*, 6 September 1982; *Daily Telegraph*, 6 September 1982; *Guardian*, 6 September 1982.

[23]M. Smith in *Daily Telegraph*, 4 August 2001; Duke of Richmond in *Daily Telegraph*, 10 August 2001; T. Purnell in *Daily Mirror* TV Supplement, 10 December 1996. On Bader and the Top 100 Britons BBC poll see *Daily Telegraph*, 22 August 2002;

http://www.links4kids.co.uk/top100britons.htm (accessed 27 August 2003). On the Bader myth as anachronistic see Smallweed in *Guardian*, 11 August 2001. On complaints about the *Secret Lives* programme see D. Sarkar (by no means uncritical of Bader in his own work) quoted in http://www.freedom.org.uk/mag/issuea03/page03d.htm (accessed 23 August 2003); non-attributed letter quoted in http://members.lycos.co.uk/jadastra/Bader.html (accessed 23 August 2003), p. 5. On the *Secret Lives* programme not being able to dent the myth see Connelly, *We Can Take It*, pp. 105–06. Video histories have been much more respectful. See *Hunters in the Sky: Struggle for Supremacy* (Anthony Potter Productions, 1991), in which Bader is described as 'a special kind of hero to the British people' who 'exemplifies the courage that won the Battle of Britain', or *Great Heroes of World War II* (Vision Video Ltd, 1995), in which Bader is described as 'one of the greatest characters of the war, and one of the finest leaders.' On the biographies see bibliography [in reference to reviewers' admiration even when some of the 'warts and all' Bader was revealed see also H. Massingberd in the *Spectator*, 14 November 1981, p. 19]; see also Richard Garrett, *Sky High* (London: Weidenfeld and Nicolson, 1991), pp. 1, 154–74. On the dangers of sending up Bader see S. Fry on T. Slattery, *Daily Mirror*, TV Supplement, 11 February 1995, pp. 2–3. On Bader's belief in reincarnation see J. Russell in http://www.geocities.com/Athens/Oracle/6840/bader.html (accessed 12 February 2004).

Conclusion

He could be a right bastard at times, but we all loved him.

Patrick 'Paddy' Barthropp, 2005[1]

Douglas Bader was a great man. But like many others who achieve greatness, he had major flaws. Indeed it might well be said that his great character strengths – the need to succeed, the refusal to admit doubt, the desire to dominate and lead – could sometimes be his worst character weaknesses.

On the one hand he could inspire admiration, confidence, and loyalty among many of those who knew him. On the other hand he could generate feelings amongst others with whom he came in contact that might border on outright loathing. 'Like other strong and dominant leaders,' as his friend Laddie Lucas explained to readers of the *Guardian* the day after Bader died, 'his defiant character and dogmatic personality provoked all the extremes of human emotion – intense devotion, friendship, loyalty and support, and then again criticism, controversy, exasperation and even dislike.' A complete lack of uncertainty can help inspire those lacking confidence, but not all that Bader was certain about, especially in relation to operations, was based on a sound understanding of the wider context. He thought of the Battle of Britain in terms of a 'Battle for London': but there was much more to it than that, as the problems generated by the No. 12 Group Wing indicate.

Once he was captured Bader understandably wanted both to annoy the Germans and to escape, but at times either did not understand or did not care that the former aim might impede the latter goal and that his actions might have negative consequences for those around him.

Throughout the war he could be very relaxed and funny, but also sometimes breathtakingly aggressive and rude. Bader was a man of great loyalty to those he admired and considered friends;

yet as his unwitting role in the struggle for power within Fighter Command indicated, his outspokenness could be manipulated by less straightforward figures for their own ends.[2]

Do these flaws make Douglas Bader a lesser mortal? They certainly suggest that the legend built up after the war obscured as much as it revealed about the man. Bader himself, to be sure, was at times uneasy about the way in which his persona had apparently been hijacked and altered by Kenneth More, and never pretended to be anything other than what he had always been. His personal achievements still ought to be celebrated, but perhaps with more emphasis on the way in which he inspired those who had lost limbs – the work for which he was knighted – and less in reference to his fighting role. A single encounter can stand for countless others as an example of the way Bader often operated in the former sphere.

In 1956, at the age of twelve, David Butler lost a hand and both legs in a bomb blast. While recovering in hospital he wrote to the hero of *Reach for the Sky* asking if he would visit him. Bader came on several occasions, providing practical advice as well as an in-the-flesh example of what might be done to recover. 'I asked him what the artificial legs were like to wear and how they worked', Butler related. 'He told me all about them and how to use them... It was a great help to talk to someone like Douglas, to learn all about the legs, how they are fixed on, what sort of difficulties you are likely to meet.' Like his mentor, Butler learned to walk much sooner than was usually the case, and went on to dance, drive, and swim. 'I very much admire Bader,' Butler concluded. 'When you see what he has been able to achieve, you go and try to do it yourself.'[3]

This was the man at his very best: straightforward, fearless, a perambulating inspiration for those unlucky enough to have lost legs and thus be left open to self-doubt about their future. Jittery fighter pilots might have taken comfort from his example in 1940–41, but over his lifetime it was individual civilians – above all the youngsters who instantly took to his uncomplicated view of life ('like a schoolboy, really' was how his sister-in-law remembered him) – who gained most from a few bluff words from Douglas Bader.[4]

Enough time has passed for the wartime career of Douglas Bader in the Royal Air Force to be put in proper historical perspective without diminishing the man's many virtues as a role model. Douglas Bader in real life simply was not the *Boy's Own* hero that the public came to believe in; so perhaps it is not an entirely bad thing that the legend, like the proverbial old soldier, is apparently fading away. 'Most of them won't have heard of Kenneth More let alone Douglas Bader', a youngish historian recently commented in reference to the youth of today. Yet he was and remains a truly remarkable figure. As his friend Dermot Boyle once rightly said, Douglas Bader – warts and all – was a true embodiment of the RAF motto, *Per Ardua ad Astra*.[5]

Notes

[1]P. Barthropp in *Britain's War Heroes: Douglas Bader, Fighter Ace* (Blakeway Associates, 2005).

[2]*Guardian*, 6 September 1982. On Bader thinking of the Battle of Britain in terms of a Battle for London see Margaret Duggan (ed.), Padre in Colditz (London: Hodder and Stoughton, 1978), p. 202.

[3]D. Butler in John Frayn Turner, *Douglas Bader* (Shrewsbury: Airlife, 2001 edn), pp. 217, 215.

[4]J. Lucas in *Britain's War Heroes: Douglas Bader, Fighter Ace* (Blakeway Associates, 2005). On Bader working for the limbless see John Frayn Turner, *The Bader Tapes* (Bourne End: Kensal, 1986), chs. 11, 14.

[5]Mark Connelly, *We Can Take It!* (London: Longman, 2004), p. 301; see *First of the Few: The True Story* (Dowty Group, 1997); C. F. Currant in *Aviation Heroes of World War II: The Battle of Britain* (Greenwich Workshop, 1990); Turner, *Douglas Bader*, p. 205. With reference to the Bader legends perhaps *not* fading see how he has inspired a song by a youthful rock band (see http://www.ectospaz.bravehost.com/douglas.htm (accessed 27 January 2005).

BIBLIOGRAPHY

Unpublished Official Documents

The National Archives

AIR 2, 4, 10, 16, 20, 22, 25, 27, 28, 29, 43, 41, 50; CAB 106, 120; DR 4, PIN 38, WO 32, 208, 224, 344.

BBC Written Archives

Script for 'The World Goes By' broadcast by D. Bader, 12 February 1941.

Unpublished Interviews

Andrew, J. (BBC); Armitage, D. (IWMSA); Ash, W. (IWMSA); Bader, D. (IWMSA; http://home.tiscali.be/ed.ragas/awshistory/awsbader. html [accessed 12 February 2004]; http://www.geocities.com/Athens/ Oracle/6840/bader.html [accessed 12 February 2004]); Bartley, A.C. (IWMSA); Bateson, R. (IWMSA); Bowering, B.H. (IWMSA); Bracken, H. (IWMSA); Broadhurst, H. (IWMSA); Brown, C.B. (IWMSA); Chapman, E.F. (IWMSA); Cox, D.G.S.R. (IWMSA); Cox, J. (IWMSA); Crawford, D. (AWM); Deere, A. (IWMSA); Dundas, H. (IWMSA); Edlmann, E. L. (IWMSA); Fleming, T. (IWMSA); Goodson, J.A. (IWMSA); Haig, D. (LC); Hutchinson, I. (IWMSA); Ironside, H. (CSVA); Johnson, J. (IWMSA); Jones, R.L. (IWMSA); Loder, R. [IWMSA); Moran, J.M. (IWMSA); Morison, W. (BBC); Pitt, E. (BBC); Pringle, J.C. (IWMSA); Purdon, C. (IWMSA); Rose, N. (IWMSA); Siska, A. (LC); Stapleton, B. G. (MGM – 'Recollections of an RAF Squadron Leader' featurette with 2004 Special Edition DVD of feature film *Battle of Britain* (1969)); Stevens, W. (IWMSA); Unwin, G.C. (IWMSA); Welch, P. (IWMSA); Wilson, J.C. (IWMSA); Winskill, A.L. (IWMSA); Wolfendale, J. (BBC); Woolley, E. M. (IWMSA); Young, J.R.C. (IWMSA).

Unpublished Memoirs, Diaries, Papers and Letters

Ambrose, R. (IWM); Austin, A.B. (IWM); Bader, D. (RAFM; BBCWA; RAFCA; SESA; BFI); Bowling, H. (RAFM); Bracken, H. (IWMSA); Campbell, C.N.S. (IWM); Churchill, W.S. (CCC); Cunningham, W. (SPM); Dashwood, O.M. (SPM); Dean, M. (LHC); Douglas, S. (IWM); Eadon, M. (LHC); Frith, L. (IWM); Fowler, H.N. (IWM); Hollingdale, L.M.E. (IWM); Howard-Williams, P.I. (IWM); Johnson, J. (RAFM); Leigh-Mallory, T. (RAFM); Liddell Hart, B.H. (LHC); Morton, P.A. (RAFM); Morton, R.A. (IWM); Neale, N.G. (IWM); Park, K. (RAFM); Ralph, W. (SPM); Stephens, W.L. (IWM); Stevens, W. (IWMSA); Walker, D. H. (UNB); Welch, P. (IWMSA); Wilson, J.C. (IWMSA); Winskill, A.L. (IWMSA); Woolley, E. M. (IWMSA); Young, J.R.C. (IWMSA).

Newspapers and Magazines

Colditz Society Newsletter; Daily Express; Daily Mail; Daily Mirror; Daily Telegraph; Film and Filming; Guardian; Journal of the Royal Air Force College; Kinematograph Weekly; New York Journal-American; New Zealand Herald; New York Times; News of the World; Royal Air Force Quarterly; Sight and Sound; Spectator; St Edward's School Chronicle; Sunday Express; Time; The Times; Times Literary Supplement; Yorkshire Post Magazine.

Published Primary Sources:

'Blake' [Ronald Adam], *Readiness at Dawn* (London: Gollancz, 1941).

Air Historical Section (Department of National Defence, Canada), *Among the Few: A sketch of the part played by Canadian airmen in the Battle of Britain (July 10th – October 31st, 1940)* AFP 49 (Ottawa: Department of National Defence, 1948).

Air Ministry, *We Speak from the Air: Broadcasts by the RAF* (London: HMSO, 1942).

Allen, H.R., *Battle of Britain: The Recollections of H.R. 'Dizzy' Allen DFC* (London: Barker, 1973).

Ash, William with Brendan Foley, *Under the Wire: The Wartime Memoir of a Spitfire Pilot, legendary escape artist and 'Cooler King'* (London: Bantam, 2005).

Ashman, R.V., *Spitfire Against the Odds* (Wellingborough: Patrick Stephens, 1989).

Austin, A.B., *Fighter Command* (London: Gollancz, 1941).

Bader, Douglas, *Fight for the Sky: The Story of the Spitfire and the Hurricane* (London: Sidgwick and Jackson, 1975 edn.).

Bader, Douglas (ed.), *My Favourite Stories of Courage* (London, 1963).

Bader, Douglas 'Fighter Pilot', *Boys' Book of the Air*, E. Leyland and T.E. Scott-Chard, eds. (London: Edmund Ward, 1957).

Bailey, Jim, *The Sky Suspended: A Fighter Pilot's Story* (London: Hodder and Stoughton, 1957).

Balfour, Harold, *Wings Over Westminster* (London: Hutchinson, 1973).

Barclay, George, *Fighter Pilot: A Self-Portrait* Humphrey Wynn, ed. (London: Kimber, 1976).

Barthropp, Patrick, *Paddy: The Life and Times of Wing Commander Patrick Barthropp* (Hailsham: JK&H, 2001).

Bartley, Anthony, *Smoke Trails in the Sky: From the Journals of a Fighter Pilot* (London: Kimber, 1984).

Bates, H.E. 'The Battle of Britain', in *Slipstream: a Royal Air Force Anthology* (London: Eyre and Spottiswoode, 1946).

Beamont, Roland, *Phoenix into Ashes* (London: Kimber, 1968).

Bennett, Alan, *Writing Home* (London: Faber, 1994).

Braham, J.R.D. *'Scramble!'* (London: Kimber, 1985 edn.).

Branson, Richard, *Losing My Virginity* (London: Virgin, 1998).

Burton, Ernie, *Go Straight Ahead: The Battle of Britain Diaries of 222 (Natal) Squadron* (Evensham: Square One Publications, 1996).

Clark, Alan, *Diaries* (London: Weidenfeld and Nicolson, 1993)

Collier, Richard, *The Past is a Foreign Country* (London: Allison & Busby, 1996).

Crook, D.M., *Spitfire Pilot* (London: Faber, 1942).

Cross, Kenneth with Vincent Orange, *Straight and Level* (London: Grub Street, 1993).

Deere, Alan, *Nine Lives* 2nd edn. (Canterbury: Wingham, 1991).

David, Dennis, *My Autobiography* (London: Grub Street, 2000).

Dezarrois, André (ed.), *The Mouchotte Diaries, 1940–1943*, J. P. Stead, trans. (London: Staples, 1956).

Doe, Bob, *Fighter Pilot* (Chislehurst: CCB, 2004 edn.).

Douglas, Sholto, with Robert Wright, *Years of Command: The Second Volume of the Autobiography of Sholto Douglas* (London: Collins, 1966).

Duggan, Margaret (ed.), *Padre in Colditz: The diary of J. Ellison Platt* (London: Hodder and Stoughton, 1978).

Duke, Neville, *Test Pilot* (London: Grub Street, 1992).

Duncan Smith, W.G.G., *Spitfire into Battle* (London: John Murray, 1981).

Dundas, Hugh, *Flying Start: A Fighter Pilot's War Years* (London: Stanley Paul, 1988).

Dunn, William R., *Fighter Pilot: The First American Air Ace of World War II* (Lexington, KY: University Press of Kentucky, 1982).

Eggers, Reinhold, *Colditz: The German Story*, Howard Gee, trans. (London: Robert Hale, 1961).

Ferguson, Ion, *Doctor at War* (London: Christopher Johnson, 1955).

Forbes, Athol and Hubert Allen (eds), *Ten Fighter Boys* (London: Collins, 1942).

Foxley-Norris, Christopher, *A Lighter Shade of Blue: Lighthearted Memoirs of an Air Marshal* (London: Ian Allan, 1978).

Frankland, Noble, *History at War: The Campaigns of an Historian* (London: DLM, 1998).

Franks, Norman (ed.), *The War Diaries of Neville Duke: The Journals of Squadron Leader N.F. Duke, 1941–44* (London: Grub Street, 1995).

Galland, Adolf, *The First and the Last*, Mervyn Savill, trans. (New York: Henry Holt, 1954).

'R.A.F. Casualty' [Tom Gleave], *"I Had a Row with a German"* (London: Macmillan, 1941).

Gleed, Ian, *Arise to Conquer* (New York: Random House, 1942).

Gray, Colin, *Spitfire Patrol* (London: Hutchinson, 1990).

Gnys, Wladek, *First Kill: A Fighter Pilot's Autobiography* (London: Kimber, 1981).

Guthrie, David (ed.), *Spitfire Squadron* (London: Hale, 1978 edn.).

Haig, Earl, *My Father's Son: The Memoirs of Major the Earl Haig* (London: Leo Cooper, 2000).

Hall, Roger, *Clouds of Fear* (Folkestone: Bailey Brothers and Swinfen Ltd., 1975).

Hillary, Richard, *The Last Enemy* (London: Macmillan, 1942).

Hodgkinson, Colin, *Best Foot Forward: The Autobiography of Colin Hodgkinson* (London: Odams, 1957).

Holliday, J.E. (ed.), *Stories of the RAAF POWs at Lamsdorf* (Holland Park, Queensland: Lamsdorf POWs Association, 1992).

Holmes, Ray, *Sky Spy: From Six Miles High to Hitler's Bunker* (Shrewsbury: Airlife, 1989).

Houart, Victor (ed.), *Lonely Warrior: The Journal of Battle of Britain Fighter Pilot Jean Offenberg* (London: Souvenir, 1956).

House of Commons Debates, 5ᵗʰ–6ᵗʰ Series

Hunt, Lloyd (ed.), *We Happy Few* (Ottawa: Canadian Fighter Pilots' Association, 1986).

Hunter, William James, *From Coastal Command to Captivity* (Barnsley: Leo Cooper, 2003).

James, B.A., *Moonless Night* (London: Kimber, 1983).

James, Clive, *Visions Before Midnight: Television Criticism from the Observer, 1972–76* (London: Cape, 1977).

Johnson, J.E. (Johnnie) and P.B. (Laddie) Lucas, *Winged Victory: Reflections of two Royal Air Force Leaders* (London: Stanley Paul, 1995).

Johnson, J.E. 'Johnnie', *Wing Leader* (London: Chatto and Windus, 1956).

Johnstone, Sandy, *Enemy in the Sky: My 1940 Diary* (London: Kimber, 1976).

Jonsson, T.E. 'Tony', *Dancing in the Skies* (London: Grub Street, 1994).

Joubert, Philip de la Ferté, *The Fated Sky: An Autobiography* (London: Hutchinson, 1952).

Kelly, Terence, *The Nine Lives of a Fighter Pilot* (Shrewsbury: Airlife, 2003).

Kelly, Terence, *Hurricane and Spitfire Pilots at War* (London: Kimber, 1986).

Kennington, Eric, *Drawing the R.A.F.: A Book of Portraits* (London: Oxford University Press, 1942).

Kent, J.A., *One of the Few* (London: Kimber, 1971).

Kingcome, Brian, *A Willingness to Die* (Stroud: Tempus, 1999).

Langdale Kelhan, R.D., *Artificial Limbs in the Rehabilitation of the Disabled* (London: HMSO, 1957).

Lucas, Laddie (ed.), *Thanks for the Memory: Unforgettable Characters in Air Warfare, 1939–45* (London: Stanley Paul, 1989).

Lucas, Laddie, *Five Up: A Chronicle of Five Lives* revised edn (Canterbury: Wingham, 1991).

Lucas, Laddie (ed.), *Wings of War: Airmen of All Nations Tell Their Stories, 1939–1945* (London: Hutchinson, 1983).

MacDonell, A.R.D., *From Dogfight to Diplomacy: A Spitfire Pilot's Log, 1932–1958* (Barnsley: Pen and Sword, 2005).

Mackenzie, K.W., *Hurricane Combat: The Nine Lives of a Fighter Pilot* (London: Grenville, 1990 edn).

Mackenzie, Ron, *An Ordinary War, 1940–1945* (Wangaratta, Victoria: Shoestrong, 1995).

McFarlane, Brian (ed.), *An Autobiography of British Cinema: as told by the filmmakers and actors who made it* (London: Metheun, 1997).

Ministry of Pensions, *Artificial Limbs and their Relation to Amputations* (London: HMSO, 1939).

Monks, N., *Squadrons Up!* (London: Gollancz, 1940).

More, Kenneth, *More or Less* (London: Hodder and Stoughton, 1978).

Morison, Walter, *Flak and Ferrets: One Way to Colditz* (London: Sentinel, 1995).

Munro, Raymond Z., *The Sky's No Limit* (Toronto: Key Porter, 1985).

Neil, Tom, *Gun-Button to 'Fire'* (London: Kimber, 1987).

Olive, Gordon and Dennis Newton, *The Devil at 6 O'clock: An Australian Ace in the Battle of Britain* (Loftus, NSW: Australian Military History Publications, 2001).

Orde, Cuthbert, *Pilots of Fighter Command: Sixty-Four Portraits* (London: Harrap, 1942).

Oxspring, Bobby, *Spitfire Command* (London: Kimber, 1984).

Page, Geoffrey, *Shot Down in Flames: A World War II Fighter Pilot's Remarkable Tale of Survival* (London: Grub Street, 1999 edn.).

Paice, Albert and Alwyn Ward, *For the Love of Elizabeth: The Memoir of Albert Paice* (privately published, 1984).

Pape, Richard, *Boldness be my Friend* (London: Elek, 1953).

Philpot, Oliver, *Stolen Journey* (London: Hodder and Stoughton, 1950).

Poole, Jack S., *Undiscovered Ends* (London: Cassell, 1957).

Pringle, Jack, *Colditz Last Stop: Four Countries, Eleven Prisons, Six Escapes* (Lewes: Temple House, 1995 edn.).

Prittie, T.C.F. and E. Edwards, *Escape to Freedom* (London: Hutchinson, 1953).

Quarrie, R.G.M. *Oflag* (Durham: Pentland, 1995).

Quill, Jeffrey, *Spitfire: A Test Pilot's Story* (London: Murray, 1983).

Reid, P.R., *The Colditz Story* (London: Hodder and Stoughton, 1952).

Richards, Denis, *It Might Have Been Worse: Recollections 1941–1996* (London: Smithson Albight, 1998).

Richey, Paul and Norman Franks, *Fighter Pilot's Summer* (London: Grub Street, 1993).

Richey, Paul, *Fighter Pilot: A Personal Record of the Campaign in France, September 8th, 1939 to June 13th, 1940* (London: Batsford, 1941).

Rogers, Jim, *Tunnelling into Colditz* (London: Hale, 1986).

Rudel, Hans Ulrich, *Stuka Pilot* Lynton Hudson, trans. (Dublin: Euphorion, 1953).

Sager, Arthur, *Line Shoot: Diary of a Fighter Pilot* (St. Catherine's, ON: Vanwell, 2002).

Sampson, R.W.F. with Norman Franks, *Spitfire Offensive: A Fighter Pilot's War Memoir* (London: Grub Street, 1994).

Scott, Desmond, *One More Hour* (London: Hutchinson, 1989).

Silver, L. Ray, *Last of the Gladiators: A World War II Bomber Navigator's Story* (Shrewsbury: Airlife, 1995).

Simpson, Allan (ed.), *So Few* (Ottawa: Canadian Fighter Pilots' Association, 1983).

Sutton, Barry, *The Way of a Pilot: A Personal Record* (London: Macmillan, 1943).

Taylor, Frank, *Barbed Wire and Footlights: Seven Stalags to Freedom* (Braunton: Merlin, 1988).

Torday, Jane (ed.), *The Coldstreamer and the Canary: Letters, Memories and Friends of Roger Mortimer, Prisoner of War No. 481, 1940–1945* (Hexam: Black Cat, 1995).

Townsend, Peter, *Duel in the Dark* (London: Harrap, 1986).

Townsend, Peter, *Time and Chance: An Autobiography* (London: Collins, 1978).

Vigors, Tim *Life's Too Short to Cry: The Compelling Memoir of a Battle of Britain Ace* (London: Grub Street, 2006).

Walker, David, *Lean, Wind Lean: A Few Times Remembered* (London: Collins, 1984).

Wellum, Geoffrey, *First Light* (London: Penguin, 2003 edn.).

Whitehead, Don, *"Beachhead Don": Reporting the War from the European Theater, 1942–1945* (New York: Fordham University Press, 2004).

Published Secondary Sources:

Addison, Paul and Jeremy Crang (eds), *The Burning Blue: A New History of the Battle of Britain* (London: Pimlico, 2000).

Andrews, Allen, *The Air Marshals* (London: Macdonald, 1970)

Axell, Albert, *Russia's Heroes* (London: Constable, 2001).

Ayling, Keith, *They Fly for Victory* (New York: Nelson, 1943).

Baker, David, *Adolf Galland: The Authorised Biography* (London: Windrow and Greene, 1996).

Barker, Ralph, *That Eternal Summer: Unknown Stories from the Battle of Britain* (London: Collins, 1990).

Bashow, David L., *All the Fine Young Eagles: In the Cockpit with Canada's Second World War Fighter Pilots* (Toronto: Stoddart, 1996).

Bère, R. de la, *A History of the Royal Air Force College Cranwell* (Aldershot: Polden, 1934).

Bickers, Richard Townshend, *Ginger Lacey: Fighter Pilot* (London: Pan, 1969 edn.).

Bishop, Patrick, *Fighter Boys: The Battle of Britain, 1940* (London: Harper Collins, 2003).

Boog, Horst (ed.), *The Conduct of the Air War in the Second World War* (Oxford: Berg, 1992).

Bower, Chaz, *Fighter Pilots of the RAF, 1939–1945* (Barnsley: Leo Cooper, 2001 edn.).

Bowyer, Michael J. F., *2 Group R.A.F.: A Complete History* (London: Faber, 1974).

Boyle, Andrew, *Trenchard* (London: Collins, 1962).

Brickhill, Paul, *Reach for the Sky: The Story of Douglas Bader* (London: Collins, 1954).

Brown, Peter, *Honour Restored: The Battle of Britain, Dowding and the Fight for Freedom* (Stroud: Spellmount, 2005).

Bryant, Arthur, *The Battle of Britain* (Manchester: Grove, 1948).

Bungay, Stephen, *The Most Dangerous Enemy: A History of the Battle of Britain* (London: Aurum, 2000).

Burns, Michael G., *Bader: The Man and his Men* (London: Cassell, 1998 edn.).

Caine, Philip D., *Eagles of the RAF: The World War II Eagle Squadrons* (Honolulu: University Press of the Pacific, 2002 reprint).

Caldwell, Donald, *The JG 26 War Diary: Volume One, 1939–1942* (London: Grub Street, 1996).

Caldwell, Donald L., *JG 26: Top Guns of the Luftwaffe* (New York: Orion, 1991).

Carpenter, Humphrey, *That was Satire, That Was: The Satire Boom of the 1960s* (London: Gollancz, 2000).

Caygill, Peter, *Spitfire Mark V in Action: RAF Operations in Northern Europe* (Shrewsbury: Airlife, 2001).

Chancellor, Henry, *Colditz* (London: Hodder and Stoughton, 2001).

Charlton, L.E.O., *Britain at War: The Royal Air Force: From September 1939 to December 1940* (London: Hutchinson, 1941).

Clarke, R.W., Sterne, J.C., Smith, J.E. E., *The Hundred Days that Shook the World* (Hemel Hampstead: Christopher Marlowe, 1969).

Clutton-Brock, Oliver, *Footprints on the Sands of Time: Bomber Command Prisoners of War in Germany, 1939–1945* (London: Grub Street, 2003).

Coleman, Terry *Olivier* (New York: Henry Holt, 2005).

Collier, Basil, *The Defence of the United Kingdom* (London: HMSO, 1957).

Collier, Basil, *Leader of the Few: The Authorised Biography of Air Chief Marshal the Lord Dowding of Bentley Priory* (London: Jarrolds, 1957).

Collier, Richard, *Eagle Day: The Battle of Britain, August 6th – September 15th1940* illustrated edn (London: Dent, 1980).

Connelly, Mark, *We Can Take It! Britain and the Memory of the Second World War* (London: Longman, 2004).

Cossey, Bob, *A Tiger's Tale: The Story of Battle of Britain Fighter Ace Wing Commander John Connell Freeborn* (Hailsham: J&KH, 2002).

Coughlin, Tom, *The Dangerous Sky: Canadian Airmen in World War II* (London: Kimber, 1968).

Cull, Brian and Roland Symonds, *One-Armed Mac: The Story of Squadron Leader James MacLachlan* (London: Grub Street, 2003).

Cull, Nicholas J., *Selling War: The British Propaganda Campaign Against American 'Neutrality' in World War II* (New York: Oxford University Press, 1995).

Darlow, Steve *Five of the Few: Survivors of the Battle of Britain and the Blitz Tell Their Story* (London: Grub Street, 2006).

Davidson, Martin and James Taylor, *Spitfire Ace* (London: Channel 4, 2003).

De Groot, Gerard J., *Liberal Crusader: The Life of Sir Archibald Sinclair* (London: Hurst, 1993).

Dudgeon, James M. *'Mick': The Story of Major Edward Mannock* (London: Hale, 1981).

Dunmore, Spencer, *Above and Beyond: The Canadians' War in the Air, 1939–45* (Toronto: M&S, 1996).

Deighton, Len, *Fighter: The True Story of the Battle of Britain* (London: Cape, 1977).

Dunn, Bill Newton, *Big Wing: The biography of Air Chief Marshal Sir Trafford Leigh-Mallory* (Shrewsbury: Airlife, 1992).

Durand, Arthur A., *Stalag Luft III: The Secret Story* (Baton Rouge, LA: Louisiana State University Press, 1988).

Fajtl, František, *Hdrina Století: příběh beznohého válečného stíhače RAF Douglase Badera* (Prague: Naše vojsko, 1994).

Fiedler, Arkady, *Squadron 303: The Story of the Polish Fighter Squadron with the R.A.F.* (London: Peter Davies, 1942).

Flint, Peter, *Dowding and Headquarters Fighter Command* (Shrewsbury: Airlife, 1996).

Foot, J. R. M. and J.M. Langley, *MI9: The British secret service that fostered escape and evasion 1939–1945 and its American counterpart* (London: Bodley Head, 1979).

Foreman, John, *Fighter Command Air Combat Claims, 1939–45: Volume One, 1939-1940* (Walton-on-Thames: Red Kite, 2003).

Foreman, John, *Battle of Britain: The Forgotten Months, November and December 1940* (New Malden: Air Research Publications, 1988).

Forrester, Larry, *Fly for Your Life: The Story of R. R. Stanford Tuck* (Garden City, NY: Nelson Doudleday, 1978 edn.).

Franks, Norman and Mike O'Connor, *Number One in War and Peace: The History of No. 1 Squadron 1912–2000* (London: Grub Street, 2000).

Franks, Norman, *Buck McNair: Canadian Spitfire Ace* (London: Grub Street, 2001).

Franks, Norman, *Air Battle Dunkirk, 26 May–3 June 1940* (London: Grub Street, 2000).

Franks, Norman, *RAF Fighter Command, 1936–1968* (Sparkford: Patrick Stephens, 1992).

Franks, Norman, *Sky Tiger: The Story of Group Captain Sailor Malan* (London: Kimber, 1980).

Franks, Norman, *Wings of Freedom: Twelve Battle of Britain Pilots* (London: Kimber, 1980).

Franks, Norman, *Fighter Leader: The Story of Wing Commander Ian Gleed* (London: Kimber, 1978).

Gammon, Victor F., *Not All Glory!: True Accounts of RAF Airmen Taken Prisoner in Europe, 1939–1945* (London: Arms and Armour, 1996).

Garrett, Richard, *Sky High: Heroic Pilots of the Second World War* (London: Weidenfeld and Nicolson, 1991).

Gelb, Norman, *Scramble: A Narrative History of the Battle of Britain* (San Diego, CA: HBJ, 1985).

Gretzyngier, Robert in assoc. with W. Matusiak, *Poles in Defence of Great Britain, July 1940-June 1941* (London: Grub Street, 2001).

Halfpenny, Bruce Barrymore, *Fight for the Sky* (Wellingborough: Patrick Stephens, 1986).

Halliday, Hugh, *No. 242 Squadron, The Canadian Years: The Story of the R.A.F.'s 'all-Canadian' Fighter Squadron* (Stittsville, ON: Canada's Wings, 1981).

Hancock, Rutherford M., *Flight Cadet* (Edinburgh: Pentland, 1996).

Haslam, E.B., *The History of Royal Air Force Cranwell* (London: HMSO, 1982).

Hearn, Peter, *Flying Rebel: The Story of Louis Strange* (London: HMSO, 1994).

Hearn, Peter, *Sky High Irvin: The Story of a Parachute Pioneer* (London: Hale, 1983).

Hill, R.D., *A History of St. Edward's School* (Oxford: St. Edward's School Society, 1963).

Jackson, Robert, *Douglas Bader: A Biography* (London: Barker, 1983).

James, John, *The Paladins: A Social History of the RAF up to the outbreak of World War II* (London: Macdonald, 1990).

James, T.C.G., *The Growth of Fighter Command, 1936–1940*, Sebastian Cox, ed. (London: Cass, 2002).

James, T.C.G., *The Battle of Britain*, Sebastian Cox, ed. (London: Cass, 2000).

Johnson, J.E. and P.B. Lucas, *Glorious Summer: The Story of the Battle of Britain* (London: Stanley Paul, 1990).

Jones, Ira, *Tiger Squadron* (London: Allen, 1954).

Kingsley, Hillary and Geoff Tibbals, *Box of Delights: The Golden Years of Television* (London: Macmillan, 1989).

Klinkowitz, Jerome, *Their Finest Hours: Narratives of the R.A.F. and Luftwaffe in World War II* (Ames, IA: Iowa State University Press, 1989).

Laffin, John, *Swifter than Eagles: The Biography of Marshal of the Royal Air Force Sir John Maitland Salmon* (Edinburgh: Blackwood, 1964).

Lanchberry, Edward, *Against the Sun: The Story of Wing Commander Roland Beamont* (London: Cassell, 1955).

Lane, Richard, *The Golden Age of Australian Radio Drama, 1923–1960: A History through Biography* (Melbourne: Melbourne University Press, 1994).

Lucas, Laddie, *Out of the Blue: The Role of Luck in Air Warfare, 1917–1966* (London: Hutchinson, 1985).

Lucas, Laddie, *Flying Colours: The Epic Story of Douglas Bader* (London: Wordsworth, 2001 edn.).

Masters, David, *"So Few": The Immortal Record of the Royal Air Force* (London: Eyre and Spottiswoode, 1941).

McKee, Alexander, *Strike From the Sky: The Story of the Battle of Britain* (Boston: Little Brown, 1960).

Morris, Richard. with Colin Dobinson, *Guy Gibson* (London: Viking, 1994).

Mosley, Leonard, *The Battle of Britain: The Making of a Film* (London: Weidenfeld and Nicolson, 1969).

Murphy, Robert, *British Cinema and the Second World War* (London: Continuum, 2000).

Nichol, John and Rennell, Tony, *The Last Escape: The Untold Story of Allied Prisoners of War in Germany 1944–45* (London: Viking, 2002).

Nicholas, Siân, *The Echo of War: Home Front propaganda and the wartime BBC, 1939-45* (Manchester: Manchester University Press, 1996).

Orange, Vincent, *Park: The Biography of Air Chief Marshal Sir Keith Park* (London: Grub Street, 2001 edn.).

Orange, Vincent, *The Road to Biggin Hill: A Life of Wing Commander Johnny Checketts* (Shrewsbury: Airlife, 1986).

Overy, Richard, *The Battle* (London: Penguin, 2000).

Parker, Matthew, *The Battle of Britain, July-October 1940: An Oral History of Britain's 'Finest Hour'* (London: Headline, 2000).

Price, Alfred, *Battle of Britain Day: 15 September 1940* (London: Greenhill, 1999 edn).

Probert, Henry and Sebastian Cox (eds), *The Battle Re-Thought: A Symposium on the Battle of Britain* (Shrewsbury: Airlife, 1991).

Ramsey, Winston G. (ed.), *The Battle of Britain Then and Now* (London: Battle of Britain Prints, 1987 edn.).

Ray, John, *The Battle of Britain, New Perspectives: Behind the Scenes of the Great Air War* (London: Brockhampton, 1999 edn).

Reid, P.R., *The Latter Days* (London: Hodder and Stoughton, 1953).

Revell, Alex, *The Vivid Air: Gerald and Michael Constable Maxwell, Fighter Pilots in Both World Wars* (London: Kimber, 1978).

Richards, Denis, *Portal of Hungerford: The Life of Marshal of the Royal Air Force Viscount Portal of Hungerford* (London: Heinemann, 1977).

Richards, Denis, *Royal Air Force, 1939–1945: Volume I, The Fight at Odds* (London: HMSO, 1953).

Rollings, Charles, *Wire and Worse: RAF Prisoners of War in Laufen, Biberach, Lübeck and Warburg, 1940–42* (Hersham: Ian Allan, 2004).

Ross, David, Bruce Blanche, Bill Simpson, *'The Greatest Squadron of them All': The Definitive History of 603 (City of Edinburgh) Squadron, RAauxAF: Vol. II, 1941-To Date* (London: Grub Street, 2003).

Ross, David, *Richard Hillary: The Definitive Biography of a Battle of Britain Fighter Pilot and Author of* The Last Enemy (London: Grub Street, 2000).

Ryde, Peter, *Out on a Limb: A Celebration of the British Limbless Ex-Service Men's Association Golden Jubilee 1932–1982* (Norwich: British Limbless Ex-Service Men's Association, 1982).

Sarkar, Dilip, *Johnnie Johnson: Spitfire Top Gun, Part I* (Worcester: Ramrod, 2002).

Sarkar, Dilip, *Battle of Britain: Last Look Back* (Worcester: Ramrod, 2002).

Sarkar, Dilip, *Douglas Bader: An Inspiration in Photographs* (Worcester: Ramrod and Douglas Bader Foundation, 2001).

Sarkar, Dilip, *Bader's Duxford Fighters: The Big Wing Controversy* (Worcester: Ramrod, 1997).

Sarkar, Dilip, *Bader's Tangmere Spitfires: The Untold Story, 1941* (Sparkford: Patrick Stephens, 1996).

Sarkar, Dilip, *A Few of the Many: Air War 1939–45: A Kaleidoscope of Memories* (Worcester: Ramrod, 1995).

Sarkar, Dilip, *Spitfire Squadron: No. 19 Squadron at War 1939–41* (New Malden: Air Research, 1990).

Saunders, Andy, *Bader's Last Flight: An In-Depth Investigation of a Great WWII Mystery* (London: Grub Street, 2007).

Shores, Christopher and Clive Williams, *Aces High: A Tribute to the Most Notable Fighter Pilots of the British and Commonwealth Forces in World War II* (London: Grub Street, 1994).

Sims, Edward, *The Fighter Pilots: A Comparative Study of the Royal Air Force, the Luftwaffe and the United States Army Air Force in Europe and North Africa, 1939–45* (London: Cassell, 1967).

Smith, Malcolm, *Britain and 1940: History, Myth and Popular Memory* (London: Routledge, 2000).

Smith, Malcolm, *British Air Strategy Between the Wars* (Oxford: Oxford University Press, 1984).

Smith, Richard C., *Al Deere: The Authorised Biography* (London: Grub Street, 2003).

Smith, Richard C., *Hornchurch Eagles: The Life Stories of Eight of the Airfield's Distinguished WWII Fighter Pilots* (London: Grub Street, 2002).

Smith, Richard C., *Hornchurch Scramble: The Definitive Account of the RAF Fighter Airfield, its Pilots, Groundcrew and Staff: Volume One, 1915 to the end of the Battle of Britain* (London: Grub Street, 2000).

Smith, Sydney, *Wings Day: The Man who led the RAF's epic battle in German Captivity* (London: Collins, 1968).

Sorel, Nancy Caldwell, *The Women Who Wrote the War* (New York: Arcade, 1999).

Spicer, Andrew, *Typical Men: The Representation of Masculinity in Popular British Cinema* (London: Tauris, 2001).

Spick, Mike, *Allied Fighter Aces: The Air Combat Tactics and Techniques of World War II* (London: Greenhill, 1997).

Spick, Mike, *The Ace Factor: Air Combat and the Role of Situational Awareness* (Shrewsbury: Airlife, 1988).

Spooner, Tony, *Night Fighter Ace* (Stroud: Sutton, 1997).

Stokes, Doug, *Wings Aflame: The Biography of Group Captain Victor Beamish* (Manchester: Crecy, 1988 edn.).

Stokes, Doug, *Paddy Finucane: Fighter Ace* (London: Kimber, 1983).

Terraine, John, *The Right of the Line: The Royal Air Force in the European War 1939-1945* (London: Sceptre, 1988 edn.).

Thomas, Hugh, *Spirit of the Blue: Peter Ayerst: A Fighter Pilot's Story* (Stroud: Sutton, 2004).

Tidy, Douglas, *I Fear No Man: The Story of No 74 (Fighter) Squadron Royal Flying Corps and Royal Air Force (The Tigers)* (London: Macdonald, 1972).

Treglown, Jeremy, *Roald Dahl: A Biography* (London: Faber, 1994).

Turner, John Frayn, *Douglas Bader: A Biography of the Legendary World War II Fighter Pilot* (Shrewsbury: Airlife, 2001 edn.).

Turner, John Frayn, *The Bader Tapes* (Bourne End: Kensal, 1986).

Turner, John Frayn, *The Bader Wing* (Tunbridge Wells: Midas, 1981).

Van Riper, A. Bowdoin, *Imagining Flight: Aviation and Popular Culture* (College Station, TX: Texas A&M Press, 2004).

Vance, Jonathan F., *A Gallant Company: The Men of the Great Escape* (Pacifica, CA: Pacifica Military Books, 2000).

Walker, Oliver, *Sailor Malan: A Biography* (London: Cassell, 1953).

Waugh, Eileen, *No Man an Island: A Biography of Peter Spencer* (London: Triton, 1970).

Wayne, Ralph, *Aces, Warriors & Wingmen: Firsthand Accounts of Canada's Fighter Pilots in the Second World War* (Mississauga, ON: John Wiley, 2004).

Webster, Charles and Noble Frankland, *The Strategic Air Offensive Against Germany, 1939–1945, Vol. 1* (London: HMSO, 1961).

Willis, John, *Churchill's Few: The Battle of Britain Remembered* (London: Michael Joseph, 1985).

Wilson, A.J., *Sky Sweepers* (London: Jarrolds, 1942).

Wilson, Eunice, *Dangerous Sky: A Resource Guide to the Battle of Britain* (Westport, CT: Greenwood, 1995).

Wood, Derek and Derek Dempster, *The Narrow Margin: The Battle of Britain and the Rise of Air Power 1930–40* (London: Hutchinson, 1961).

Wright, Robert, *Dowding and the Battle of Britain* (London: Macdonald, 1969).

Wyndham, Charles, *Douglas Bader: A Great Air Ace* (London: Blackie, 1966).

Zimmerman, David, *Britain's Shield* (Stroud: Sutton, 2001).

Zuk, Bill with Janusz Zurakowski, *egend in the Skies* (St Catherines, ON: Vanwell, 2004).

Articles

Chesshyre, Robert, 'We Can Be Heroes', *Saga Magazine* August (2004), pp. 90–96.

Cook, Tricia, 'In a Class of its own', *Everybody's War* 10 (2004), p. 73.

Cox, Sebastian, 'The Sources and Organisation of RAF Intelligence and Its Influence on Operations', in Horst Boog (ed.), *The Conduct of the Air War in the Second World War: An International Comparison* (Oxford: Berg, 1992), pp. 553–79.

Cox, Sebastian, 'A Comparative Analysis of RAF and Luftwaffe Intelligence in the Battle of Britain, 1940', *Intelligence and National Security* 5 (1990), pp. 425–43.

Haslam, E.B., 'How Lord Dowding came to leave Fighter Command', *Journal of Strategic Studies* 4 (1981), pp. 175–86.

Harvey, Michael, 'A Study in Heroism: Douglas Bader', *Silver Jacket*, 24 (1955), pp. 10-11.

Omissi, David Enrico, 'The Hendon Air Pageant, 1920–37' in John M. Mackenzie (ed.), *Popular Imperialism and the Military* (Manchester: Manchester University Press, 1991), pp. 198–220.

Price, Alfred, 'Battle of Britain Day', *Royal Air Force Historical Society Journal*, 29 (2005), pp. 5–16.

Saunders, Andy, 'Who Downed Douglas Bader?', *After the Battle* 125 (2004), pp. 2–25.

Video Documentaries

Aviation Heroes of World War II: The Battle of Britain (Greenwich Workshop, 1990).

Britain's War Heroes: Douglas Bader, Fighter Ace (Blakeway Associates, 2005).

Escape from Colditz (Windfall Films, 2000).

Fighting the Blue (ASA Productions (UK), 2005).

First of the Few: The True Story (Dowty Group, 1997).

Great Heroes of World War II (Vision Video, 1995).

Hunters in the Sky: Struggle for Supremacy (Anthony Potter Productions, 1991).

Hunters in the Sky: The Great Defenders (Anthony Potter Productions, 1991).

Secret Lives: Douglas Bader (Twenty Twenty Productions, 1996).

Spitfire: Power, Grace and Glory (DD Video, 1998).